Advance Praise for
The Tough Standard

"In their book, *The Tough Standard*, Levant and Pryor practically rip the topics from today's headlines and situate the troubling events of men's violence in a strong theoretical and empirical body of work, bringing light—instead of just heat—to the issues they address. It is a must-read as a resource to understand and engage in critical issues affecting our lives, families, and the fabric of society in the United States."

**—James R. Mahalik, PhD, MA, Professor,
Lynch School of Education and Human Development, Boston College**

"Most acts of sexual assault and gun violence are perpetrated by men, yet most men are not violent. How then do we explain the connection between men and violence without condemning men? In this book, Ron Levant and Shana Pryor skillfully address this conundrum, by shifting the focus of analysis to masculinity. This book has the perfect blend of contemporary issues (e.g., the #MeToo movement), science, theory, and practical examples. I highly commend it to anyone who seeks to understand the complex relationship between gender and violence."

**—Joel Wong, PhD, Professor of Counseling Psychology,
Indiana University**

"Take a deep breath and prepare to hold yourself and your community accountable. *Tough Standard* takes an honest and well-researched look at the implications of modern masculinity. Accessible to both researchers and nonacademics alike, *Tough Standard* pulls back the veil to reveal how we are all impacted—and indeed complicit—in the construction of modern masculinity. As we look to heal and move forward in a positive way, *Tough Standard* offers invaluable insights and tools to get us there. It's a comprehensive, thoughtful, and profound piece of work. A fine compilation of a lifetime of research and beautifully linked to the political and cultural moments of our time."

**—Cleo Stiller, author of *Modern Manhood* and Peabody
Award-nominated television host**

"Between the Gillette ad that prompted a firestorm of criticism and the flood of 800-word sometimes simplistic blogs about manhood, it's easy to lose sight of what the evidence says about masculinity and its links to violence. In *The Tough Standard*, Levant and Pryor do a stellar job of presenting how masculinity shapes violence in our lives and what to do about it. In a historic moment when even talking about 'masculinity' becomes incendiary, they lay out their argument with deeply personal stories and always with empathy."

—Gary Barker, PhD, CEO and Founder,
Promundo-US

"Ron Levant and Shana Pryor have pulled off an astonishing piece of scholarship: synthesizing decades of research on men and masculinities into a book that is both rigorously researched and readily accessible to the lay reader. Levant is one of the fathers of the psychology of men and masculinities discipline who for more than four decades has addressed—as he brilliantly does with his coauthor in this important new book—the full range of the male lived experience, from examining men's sexual and domestic violence and addressing manhood in the #MeToo era to sensitively considering men's health (including depression and trauma). It explores the strain facing men of color and the struggles of white working class men. Acknowledging both the joys and challenges of fatherhood and boys on the journey to manhood, it contextualizes the patriarchal yoke stifling males (as it continues to oppress women and girls). Drawing on foundational research that marked the early days of the study of men and masculinities (Levant coedited A New Psychology of Men 25 years ago)—and seamlessly integrating insights from both academic and activist efforts of more recent times—The Tough Standard will no doubt become an essential guide for men navigating their way through the treacherous waters of traditional masculinity enroute to a profeminist port where the future is more than female—it is welcoming to male allies."

— Rob Okun, Editor & Publisher, Voice Male magazine,
the Magazine for Changing Men

"In a nation awash in violence, Ron Levant and Shana Pryor's wise book contains a vital message for the moment: Men may be the perpetrators of almost all of this violence, but they are not the only ones at fault. Rather, reared to strongly endorse masculine norms, they learn habits that often harm women, children, the earth, and themselves. Dr. Levant understands that traditional masculinity can be positive with its emphasis on protecting and supporting others. But too often, protection becomes possession, support becomes suppression, and men use their physicality to dominate. Dr. Levant and Ms. Pryor are neither apologists nor prosecutors of men. In this ultimately hopeful book, they contend that given more and better options, most men would choose a type of masculinity that heals rather than harms."

—Neil Chethik, BSJ, Executive Director, Carnegie Center for
Literacy & Learning; Author, FatherLoss: How Sons of all
Ages Come to Terms With the Deaths of Their Dads and VoiceMale:
What Husbands Really Think About Their Marriages,
Their Wives, Sex, Housework, and Commitment

view of the challenges that men face in meeting 'the tough standard'—today's changing, diverse, and often contradictory expectations for them."

—**Joseph H. Pleck, PhD, Professor Emeritus, University of Illinois**

"This is a critically important work from a leading scholar and founder of our modern psychology of masculinities. The authors synthesize decades of research across various disciplines to help us better understand how masculinities and violence intersect in the lives of some men. Using their experiences, Levant and Pryor wrote a book that is provocative, incisive, and relevant for us who work with masculinities."

—**William Ming Liu, PhD, Professor, University of Maryland
and Editor,** *Psychology of Men and Masculinities*

"We are well past the time for a serious discussion about the connection between masculinity and violence. Ron Levant and Shana Pryor are the perfect guides for an honest and evidence-based discussion about what is one of the most pressing concerns facing modern society. This is a thoughtful and intelligent book that helps the reader understand the underlying concerns that are much deeper than the common discourse about violence. At some point we all have to take a deep look at the culture of violence that influences us all and has vast consequences for many men."

—**Matt Englar-Carlson, PhD, Professor, Department of Counseling,
California State University, Fullerton**

"In *The Tough Standard: The Hard Truths About Masculinity and Violence*, Dr. Ron Levant and Shana Pryor take decades of authoritative work on masculinity in American men and describe how it can and has led to violence, as well as to economic stagnation and other social pathologies. At this moment of extensive feminist reawakening and intensification, by way of the #MeToo movement, and the importance of inclusiveness and intersectionality, Dr. Levant and Shana Pryor's findings feel essential for men, women, and the culture."

—**John Kelly, author of** *The Graves Are Walking: The Great Famine and
the Saga of the Irish People* **and** *The Great Mortality: An Intimate History
of the Black Death, the Most Devastating Plague of All Time*

"*The Tough Standard* is the new standard for understanding the shaping of masculinity and the risks of rigid overadherence to traditional norms. This critical volume also addresses the role of masculinity in modern social challenges, from gun violence to untreated trauma. An essential tool to understand today's social problems and their links to gender socialization."

—**Mike C. Parent, PhD, Assistant Professor,
University of Texas at Austin**

"*The Tough Standard* is the most important book on men and mascu
available today, and it couldn't come at a more opportune moment. At a
when sex and gender issues are confusing and conflicted, Dr. Levant and
Pryor offer a scientifically sound exploration of what it means to be a go
man in today's world. Drawing on 45 years of experience as a leader in the fiel
of men and masculinities, Dr. Levant gives us a book that will change lives for the
better. Unlike many evidence-based experts, he shares his own personal journey
as a husband, father, and a man. I highly recommend this book for all those who
want to understand why men are the way they are and how we can expand our
understanding of masculinity to become our best selves."

—**Jed Diamond, PhD, author of *12 Rules for Good Men***
and *The Irritable Male Syndrome*

"A provocative, insightful, and useful book that is timely in addressing how men's
violence permeates our world. Levant and Pryor's excellent data-based analysis
on how masculinity ideology and gender role conflict/stress contribute to men's
violence toward others is significant in identifying what has been left out of many
critical discussions on a national level and in men's and women's lives. This book
is highly recommended to anyone wanting to understand the role that violent
masculinity plays in explaining America's number one problem—violence
against other human beings."

—**James M. O'Neil, PhD, Professor of Educational Psychology,**
Department of Educational Psychology, Neag School
of Education, University of Connecticut, and a licensed
psychologist in private practice in South Windsor, CT

"What do men do when long-established concepts of masculinity no longer define the American male? In the workplace, the home, and even the military—
perhaps the last bastion of traditional American masculinity—the roles of men
are increasingly challenged. There are no easy answers to the complex and
changing definition of masculinity, and Levant and Pryor do not pretend to present any. By a careful dissection of elements of traditional masculine identity,
this book provides some insight into how such attitudes have shaped American
men. The authors do a service by providing the reader not with answers but
with framework for further discussion."

—**Morgan T. Sammons, PhD, ABPP, Executive Officer,**
The National Register of Health Service Psychologists

"A masterful analysis of what we *know*, what we *need to know*, and what we *need
to do* about the connection between masculinity and violence. Levant and Pryor
provide an essential understanding of male sexual and gun violence that is sensitive to racial/ethnic, cultural, and class differences. In addition, they offer insight into some tricky conceptual issues about masculinity and a sympathetic

"A timely book that is packed with research and insights from a distinguished career in studying men and masculinity. Levant and Pryor do not shy away from controversial topics like gun violence, suicide, and sexual assault, and they offer realistic and urgent solutions to help promote health in boys and men."

—Kate Richmond, PhD, Associate Professor of Psychology, Director of Women & Gender Studies, Muhlenberg College

"Dr. Ron Levant has devoted his impressive career to understanding and helping men. In this new volume, he reviews and synthesizes his substantial publication record with the available literature, providing new insights on a body of research and therapeutic work that spans four decades. *The Tough Standard* provides provocative evidence about how America's traditional definition of masculinity contributes to men's violence against others and themselves."

—Andrew P. Smiler, PhD, Therapist, and Author of *Dating and Sex: A Guide for the 21st Century Teen Boy* and Editor, Online Publications, Society for Research on Adolescence

The Tough Standard

The Hard Truths about Masculinity and Violence

RONALD F. LEVANT

AND

SHANA PRYOR

OXFORD
UNIVERSITY PRESS

OXFORD
UNIVERSITY PRESS

Oxford University Press is a department of the University of Oxford. It furthers
the University's objective of excellence in research, scholarship, and education
by publishing worldwide. Oxford is a registered trade mark of Oxford University
Press in the UK and certain other countries.

Published in the United States of America by Oxford University Press
198 Madison Avenue, New York, NY 10016, United States of America.

Library of Congress Cataloging-in-Publication Data
Names: Levant, Ronald F., author. | Pryor, Shana, author.
Title: The tough standard : the hard truths about masculinity and violence /
Ronald F. Levant, Shana Pryor.
Description: New York, NY : Oxford University Press, [2020] |
Includes bibliographical references and index. |
Identifiers: LCCN 2019044733 (print) | LCCN 2019044734 (ebook) |
ISBN 9780190075873 (hardback) | ISBN 9780190075897 (epub)
Subjects: LCSH: Masculinity. | Men—Psychology. | Men—Social conditions. |
Violence in men.
Classification: LCC BF692.5 .L49 2020 (print) | LCC BF692.5 (ebook) |
DDC 155.3/32—dc23
LC record available at https://lccn.loc.gov/2019044733
LC ebook record available at https://lccn.loc.gov/2019044734

1 3 5 7 9 8 6 4 2

Printed by Sheridan Books, Inc., United States of America

CONTENTS

ACKNOWLEDGMENTS

We wish to acknowledge the contributions of Gary Brooks, Chris Liang, Ryon McDermott, Louise Silverstein, and Joel Wong, who read drafts and offered critiques. I (RL) want to acknowledge my collaborators and students, too numerous to mention by name, who have provided nonstop stimulation and companionship over the last 4+ decades. I also want to thank members of American Psychological Association Division 51, the Society for the Psychological Study of Men and Masculinities, with whom I (RL) have had an ongoing conversation about men and masculinities over 25 years. Finally, I want to thank my family for their forbearance throughout the long and arduous process of co-authoring this book, particularly my life-mate and wife, Carol Slatter, who supported me during the writing process, and my daughter Caren and grandsons Adrian and Jeremy, who offered encouragement.

I (SP) want to thank Kristin Silver for suggesting that I help write this book. I also want to thank Taylor Ceroni who is always there to support me and who will always be my role model. I will be eternally grateful for my Nervous Dog Coffee Bar crew: Devynn Campbell-Halfaker, Ginelle Wolfe, and Alyssa Eversmeyer for always uplifting my spirits and helping me to work every Sunday morning. I want to thank Steve Antonucci for his willingness to sit with me for hours in deep discussion about topics related to this book. Finally, I want to thank my good friend Laurel Glaze for her constant presence in my life and who has always encouraged me to read.

1

Masculinity and the Present Cultural Moment

The time has come in our culture for a serious examination of the role of masculinity in sexual and gun violence—topics which have assumed a very high profile in U.S. society of late. Masculinity is a complicated and problematic phenomenon. We will also look at the role of masculinity in other contemporary social problems, such as the economic stagnation of White working-class men. In addition, there are long-standing issues of men's greater mortality than women and their unremitted suffering from mental illnesses and trauma due both to their reluctance to seek help and other people's use of a masculinist perspective to presume that men do not hurt. Because masculinity is a cultural idea and there are many different subcultures in the United States, we will discuss different versions of masculinity, or as they are often referred to—masculinities—and how they have been studied, based on cultural dimensions such as race, ethnicity, social class, sexual orientation, gender identity, and age/developmental stage. In summary, we will identify a relatively unacknowledged factor—masculinity—that influences certain high-profile contemporary social problems, analyze the nature of its influence, discuss the evidence that supports the role of masculinity in these problems, and, most important, address solutions.

What Is Masculinity?

The term *masculinity* is understood in somewhat different ways by different cultural and demographic groups in our society, as we have just noted, but there are two major conceptual orientations to the use of this term. It is important to discuss these orientations at the outset and define the way we will use the term.

Masculinity Is Synonymous with Being Male

Most scientists recognize that human behavior results from an intricate interaction between nature and nurture, but most will also acknowledge that we are a long way away from knowing exactly how that works out in any specific instance. Some people ignore this dual causation and believe that nature is the only important determinant. Such folks tend to think that masculinity is synonymous with being biologically male. Examples abound, but here is one from a recent article in *Psychology Today*, in which Saad (2018) stated: "Women are attracted to 'toxic masculine' male phenotypes that correlate with testosterone."

Hence, in criticizing masculinity, readers who view masculinity as synonymous with being biologically male may misunderstand our intentions and think that we are denouncing men. *We are not.* In fact, we feel quite a bit of empathy and compassion for boys and men in general and, in particular, for those boys and men whom we believe are imprisoned by masculinity. We use this prison metaphor throughout the book because (as we will explain in more detail in the following discussion) masculinity is understood to be obligatory by most men at some point in their lives, usually when they are children. For me (RL) my empathy and compassion stems in part from the fact that I was in that situation myself and had to struggle mightily to get out. Not only was I brought up in a working-class home and neighborhood where I conformed to traditional masculine norms, which took me many years and a 4-year course of psychoanalysis to work my way out of. But also, from the vantage point of over four decades of research, teaching, and clinical practice in the psychology of men and masculinities, I understand the powerful grip that masculinity has on many boys and men, and I will convey that understanding in this book. I have done research on boys' and men's adherence to masculine norms and on the socialization of boys to harden their hearts and restrict the expression of vulnerable and caring emotions. As a licensed psychologist, I focused my practice on traditional men. I have counseled many men seeking to overcome the effects of their socialization and open up their hearts to their families and regain their freedom. And I have taught many generations of students in these topics.

As a woman, I (SP) have seen the dark side of masculinity. As a sexual assault survivor, a daughter, a sister, and a psychologist-in-training, I have experienced how masculinity can negatively impact not only men themselves but also the people around them. I specialize in investigating and treating men who have experienced interpersonal trauma. I have seen how masculine norms can impede the healing process that men go through when dealing with past experiences of trauma.

Another View of Masculinity

There is another, more psychological view of masculinity, which is the one we use in this book. As Bohan (1997) noted, psychology distinguishes biological sex (being male, female, or intersex) from socio-psychological gender (referring to masculinity, femininity, as well as various nonbinary identities). In this vein, we define masculinity as a set of thoughts, feelings, beliefs, and behaviors that are generally considered to be appropriate for boys and men; importantly, it also includes those that are considered inappropriate for boys and men, against which it has drawn a bright line. It is often considered to be a set of beliefs that individuals hold, which are based in socio-cultural ideologies regarding gender. Masculinity is therefore a social construction distinct from male biological sex. Definitions of masculinity vary across different cultures and historical periods. Both males and females can perform masculinity and femininity. In Chapter 2 of this volume, we go into considerable detail on contemporary masculinity ideologies and norms, and we will define what we consider the dominant form today—traditional masculinity ideology. Throughout the book, whenever we use the term *masculinity*, we are referring to this dominant form.

In this view, masculinity is not "hard-wired" due to genes and hormones, and therefore it is not essential nor inescapable for boys and men. Hence, boys and men can retain their gender identities without conforming their thoughts, emotions, and behaviors to masculine norms. This is the view we take in this book. We do so for several reasons. First, we are psychologists, not biologists nor medical physicians, and psychology is what we know. Second, psychological phenomena—thoughts, beliefs, emotions, and behaviors—are more amenable to change than genes and hormones, and change is our ultimate goal. We wish to free men from the prison of masculinity to both improve lives and benefit society.

Will a Critique of Masculinity Threaten Some Men?

Another consideration is that a serious critique of masculinity may be unsettling or even threatening for some men. In fact, a recent article was titled "The Terrifying Potential for Masculinity: The Erosion of Traditional Gender Roles Destroys Much-Needed Security: What Will Replace It" (Schuhr, 2018)? Schuhr noted:

> The erosion of traditional manliness is the flipside of female eman-
> cipation. Underlying all brands of feminism . . . is the assumption

that sex differences don't imply gender differences. While biological discrepancies are inevitable, the manifold social consequences affiliated with them are not. They are socially constructed and, thus, subject to change. The liberating potential of this insight for girls and women has always been obvious, even to women who reject it. Men, however, are left with fear and lack of direction. Masculine ideals become debatable. Identities crumble. Certainties vanish. Restrictive as they are, the rules of masculinity provide clear goals, and standards of right and wrong. Now they have disappeared, or at least their absolute validity has. What is left is confusion, and a terrifying wealth of possibilities.

Here is another example, written in the first person:

> I read an article stating a university wouldn't stand for toxic masculinity, and then went on to describe male behavior in bars: being aggressive, touching women without their permission, and asshole nonsense like that. I agreed with every statement in that particular article. Then I read an article that asked, "Why do we even put the word 'toxic' before 'masculinity?' Isn't *masculinity* alone toxic?" **It made me roll my eyes so hard they hurt.** (Timmel, 2018; emphasis added; the author is forcefully indicating his disbelief that masculinity itself is toxic[1]).

Finally, a recent example shows how criticism of masculinity can be highly disturbing to some people. The Boys and Men Guidelines Group of the American Psychological Association (2018) recently released a newly approved set of guidelines for psychological practice with boys and men. The release was followed a few months later by a magazine article in the *APA Monitor on Psychology* and a tweet about the *Monitor* article and the guidelines. The tweet used the unfortunate term *traditional masculinity*, whereas the term used in the guidelines is actually the rather academic-sounding *traditional masculinity ideology*, and it came with a precise definition. In the Twitter era, everything gets stripped of context. As a result, negative comments flooded in on Twitter, as well as from conservative news outlets. Fortin (2019) reported on writers who subscribe to view that masculinity is hard-wired due to biological factors:

> "If men are struggling more the farther we move from those traditional norms, is the answer to continue denying and suppressing a boy's

---

[1] While we do not consider masculinity to be toxic, we do consider it to be problematic.

essential nature?" David French, a senior writer for *National Review*, wrote in an article about the guidelines on Monday.

"Traditional masculinity seems to be, in this report at least, conflated with being a pig, or a creep, or a Harvey Weinstein kind of person," said Laura Ingraham on her *Fox News* show on Tuesday.

In addition, some of us who were cited in the *Monitor* article received hateful emails and threatening cell phone calls. Here is an email I (RL) received:

> Bro, are you a fifthy juden and a faggot or just a filthy juden? You look to me like you are a Kevin Spacey pedophile type but I guess according to the jew-infested APA just like fagotry, pedophilia is a normal condition unlike "toxis masculinity." You filthy cocksuckers! Inverting right to being wrong and wrong and disgusting to being right! I hope Trump declare martial law sooner rather than later, call the white men only to the National Guard and ask us to start rounding up little whiny faggots like yourself in 4 in the morning in windowless vans!

We do understand that our thesis may be unsettling to some readers, even deeply so as the previously quoted email suggests. Such readers may wonder what is left after masculinity is critiqued and problematized. We agree that alternative ways to be a man are not very visible at all. This is why our final chapter is devoted to solutions, in which we discuss sources that promote healthy ways to be a boy or man.

So, long story short, we are not condemning men. We are simply stating that a socialized gender role with associated norms, namely masculinity, is an important contributing factor in several serious contemporary social problems. We spend the next three chapters focused squarely on masculinity. We discuss the psychological construct of masculinity in detail in Chapter 2, including the larger theoretical framework in which it is embedded, how masculinity is conceptualized and measured in the scientific study of men and masculinities, and what seems to account for its destructive effects. We will also take up the controversial topic of "toxic masculinity." This will be followed by Chapter 3, which details the theorized consequences of socializing boys and requiring men to conform to traditional masculine norms, and then Chapter 4, which summarizes the research on the outcomes of endorsing or conforming to traditional masculine norms and of experiencing gender role conflict or stress.

What Is the Present Moment?

There is an ancient Chinese curse: "May you live in interesting times." The present cultural moment that we are living in is certainly interesting—at times much too much so -- and indeed, curse-worthy. It is the result of the public's varying, and often polarized, reactions to the exposure of numerous high-power men as sexual predators and abusers, as well as to unremitting gun violence, particularly mass shootings, many of which have occurred at schools. In addition, the economic stagnation of working-class men is also playing a role in today's turbulence. Together, these phenomena have created a new iteration of the masculinity crisis first identified in the 1980s (Kimmel, 1987). According to Ruiz (2018), "masculinity is having a moment. There's a movement for a more expressive, more inclusive definition of manhood."

Sexual Violence

The cultural moment that we are responding to has arrived courtesy of the #MeToo movement, in which waves of women from various industries and sectors of society have summoned the courage to publicly confront their powerful harassers and abusers. This movement was founded in 2006 by Tarana Burke, an African American woman who began using the phrase "Me Too" to raise awareness of the pervasiveness of sexual abuse and assault in society. The phrase developed into a broader movement following the 2017 use of #MeToo as a hashtag for the exposés of Hollywood, the infamous "casting couch," and Harvey Weinstein and continued on from there. It spawned the Time's Up movement against sexual harassment, which was founded by Hollywood celebrities in response to the Weinstein effect and #MeToo. It has resulted in the conviction of Bill Cosby and the accusation of then–Supreme Court nominee Bret Kavanaugh of sexual assault. By October 2018, #MeToo had brought down 201 powerful men, and nearly half of their replacements were women (Carlsen et al., 2018). The *Chicago Tribune* published a timeline of the #MeToo movement from 2006 to 20169, which may be of interest to readers (Chicago Tribune Staff, 2019).

One critique of the media response to the #MeToo movement is that it has focused on celebrity White women and ignored the complaints of Black and other low-wage women workers. For example, Jones (2018) commented:

Though the #MeToo hashtag was created by a Black woman more than a decade ago, the faces of the cause have often been White and affluent, and the industries receiving the most media scrutiny have been the rarefied worlds of Hollywood and TV journalism. And yet it is Black women in particular and female employees of restaurants, factories and other blue-collar workplaces who bear the brunt of sexual harassment and abuse.

However some of this may be changing as a result of Lifetime's six-part documentary *Surviving R. Kelly*. According to Tillet and Tillet (2019), "for 20 years, Black girls and women accused the R&B singer Robert Kelly of sexually assaulting minors. Yet he still enjoyed enormous success." They further state:

The backlash against R. Kelly includes high-profile celebrities and everyday fans, as well as prosecutors in Atlanta and Chicago who are looking into the allegations and asking potential victims and witnesses to come forward. And it builds on the #MuteRKelly campaign; the cancellation of his concert last spring in Chicago, his hometown; and a statement by the Women of Color of Time's Up demanding that companies like RCA Records, Spotify and Apple Music stop doing business with him.

The pushback has succeeded. On February 22, 2019, after weeks of renewed scrutiny, Kelly was indicted in Chicago, accused of aggravated criminal sexual abuse involving 10 counts over four victims, three of whom were underage at the time of the alleged abuse.

Furthermore, it is noteworthy that low-wage restaurant workers and women of color are leading the charge. Quart (2018) noted:

Last Tuesday [September 18, 2108], McDonald's workers in 10 US cities walked off the job to protest against pervasive sexual harassment. A week earlier, female janitors in California marched 100 miles from San Francisco to the state capitol in Sacramento to support anti-harassment legislation. The janitors' union, SEIU, in partnership with the East LA Women's Center, has been quietly training women in self-defense and promoting peer-to-peer anti-harassment workshops and an assault crisis hotline.

These legitimate criticisms notwithstanding, the #MeToo movement has accomplished what heretofore had seemed improbable, namely, that the women's accusations of events that took place 10, 15, or even as long as 36[2] years ago were

[2] Dr. Christine Blasé Ford accused Brett Kavanaugh of a sexual assault that took place 36 years before the allegation was made.

believed by a large segment of the population. Invoking a feminist slogan from the 1960s, *the personal had in fact become political.*

As an indication of these changes wrought by #MeToo, Southall (2018) reported that rape reports in New York City are up sharply, and Mayor de Blasio suggested that it might be due to #MeToo:

> Reported rapes in New York City have risen for 16 consecutive months since last fall, when allegations of sexual misconduct against the movie producer Harvey Weinstein ignited a global reckoning about sexual harassment and assault, especially in the workplace. Mayor Bill de Blasio said the numbers appear to reflect a cultural shift in attitudes about sex crimes. . . . "I think the #MeToo movement is a part of it . . . victims— survivors— . . . know that they should come forward, that it's important, that they'll be protected, they'll be supported." (p. A19)

This movement is clearly aimed at abusive men, as well as the systems of enablement in the workplace and society at large. On this point, a Washington Post–Schar School poll (Rubin, 2018) found sharp partisan divisions on views about accusations of sexual assault in the wake of Brett Kavanaugh's confirmation to the Supreme Court. Kavanaugh's aggressive grievance-driven performance before a Senate committee seems to have turned the tide for the Republicans against a credible woman accuser. Overall, 57% of battleground district voters say they are concerned that men they are close to might be unfairly accused of sexual assault, reflecting a conservative point of view. However, a far larger number, 78%, say they are concerned that women in this country are not believed when they report that they were sexually assaulted. Overall, by 59% to 41%, Americans say the bigger problem is that women who report that they were sexually assaulted are not believed.

As we as a society move forward in this conversation on what constitutes consent for sexual activity, it is important to highlight the ambiguities that occur. One example is the case of Aziz Ansari, a popular comedian and actor, who was accused of sexual misconduct by a women pseudonymously named Grace, in an article on the website *Babe* (Way, 2019). He was shocked by the account, having felt that encounter was consensual. He not only issued a letter of apology but also addressed the situation in a pop-up comedy show. According to an article in *Vox*, "he admitted that the allegation against him was 'a terrifying thing to talk about.' However, he said, 'It made me think about a lot, and I hope I've become a better person'" (North, 2019). Another example is the case of former Senator Al Franken, which Mayer (2019) recently reconsidered. She argued that Franken's Senate Democratic colleagues judged him too quickly and harshly. We will explore in detail masculinity's role in sexual violence in Chapter 6.

Gun and Other Physical Violence

The category of gun and other physical violence addressed in this book includes school and other mass shootings; the killing of unarmed Black men by White police officers; hate crimes like the attacks on Black churches, Jewish synagogues, and LGBTQ persons; and domestic/intimate partner violence.[3] We will discuss this in detail in Chapter 5, but will comment here on the way that school and other mass shootings have contributed to the present moment and also discuss some broader issues.

Adding to the present moment, but coming from a different direction, is the movement March for Our Lives, started by the Marjory Stoneman Douglas High School students (such as Emma González, David Hogg, and Delaney Tarr) in Parkland, Florida, who survived the February 14, 2018, mass shooting there. Although the shooter was male, as are most mass shooters (from 1982 to 2017, only three American mass shooters have been women, whereas 93 have been men; Epps, 2018), this particular movement rarely comments on the gender of the shooter and has only recently mentioned masculinity as a factor, but rather has focused on gun control or mental illness.

Most Physical Violence Is Committed by Males, but Are All Males Violent?

Consider the fact that most of these criminal acts of physical violence are committed by boys and men; in fact, 87% of violent crime in the United States is committed by males, and most of that by White men (U.S. Department of Justice, 2016). *That does not mean that most males are violent.* Although the jury is still out on what causes violence, some think that the propensity to act violently is due to the "red triad" of personality traits, which includes (a) amorality, (b) being thin-skinned and not taking criticism well, and (c) being hot-headed and quick to get angry and aggressive (Pitt, 2016). If true (and as we discuss shortly, there is reason to doubt that it is), personality traits such as these would likely not be normally distributed throughout the population, but rather highly skewed to the lower, nonviolent part of the distribution. Those who actually behave violently are, in fact, a tiny minority, whose scores on such tests would be are in the extreme high end of the distribution.

---

[3] Guns are often used by men to commit suicide, but we will take up this point when we discuss men's mental health.

Personality Traits or the Social Situation?

Furthermore, social psychologists have shown that personality traits are poor predictors of people's actual behavior, which would be even more true with very low frequency behaviors such as violence. In fact, based on numerous studies over many decades of the relationships between various personality traits and their corresponding behaviors, Ross and Nisbett (2011) have estimated that, at most, personality traits account for 9% of the variation in their corresponding behaviors. That is, scores on a measure of a personality trait—say, independence—will only weakly explain whether participants will behave independently in any given situation. Much more of the variation in behavior is accounted for by the power of the social situation. It should be noted though that psychological research typically accounts for less than 50% of the variance in the variables of interest. In the present case concerning male violence, the social situation in question would be the socio-cultural ideologies about masculinity, which create compelling expectations for how boys and men should think, act, and feel.[4]

The Role of Biology

As we have previously touched on, some might argue that men's greater perpetration of violent acts is due to innate biological factors that make men more violent than women, and they might invoke the controversial role of testosterone. It is controversial for several reasons. First, people of all genders have both testosterone and estrogen circulating in their blood streams. Second, as MacArthur Grant recipient Robert Sapolsky (2104) has noted, there is no dose–response effect. That is, in studies of nonhuman primates, the animals show the same level of aggression whether the level of testosterone is manipulated from 20% to 200%, although aggression does decrease when testosterone is reduced to zero. Sapolsky theorized that testosterone has a permissive effect, meaning that some testosterone is required for aggression to occur, but it in no way completely explains aggression. Third, in studies of testosterone's effects, correlation—the association of a biological factor with a behavior—is often mistaken as evidence of causation. Sapolsky's work on testosterone further suggests that it might not always cause increases in aggression but that aggression may result in increased

---

[4] We realize that some social psychologists might take issue with this statement, arguing that ideologies are not social situations. However, an examination of situations created in iconic experiments such as Milgram's obedience study reveals that the results were obtained because participants *believed* that the fake shocks were real, just like boys and men *believe* that masculinity is obligatory.

levels of testosterone. For example, a well-known correlation is that testosterone is higher in juvenile delinquent boys as compared to normal boys. Did testosterone cause the delinquency, or was it the other way around—delinquency elevates testosterone? We really cannot say based on present evidence.

However, even if it were to be proven that males did have a greater biological propensity for violence, we also know from studies of both human and nonhuman animals that any propensity for violence can be modified and even subdued by social and psychological factors. For example, Old World monkeys use violence to establish a dominance hierarchy. But with these monkeys, there is less violence when there is a dominant male. In contrast to the biological perspective, we will show that physical and sexual violence is influenced by the outmoded yet still influential definition of masculinity, although (as will be shown in Chapters 5 and 6) the theorized pathways of masculinity's influence are somewhat different for these two categories of violence.

Masculinity and the Economic Stagnation of White-Working Class Men

The present masculinity crisis concerns not only sexual and physical violence but also the economic stagnation of White working-class men resulting from the confluence of large-scale economic, political, and social changes. These changes include the Great Recession (dubbed at one time the "Mancession" because of its disproportionate effect on men), technological and productivity advances, globalization of the economy and the rise of China and India, weakening of labor unions and the resulting loss of high paying union jobs, and growing income disparity.

Earlier stages of these changes were described by Hanna Rosin (2012) in her provocatively titled book, *The End of Man and the Rise of Women,* and even earlier by Susan Faludi (1999) in *Stiffed: The Betrayal of the American Man.* Two articles on this topic appeared more recently in *The Economist* ("Men Adrift," 2015; "The Weaker Sex," 2015). According to "Men Adrift," "jobs that used to take 100 men now take 10. . . . A strong set of hands is no longer enough." Furthermore, blue-collar jobs now take more skill than they used to. In addition, the problem is not just due to changes in the labor market; it is also due to the poorer performance of boys in school compared to girls.

Giridharadas (2018) put it this way:

> Globalization, the internet, automation, mass migration, the emergence of India and China, the financial crisis of 2008, the rise of women

and their displacing of men in more service-oriented economies, the civil rights movement and the emancipation of other groups and the loss of status for White people—these are just some of what we have lived through of late. Yes, the world has gotten better for hundreds of millions. But Fukuyama reminds us that across much of the West, people have suffered dislocation and elites have captured the fruits.

Economists Autor, Dorn, and Hanson (2018) argued that adverse trade shocks, like a surge of imports from China, "differentially reduce employment and earnings of young adult males" and "heighten male idleness and premature mortality." These changes have resulted in unemployment or underemployment of White working-class men. According to "The Weaker Sex" (2015), "In America pay for men with only a high-school certificate fell by 21% in real terms between 1979 and 2013; for women with similar qualifications it rose by 3%. Around a fifth of working-age American men with only a high-school diploma have no job." This has resulted in huge sense of grievance, which plays a prominent role in our country's current political turbulence. Claire McCaskill, the former Democratic senator from Missouri who was recently defeated in her re-election campaign, was interviewed on the podcast *The Daily* (Tavernise, 2018). She had an interesting insight into why so many White working-class and rural people have abandoned the Democratic Party. According to her, these people see the Democrats helping women, gay men and lesbians, Blacks, and immigrants from Mexico and Central American and ask, "What about me?"

This sense of grievance may also be related to the increases in opioid addiction, overdoses, and suicide. Although a recent study argued that the supply of these drugs is a more significant cause than despair itself (Florida, 2018), just on the face of it, one would think that despair is probably a factor, although evidence supporting this has yet to emerge. On this point, a recent study linked chronic opioid use with a preference for Donald Trump in the 2016 presidential election, and Trump's campaign most assuredly fanned the flames of working-class resentment (Goodwin, Kuo, Brown, Juurlink, & Raji, 2018).

The Role of Masculinity

Working-class men have been found to endorse traditional masculinity ideology more strongly than men in higher social classes (Wimer & Levant, 2013). Adherence to masculinity exacerbates these men's difficult situations in two major ways. The first is the role it plays in their unwillingness to consider jobs in fast-growing service fields that are thought of as feminine, the so-called pink-collar jobs, such as in health care, child care, elder care, education, bookkeeping, sales, and food preparation—endeavors some of which are performed as the unpaid work of housewives. Rosin (2012) noted that of the 30 occupations expected to grow fastest in America in the coming years, women dominate 20: "The list of working-class jobs predicted to grow is heavy on nurturing professions, in which women, ironically, seem to benefit from old stereotypes" (p. 64). These old stereotypes are deeply ingrained in the minds of the men they marginalize; they do not see jobs centered on serving or caring as something for them. This might put men of low socioeconomic status at a disadvantage by limiting their employment options. Lupton (2000, p. 38) noted that men who do decide to enter into the female-dominated workplace experience threats to their masculinity in three ways: (a) an inability to "regenerate" their masculinity in a homosocial place of employment; (b) the fear of feminization; and (c) fear of being called gay.

Domingue et al. (2009) recently reported the results of a longitudinal study, using data from National Longitudinal Study of Adolescent to Adult Health (Add Health), which enrolled a cohort of nationally representative school students aged 11–19 years from across the USA and followed them up for 14 years. Their conclusions (p. e420):

> More masculine male respondents were downwardly mobile; they were enrolled in school for fewer years and were more likely to have lower status jobs than their less masculine same-sex school peers. [They] . . .were also more likely to have jobs in occupational categories with larger proportions of males than their same-sex school peers. Gendered behaviour was not predictive of future educational and occupational attainment for female respondents.

Nixon (2009) interviewed 35 unemployed low-skilled men in the United Kingdom on their attitudes toward entry-level service work. Manual labor and interacting with other men in an all-male environment where they could swear, shout, and engage in masculine horseplay were sources of pride for many working-class men. Further, Nixon found that entry-level service work requires skills and attitudes that are antithetical to working-class men's adherence to masculinity—specifically, the need for men to act more docile and courteous to customers and their female co-workers, which they were unwilling to do, leading them to reject many forms of low-skilled service work as a future source of employment. Here are a couple of these men's statements.

> "I've got no patience with people basically. I can't put a smiley face on, that's not my sort of thing." (Colin, aged 24, unskilled manual worker; p. 315)

"Sales assistant, no, rule that out completely. . . . I suppose I'd be fright-
ened by it, never done anything like that before . . . services, it's not my cup
of tea really. . . . I think I wouldn't be good at it. Wouldn't have confidence
in it." (Jim, aged 45, former sewing machine mechanic; pp. 313–314)

We need to help working-class men come to understand and accept that traditional well-paying factory jobs are not coming back and that they can be nurses
or sales clerk and still be men.

The second way that masculinity exacerbates these men's difficulties is the role it
plays in their unwillingness to play a greater role in family work, including childcare
and housework, which might enable their employed wives to earn more, again because childcare and housework are thought of as feminine activities. According to "The
Weaker Sex" (2015), "American men without jobs spend only half as much time on
housework and caring for others as do women in the same situation, and much more
time watching television." Interestingly, Yavorsky, Cohen, and Qian (2016) found that
racial minority men are more likely than White men to occupy female-dominated
jobs at all levels of education—except highly educated Asian/Pacific Islander men—
and that these patterns are more pronounced at lower levels of education.

A ray of hope for White working-class men comes from a study done in the
United Kingdom. Roberts (2012) interviewed 24 young men employed in the
retail sector, finding (surprisingly) that young White working-class men were
able to resist traditional masculinity ideology. Participants demonstrated a more
positive attitude toward the "emotional labor" required in the service sector
than has been previously documented, while also rejecting notions of traditional
gendered domestic responsibilities as potential partners and parents. Roberts
(2012) concluded: "Congruent with other emerging research in this area, the
reference point for an 'acceptable' masculine identity appears to have shifted,
with some young working-class men's lives, at least, illustrating an attenuated or
softened version of masculinity" (p. 671).

To explore this topic in depth would require expertise in labor economics and
sociology, which is outside of our scope, so we do not have a separate chapter on
the role of masculinity in the economic stagnation of working-class men. It will
suffice to have included it here, as part of our discussion of the present moment
and masculinity crisis.

The Role of Masculinity in Men's Health, Mental Health, and Trauma

Men's health is a long-standing problem, which, surprisingly, has a low sense of
urgency, and thus it cannot be considered a part of the higher profile movements

that have created the present masculinity crisis. And this is despite the fact that there is some evidence that men's health is getting worse of late relative to women's. For example, the relative life expectancy of males as compared to females decreased 0.2 year from 2015 to 2016 (Kochanek, Murphy, Xu, & Arias, 2017). However, since it is such a serious problem, we have decided to take Rahm Emanuel's famous advice offered in the wake of the 2008 Great Recession to never let a good crisis go to waste and take advantage of the masculinity crisis to bring these issues to the forefront in the discussion.

Physical Health

Worldwide, there are significant gender gaps in morbidity and mortality, with men generally dying earlier and at a faster rate than women from various diseases (Gough & Robertson, 2017). Overall, men die 5 years earlier than women in the United States (Kochanek et al., 2017). With regard to specific causes, American men are 2.1 times more likely to die from liver disease than women and 2.7 times more likely to die from HIV/AIDS (National Center for Health Statistics, 2017). Thus, improving men's access, ability, and, above all, willingness to utilize health care is essential. Although some of these gender discrepancies may relate to biological factors, many of them are due to social and psychological variables. For men of color or sexual/gender minority men, the lack of access to good health care could be a major factor impacting their physical health, on top of the incentives to engage in health risk behaviors that masculinity creates. Importantly, there are proven relationships between men's masculinity and engaging in behaviors that put their health at risk. For example, a recent study found that for young White men, the endorsement of traditional masculinity ideology was linked with expectations of benefits from consuming highly caffeinated energy drinks, which, in turn, was linked with energy drink consumption, which finally was linked with sleep disturbance symptoms (Levant, Parent, McCurdy, & Bradstreet, 2015). We will discuss men's physical health in depth in Chapter 7.

Mental Health

Furthermore, boys and men experience the full gamut of mental health problems, in some diagnostic categories, more than girls and women and in others, less. The details will be discussed in Chapter 7. For now it is important to note that boys and men have considerable needs for mental health services, but many do not avail themselves of these services. Once again there are relationships between masculinity and negative opinions about seeking help for health issues (Addis & Hoffman, 2017). Specifically two aspects of masculinity are theorized to play a role in men's reluctance to seek physical and mental health care. One is the obligation to be self-reliant to the point of not needing help from anyone. The second is the mandate to never reveal vulnerability to anyone. Additionally, a mistrust of the mental health profession might also impact whether racial/ ethnic and sexual orientation/gender identity minority men pursue mental health care.

Trauma

The notion that men experience trauma is seldom entertained, with the exception of combat trauma. While combat trauma is indeed a terrible experience that afflicts both men and women, very few conversations are occurring about men's experiences with interpersonal trauma. Such trauma can consist of bullying, domestic/intimate partner violence, and sexual assault, three crimes usually associated with female victims. While women indeed make up the majority of victims in both of these crimes, men are also victims.

Many people do not believe that male rape is possible. This is clearly wrong— witness men's allegations as part of #MeToo that Kevin Spacey sexually abused them. Even less believed is the idea that men can be victims of domestic violence. This is, in part, because of the heteronormative assumption that couples can only be heterosexual and because people make the sexist assumption that women cannot physically hurt men. Additionally, research on sexual trauma and domestic violence does not give enough attention to the experiences of men in the LGBTQ community. This population is at risk because not only do they have to contend with being men, they also have to deal with discrimination from being gay, transgender, or queer. Recently, a few battered male shelters have opened their doors to find that many men are, indeed, in need of a shelter. It is worth noting that masculinity also plays a role in the skeptical way that other men, women, and society at large have viewed men who claimed to be victims of these tragedies. But, most important, the adherence to masculinity leaves many male survivors of these traumas reluctant to seek treatment and a supportive environment in which to heal. This topic too will be taken up in Chapter 7.

Many Masculinities

Since masculinity is a social construction and there are many different cultural and demographic groups in the United States, there are many masculinities. Thus, the question is, How do men with different identities based on age/ generational cohort, race/ethnicity, sexual orientation, gender identity, educational level (from some high school to college degree and beyond) respond to the question: "What does it mean to me to be a man today?" Another way of saying this, using the perspective of intersectionality (Crenshaw, 1991), is that a person's identity reflects not only their gender but also their race, ethnicity, social class, educational attainment, sexual orientation, age/developmental stage/generational cohort, religion, and ability status. Further, since we (unfortunately) live in a society with many "–isms," such as sexism, racism, heterosexism, agism, antisemitism, and Islamophobia, certain identities are marginalized or stigmatized. Thus, a person can have a privileged identity, such as man or White, and a marginalized identity, such as gay or woman, respectively.

Examples

For example, in regard to race/ethnicity we know that African American men viewed themselves as hindered in meeting traditional masculine norms by the systemic barriers resulting from racism, a phenomenon termed "racist gender role strain" (Rogers, Sperry, & Levant, 2015, p. 420). Due to racist gender role strain, African American men constructed a culturally unique version of masculinity and created strategies to develop identities as men. They also viewed their masculinity in a broader frame than traditional masculine norms to also include family, community, and spiritual emphases. For one thing, because the "good provider" role is impeded for Black men by racist barriers to education and employment, the masculine role of provision has been expanded to include emotional nurturance of family members.

With regard to age, how do older men (e.g., baby boomers) differ from younger men (Gen X, Gen Y, the millennials)? Anecdotally, it appears that among college educated men, millennial men differ from boomer men in at least two ways: As fathers, they are much more engaged as hands-on parents, and they have less sexual prejudice. We will discuss in detail some of what is known about different masculinities in Chapter 8.

Solutions

How can we help men who feel that they have no other choice than to be masculine and whose lives are the worse for it? In Chapter 9, we will examine a number of sources to help free men from the prison of masculinity. These include feminist, progressive, permissive, and positive masculinities; large-group awareness training; social marketing and public service announcements; gender-neutral parenting; academic sources; and psychotherapy. We will end with a case study of a man who "felt nothing" about his impending paternity.

About the Book

We present our case in several ways. The first is an overarching conceptual/the-oretical narrative, utilizing theories in the psychology of men and masculinities. Second, we draw on decades of research in the psychological, and to a lesser ex-tent in the interdisciplinary, study of men and masculinities. Although we have endeavored to tap the best studies in the field, we have tended to draw more from those arising from Ron Levant's research lab, simply because we are more familiar with them. We take you "under the hood" of the more iconic studies, explaining in accessible language what the investigators were trying to get at, how the study was conducted, the results, and what they mean. We discuss re-search investigations conducted at various times during the last 30-plus years. While we understand that older information may not be as credible as newer data, offering older information alongside the new information will show that some of these problems have been identified a long time ago and still have not been fully addressed. As the reader has seen in this chapter, we do discuss some statistics, which is the language of psychological science. However, we have endeavored to make the general presentation as accessible as we possibly can, while footnoting more detailed information for readers with greater statistical knowledge. Ideally, we would join such a review of theories and research with actual data, such as interviews with perpetrators. This is not feasible, so we draw on journalistic accounts of sexual and gun violence and other topics to com-plete the circle, showing the role that masculinity played in contemporary so-cial problems. We also use clinical case material to illustrate some of the points. Thus, we will combine professional and popular sources, much as we have done in this chapter.

2

Theories of Gender and How Masculinity Is Measured

Imagine what it was like for the psychology of men pioneers at the beginning of this field, during the emergence of the modern feminist movement. This was in the late 1960's and early 1970's, after *The Feminine Mystique* had been published and before *Ms. Magazine* was launched. Scholars like Joseph Pleck, Robert Brannon, James Harrison, Robert Staples and Jack Sawyer might have received pushback when they suggested a new psychology of men. Critics might have said: "What do you mean, a new psychology of men? Isn't all psychology the psychology of men?" And the critics would have had a great point, for psychology has long exclusively used males, and White males at that (Guthrie, 2004), in the iconic longitudinal studies of personality and development conducted by such giants in the field as Jerome Kagan and Paul Mussen. The difference was back then males were taken as proxies for the entire species, whereas the new psychology of men wanted to study the effects of men's gender. Furthermore, as we will shortly discuss, there was a dearth of good tools (theory, scales) to work with at that time.

Thus, it is important to provide some background on the psychology of gender, particularly on the evolution of theoretical frameworks regarding the psychology of gender. Hence, we will first discuss the older gender role identity paradigm (GRIP) and the early measures of gender that arose from that perspective. We will then introduce the more modern view of gender called the gender role strain paradigm, the different forms of gender role strain that are proposed by this paradigm, and current definitions and ways to measure various aspects of masculinity. We will conclude this chapter with a discussion of the controversial topic of toxic masculinity and then provide a careful qualification of what seems to account for masculinity's harmful correlates.

Gender Role Identity Paradigm

The GRIP drew from psychoanalytic theory and reigned for approximately 50 years, from about 1930 to 1980. It has been traced back to Terman and Miles (1936), who described masculinity and femininity as essentially immutable sex differences rooted in biology: "The belief is all but universal that men and women as contrasting groups display characteristic sex differences in their behavior, and that these differences are so deep seated and pervasive as to lend distinctive character to the entire personality" (pp. 1–2).

Thus, the GRIP assumed that people have a very strong psychological need to create a gender identity that matches their biological sex, which for boys was masculinity, and that optimal personality development depended on the successful appearance of that identity. Hence, psychology regarded the adoption of masculinity as essential to a boy's healthy development. The extent to which this "inherent," essential need was met was determined by how completely a person adopted their traditional gender role. The father's role in the family, also considered essential, was to model masculinity and heterosexuality for his son(s). From such a perspective, the development of appropriate gender role identity was viewed as a failure-prone process, and failure for men to achieve a masculine gender role identity was thought to result in homosexuality, negative attitudes toward women, and/or defensive hypermasculinity (Pleck, 1981). This paradigm sprung from the belief that biological sex determines gender.

Early Gender Scales

One popular early scale to measure gender was the Mf scale of the Minnesota Multiphasic Personality Inventory. The Mf scale was unidimensional and bipolar, with masculinity at one pole and femininity on the other. Thus, masculinity was defined as the opposite of femininity. The aim at the time was to ferret out homosexuality in males, which until 1973 was defined by the American Psychiatric Association as a psychological disorder. To illustrate this perspective, I (RL) in the past have used an older film on activity group therapy for boys in my group therapy course. This film depicts 14 boys in a woodshop-like room in a child guidance clinic and notes that 11 had been referred to the clinic for "effeminate behavior." We mention this to show that in the ethos of the 1940s and 1950s parents feared homosexuality in their sons, in the same way that we might fear a terrible childhood illness today, and that this heterosexism influenced how people thought about masculinity.

A shift came in the 1960s, with the development of the Bem Sex Role Inventory and the Personal Attributes Questionnaire, both of which conceptualized

masculinity and femininity in a multidimensional way—specifically as two related but distinct dimensions, in which it was possible to score high on both, a
result that was termed "androgynous." On the Bem inventory, participants were
asked to what extent a series of personality traits were true of them on a 7-point
scale, ranging from 1 (*never or almost never true*) to 7 (*always or almost always
true*). The traits for the most part represented stereotypical masculine (e.g., self-
reliant) and feminine (e.g., yielding) personality traits.

The Gender Role Strain Paradigm

During the 1970s and 1980s, a major change occurred in the psychology of
gender. Feminist scholarship on the psychology of women developed a new perspective that viewed gender roles as socially constructed, rooted in structural
power differences between men and women (Deaux, 1984; Unger, 1979). As
Gerdes (2018) pointed out, these scholars drew on earlier work by sociologists
such as Talcott Parsons and anthropologists like Margaret Mead who introduced
the idea that different cultures had different gender-based expectations for behavior. Joseph Pleck (1981) applied these insights to men in his landmark book,
The Myth of Masculinity. There, he formulated the sex role strain paradigm (later
termed the gender role strain paradigm [GRSP]; Pleck, 1995). The GRSP
is the major theoretical paradigm in the field of the psychology of men and
masculinities (Cochran, 2010; Wong, Steinfeldt, Speight, & Hickman, 2010).
I (RL) got an early boost in my work in this field in 1980, when I undertook a
postdoctoral research fellowship at the Wellesley College Center for Research
on Women with Pleck.

The GRSP views gender as socially constructed roles that arise from, and
serve to protect, the patriarchal social order. Traditional gender roles, therefore, undergird power differences between men and women by defining masculinity as dominance and aggression and femininity as submissiveness and
nurturance (Levant, 1996). According to social constructionism, masculinity
and femininity are thought of as scripts for the performance of gender, which
are independent of biological sex (West & Zimmerman, 2009). Hence, women
can perform masculinity, men can perform femininity, and both sexes can perform any combination and permutation of these gender roles (Butler, 1990).
Yet, within a patriarchal society, there are tangible rewards associated with
conforming to traditional gender roles as well as negative consequences associated with failure to conform (Pleck, 1981, 1995). Over time, traditional
gendered performances become normative and compulsory and are baked into
everything from the neural networks of individual persons to social interactions
(Fausto-Sterling, 2000).

Pleck (1981) proffered the GRSP as an alternative to the older paradigm, after providing a convincing demonstration that the GRIP not only poorly accounted for the observed data in many highly respected iconic studies on personality development, but also that such studies often arbitrarily reinterpreted the meaning of the data to provide support for the GRIP. Pleck (1981) put forth a set of theoretical propositions for the GRSP: Gender roles are defined by gender stereotypes and norms and, although they are contradictory and inconsistent, they define the dominant position of men across social contexts. The proportion of persons who violate their gender norms is high, and violation of the expected norms can lead to social condemnation and negative psychological consequences. Actual or imagined sanctions for violating gender norms leads some people to overconform to them. Violating gender norms has more severe consequences for males than for females. Certain prescribed gender norms (such as male aggression) are often dysfunctional. Each sex experiences gender role strain in its paid work and family roles. Historical change causes gender role strain.

Since the original formulation of the GRSP in 1981, there have been several clarifications. First, Pleck (1995) indicated that, although they were not explicitly mentioned in the original propositions, gender ideologies are central to the GRSP and a "vital co-factor in male role strain" (Pleck, 1995, p. 19). The term "gender ideologies" refers to culture-based beliefs about appropriate gender relations and performances. The dominant gender ideologies in a given society define the norms for gender practices. They therefore influence how parents, teachers, coaches, peers, and society-at-large socialize children and, consequently, how children think, feel, and behave in regard to gender-salient matters (Levant, 1996; Pleck, Sonenstein, & Ku, 1994a). Hence, the first proposition of the GRSP should be modified to read: Gender roles are operationally defined by gender stereotypes and norms, *which in turn are defined by the dominant gender ideologies in a given society.*

Second, while the original theory implied a social psychological foundation for gender socialization, namely social learning theory (Pleck, 1981), Levant (2011) explicitly framed the GRSP in social psychological terms, using social cognition and social influence theories and the constructs of gender roles and social norms. Thus, in the current formulation, the dominant masculinity ideology is theorized to exert social influence resulting in reinforcement of behavior consistent with local masculinity norms, punishment of behavior that violates these norms, and observational learning of masculine behavior. The pervasive masculinity ideology thus informs, encourages, and constrains boys and men to conform to (or comply with, or obey) the prevailing masculinity norms (both descriptive and injunctive) by adopting socially sanctioned (prescribed) behaviors and avoiding certain forbidden (proscribed) behaviors.

Types of Gender Role Strain

The GRSP further theorized that imposing gender roles on developing children, whose personalities may not fit their assigned gender roles (e.g., some girls are aggressive; some boys are nurturant) leads to strain. To elaborate, any personality trait, such as aggression (a male stereotyped trait) or nurturance (a female stereotyped trait), is distributed throughout the population so that some children are high on that trait, some are low, and most are in the middle. Many children's personalities do not match their gender's stereotyped personality traits. In those cases, forcing the child to conform their personality to their gender stereotype can be tremendously damaging and must be viewed as an act of great cruelty. There are three types of gender role strain: discrepancy, dysfunction, and trauma strain (Pleck, 1995).

Discrepancy Strain

Discrepancy strain results when one fails to live up to one's internalized manhood ideal, which often closely approximates traditional norms. Discrepancy strain has been theorized to result in low self-esteem among men, although evidence to support this proposition has been elusive (Rummell & Levant, 2014).

Dysfunction Strain

Dysfunction strain results when one fulfills the requirements of the masculine norms, because many of the characteristics viewed as desirable in men can have negative side effects on the men themselves and on others, including those close to them. Here are a couple of examples. First, the masculine norm of restricting the expression of emotions (termed "restrictive emotionality") has been linked to a clinical condition known as alexithymia, which literally means "without words for emotions" (Levant, Wong, Karakis, & Welch, 2015). We will discuss in Chapter 3 of this volume how the socialization of a boy's emotional expression can lead to alexithymia and the role that alexithymia plays in violence. Second, the masculine norms of toughness and being aggressive obviously play a role in violence, as does the norm of dominance in intimate partner violence. Less obviously (as will be elucidated in Chapter 6 of this volume), the masculine norm of avoiding all things feminine plays a central role in sexual violence.

Trauma Strain

The concept of trauma strain was initially applied to certain groups of men whose experiences with gender role strain were thought to be particularly harsh.

This includes professional athletes, men of color, combat veterans, and survivors of child abuse. It is also recognized that gay, bisexual, and transgender men are normatively traumatized by gender role strain by virtue of growing up in a heterosexist society. Beyond the recognition that certain classes of men may experience trauma strain, a perspective on the masculine socialization process emerged in the mid-1990s (Levant & Pollack, 1995) that viewed socialization under traditional masculinity ideology (TMI) as inherently traumatic, particularly in those socialization practices that force boys to be masculine using fear- and shame-based strategies. We will illustrate this more fully in Chapter 3 of this volume, where we discuss the effects of gender role socialization on boys.

Masculinity and How It Is Measured

In the perspective of the GRSP, masculinity is a set of cultural expectations for how boys and men should think, feel, and behave. These cultural expectations are shared broadly by people of all genders. Since masculinity is based in culture and there are many different subcultures in the United States, there are potentially many masculinities. We mentioned in Chapter 1 of this volume the racist gender role strain masculinity found among African American men. In addition, in the Latinx community there are two prominent versions—the family-oriented and chivalrous (but benevolently sexist) *caballerismo* and the aggressive, hostile sexist, and hypermasculine *machismo* (Arciniega, Anderson, Tovar-Blank, &Tracey, 2008; Ojeda & Piña, 2014). We will return to this topic in Chapter 8.

Furthermore, although it is certainly not easy, it is possible for boys and men to opt to not conform to—by actively resisting—masculine norms (e.g., Way et al., 2014) or to pick and choose which masculine norms to conform to and how they will conform. One form that this may take is "hybrid masculinities," defined as privileged "men's selective incorporation of performances and identity elements associated with marginalized and subordinated masculinities and femininities," such as those of sexual minorities (Bridges & Pascoe, 2014, p. 246). Another example is "inclusive masculinities." Drawing on various male-oriented settings (e.g., sports teams, fraternities), Anderson (2005, 2011) argued that cultural homophobia is declining, with boys and young men shown to be comfortable in having close emotional ties and expressing physical affection to other males, having positive attitudes toward gay men, and even going so far as to stigmatize homophobic comments.

Despite this potential diversity, there is one dominant masculinity in the United States that had reigned largely unopposed prior to the feminist movement of the late 1960s. However, because it is important to take culture into account, this dominant masculinity must be qualified as White, post–World

War II, Christian, cisgender,[1] heterosexual masculinity. This should be no surprise, since White is the dominant race, Christianity is the dominant religion, cisgender is the dominant gender identity, and heterosexuality is the dominant sexual orientation in the United States. The dominant masculinity remains so deeply ingrained in U.S. culture that all boys and men, regardless of race, ethnicity, religion, gender identity, sexual orientation, or any other dimension of diversity, must contend with it at some level. This version of masculinity goes by several names—traditional, hegemonic, patriarchal, or stereotypical.

The term "traditional masculinity ideology" is used more often by psychologists, whereas the term "hegemonic masculinity" is used more often by sociologists (e.g., Connell & Messerschmidt, 2005). Both constructs arise from a feminist social scientific perspective. Whereas hegemonic masculinity refers to practices that promote the dominant position of privileged men vis-à-vis subordinate and marginalized men, and the subordinate position of all women in society, TMI refers to the cultural beliefs regarding the norms that inform and sustain men's practices. The other two terms are used less frequently. In this book when we refer to masculinity we are talking about TMI.

TMI is operationally defined and measured in several closely related scales. The foundational version of a TMI scale, developed by the psychologist David Brannon (Brannon & Juni, 1984), is the Brannon Masculinity Scale (BMS), which specified four norms: that men should not be feminine ("no sissy stuff"); that men should strive to be respected for successful achievement ("the big wheel"); that men should never show weakness ("the sturdy oak"); and that men should seek adventure and risk, even accepting violence if necessary ("give 'em hell").

A current version, the Male Role Norms Inventory–Short Form (MRNI-SF), which has undergone several revisions from its original version that was derived in part from the Brannon Masculinity Scale, specifies seven norms: avoidance of femininity, negativity toward sexual minorities, self-reliance through mechanical skills, toughness, dominance, importance of sex, and restrictive emotionality (Levant, Hall, & Rankin, 2013).

The BMS, MRNI-SF, and other similar scales (such as the Male Role Norms Scale; Thompson & Pleck, 1986) are measures of TMI. They ask respondents to indicate to what extent they agree or disagree (from *strongly agree* to *strongly disagree*) with statements about how men ought or ought not to think, feel, and behave on scales ranging from zero to 4 or 1 to 7, a format that is used in most of the other scales mentioned in the following discussion. A sample item from the MRNI-SF is "Men should be detached in emotionally charged situations."

---

[1] The term "cisgender" refers to people whose gender identity matches the sex they were assigned at birth. This is in contrast to transgender or gender nonconforming people, whose gender identity either does not match the sex assigned at birth or is variable, fluid, and nonbinary.

Another widely used scale measures the extent to which participants conform to traditional masculine norms, the Conformity to Masculine Norms Inventory (CMNI; Mahalik et al., 2003). Instead of assessing beliefs, as does the MRNI-SF, the CMNI assesses self-concept. The original CMNI specified 11 norms: winning, emotional control, risk-taking, violence, dominance, playboy, self-reliance, primacy of work, power over women, disdain for homosexuality, and pursuit of status. A sample item is "Taking dangerous risks helps me to prove myself."

Two other scales tap the "strain" aspect of gender role strain. The most widely used scale in the psychology of men and masculinities is the Gender Role Conflict Scale (GRCS; O'Neil, 2008). Men's gender role conflict was hypothesized to result from masculine gender role socialization and to be experienced in men's interpersonal, career, family, and health lives. The GRCS measure four patterns of gender role conflict: success, power, and competition; restrictive emotionality; restrictive affectionate behavior between men; and conflict between work and family relations. A sample item is "Verbally expressing my love to another man is difficult for me." Finally, there is the Masculine Gender Role Stress Scale (MGRSS; Eisler & Skidmore, 1987). Masculine gender role stress refers to men's tendency to experience negative psychological (e.g., insecurity, low self-esteem, increased anger) and physiological effects (e.g., increased cardiovascular reactivity and skin conductance) from their attempts to meet societally based standards of the male role. The MGRSS has five subscales: physical inadequacy, emotional inexpressiveness, subordination to women, intellectual inferiority, and performance failure. Unlike the other scales we have just described, this scale asks participants how stressful situations that violate masculine norms would be for them on a 6-point scale ranging from *not stressful* to *extremely stressful*. A sample item is "Being outperformed at work by a woman." It can be argued that the MGRSS is a measure of discrepancy strain, because it asks men to imagine themselves in situations discrepant from their internalized manhood ideal.

Problems with the Term "Toxic Masculinity"

Before we leave the topic of defining and measuring masculinity we want to critique the term "toxic masculinity," which is increasingly used in the popular media. The other terms (traditional, hegemonic, patriarchal, stereotypical) have scientific definitions and scales to measure them, and although there is some variation as previously noted in regard to the measurement of traditional masculinity, there is considerable overlap. On the other hand, "toxic masculinity" is a mostly a popular term that is defined differently depending on the author's purpose. Here are several definitions from media sources:

Toxic masculinity is built on two fundamental pillars: *sexual conquest* and *violence*—qualities men regale as manly and virtuous. (Douglas, 2017)

Toxic masculinity is thus defined by adherence to traditional male gender roles that *restrict the kinds of emotions* allowable for boys and men to express, including social expectations that men seek to be *dominant* (the "alpha male") and limit their emotional range primarily to expressions of *anger*. ("Toxic Masculinity," n.d.[a])

A social science term that describes narrow repressive type of ideas about the male gender role, that defines masculinity as exaggerated masculine traits like being *violent, unemotional, sexually aggressive,* and so forth. Also suggests that men who act too emotional or maybe aren't violent enough or don't do all of the things that "real men" do, can get their "man card" taken away. ("Toxic Masculinity," n.d.[b])

My definition of toxic masculinity is actions or beliefs that define manhood in such contrast to femininity as to *reject and despise all things that are or are perceived to be feminine* in such a way that it becomes harmful to men and those around them. (Carley, 2018)

Toxic masculinity concerns those things that describe what it is to be a man, often things that are bad, *violent* or *aggressive.* . . . Men say that in order "to be celebrated, you need to be *tough*; you need to be *emotionless.*" (Gbadamosi, 2018)

Toxic masculinity . . . dictates that men should be *stoic* and *strong,* both *emotionally* and *physically.* (Petter, 2018)

In addition, the term has entered the professional literature. Here are two examples:

"Toxic masculinity is the constellation of socially regressive male traits that serve to foster *domination, the devaluation of women, homophobia, and wanton violence.*" (Kupers, 2005, p. 714)

Toxic masculinity is characterized by a *drive to dominate* and by *endorsement of misogynistic and homophobic views.* (Parent, Gobble, & Rochlen, 2018[2])

---

[2] Parent et al. (2018) measured toxic masculinity using three subscales of the CMNI (46-item version) that had high intercorrelations. However, only one of these (misogynistic attitudes) overlapped with the six subscales of the CMNI (94-item version) identified by Gerdes and Levant (2017) as "mostly associated with negative outcomes"—emotional control, violence, power over women, dominance, playboy, and self-reliance (p. 237).

If the reader looks over the italicized words, these several definitions of toxic masculinity taken together mention many of the norms of TMI. Given that, there seems to be no point to using the modifier "toxic." In fact it is misleading, because it implies that masculinity itself is not problematic, which is not the case.

What Is Problematic About Masculinity?

Masculinity is indeed problematic, in at least three ways. In our view, the central problem is that most boys and men are made to feel that they *must* act in ways consistent with their gender. That is, masculinity is presented as obligatory for most boys and men, and most boys and men feel they have no other choice but to conform to masculine norms. This is not true for other gender ideologies, such as femininity ideology. As we will discuss, girls and women are given much more flexibility and latitude when it comes to their performance of gender than are boys and men. Another problem is that the term "masculinity" itself serves to divide people. It elevates some people and marginalizes or "otherizes" other people. For one thing, gender is conventionally viewed as a binary (men, women), so being masculine means not being feminine, thus otherizing femininity.[3] Furthermore, the otherizing is apparent when you look at the definition of hegemonic masculinity, which is defined as a vehicle to keep men dominant over women, and White Christian cisgender straight men dominant over men of color, non-Christian men, and men of different gender and sexual orientation identities (Connell & Messerschmidt, 2005). A third problem is that the major masculinity constructs (TMI, conformity to masculine norms, gender role conflict and gender role stress) are associated with a broad range of harmful outcomes, a topic which will be discussed in detail in Chapter 5 of this volume.

Are We Saying That Masculinity Is All or Always Bad?

Although these problems are real and quite serious, *that does not mean that masculinity is all or always bad*. Indeed, it is not. There are circumstances under which some traditional masculinity norms that have been associated with negative outcomes can be positive, such as emotional control during a crisis, or aggression during a war. In addition there are some masculinity attributes that are inherently positive. This first appeared in the Positive Psychology Positive Masculinity movement, which affirmed the prosocial aspects of traditional masculinity norms. Kiselica and Englar-Carlson (2010) have suggested that

---

[3] We are indebted to Professor Michael Addis of Clark University for this insight.

clinicians apply positive psychology principles in psychotherapy with boys and men. A goal of this framework is to help boys and men learn to embrace healthy and constructive aspects of masculinity.

However, until recently, investigators have not explicitly tested whether the attributes associated with positive masculinity in fact represented cultural expectations for boys' and men's thoughts, feelings, and behaviors. McDermott et al. (2019) explored whether 79 potential positive masculinity attributes were perceived as both positive and socially expected of men (as contrasted with negative and expected of women). Of the 79 items, all but 3 were strongly rated as positive, 32 were expected more of men, 36 were expected more of women, and 11 were gender neutral. Many definitions of positive masculinity in the literature correctly represented positive social expectations of men, such as male service, bravery, honesty, loyalty, wisdom, provider, protector, and generative fathering. On the other hand, nearly all positive relational attributes (e.g., considerate, dependable, polite, encouraging and fair) were expected more of women than of men, suggesting that some interpersonal characteristics labeled as positive masculinity in prior literature may not represent gendered expectations of men in the broader culture. In addition, some attributes identified as both positive and expected of men in McDermott and colleagues (2018) study represent moderate expressions of traditional masculinity norms, a point that will become very important shortly.

However, we would be remiss if we did not issue a caution here. McDermott (personal communication, February 23, 2019) thinks that there may be a continuum with respect to masculinity. On one end, you have the misogynistic and homophobic TMI norms, which as we will shortly discuss is where we find the linkages with harmful outcomes. On the other end of the continuum, you have a pro-feminist identity, which as we will also shortly discuss, is very underdeveloped for men. McDermott et al. (2018) uncovered beliefs about social norms for men that fall somewhere between these two poles. One of their other highest loadings items was an expectation that men should respect women. Of course, that could also be benevolent sexism, as in the Latinx *caballerismo*. Additional research that closely examines the correlates of the McDermott et al. norms will help us answer this question.

Do Most Men Endorse Masculinity Norms?

It may come as a surprise to some readers, but most men do not strongly endorse TMI. Studies reported over the 16-year period from 1997 to 2013 using several successive versions of the MRNI assessed men's endorsement of TMI (Levant et al., 2003; Levant, Hall, & Rankin, 2013; Levant & Majors, 1997; Levant, Rankin, Williams, Hasan, & Smalley, 2010). These studies indicate that men (primarily White heterosexual U.S. college students, as is typical of most studies of this kind[4]) rejected most of the operationalized norms.[5] Norm rejection was defined as the average or mean score of all of the men in a given study being less than the neutral score. The neutral score represents neither endorsement nor rejection (e.g., 4 on a 7-point Likert scale, in which higher scores indicate greater endorsement. For example, Levant et al. (2010) reported mean scores and standard deviations for the total scale and subscale scores of the MRNI–Revised. This is shown in Table 2.1 in the Appendix, where it can be seen that the total scale score and 4 of the 7 subscale scores were less than 4. Thus most of the men sampled did not endorse most of the traditional norms. As noted, these results draw on the opinions of college students to represent mean (average) scores and these data tend to be nonnormally distributed, skewed toward the lower end. However, a substantial minority of men do endorse traditional norms, and some do so quite strongly. This is illustrated in Figure 2.1 (see Appendix), which shows the distribution of the scores of over 1,000 men on the MRNI-SF. The distribution is skewed to the lower end, in which the bulk of scores is below the neutral score of 4. The mean score was 3.40, the median score, at the exact midpoint of the distribution at which half the scores are higher and half lower, was 3.38, and the mode, or most frequent score, was 1. However, a not insubstantial minority scored above the mean.

Do Most Men Conform to Masculine Norms?

For comparison's sake, we also investigated the extent to which men conformed to masculine norms, using the CMNI, as previously described. As already noted, the GRSP posits that *most* men violate the norms, rather than conform to them. The evidence tends to support a weaker version of this statement—namely, that *many* men violate the norms. This is illustrated in Figure 2.2 in the Appendix, which shows the distribution of the scores of over 1,500 men on the CMNI. The distribution is less skewed to the lower end than that for the MRNI-SF. The scale scores run from 1 (*strongly disagree*) to 6 (*strongly agree*). The mean score was 3.65, slightly above the neutral point of 3.5, the median score was 3.66, and the mode, or most frequent score, was 4.

Thus, it appears based on these two samples that slightly more men report that they conform to masculine norms than do those who say they endorse TMI; however, in both cases, large percentages of men say they do not endorse

---

[4] One of the studies had a U.S. Black sample (Levant & Majors, 1997), and another had a Russian White sample (Levant et al., 2003), but for the sake of consistency we report only the data for U.S. White men.

[5] They either rejected 4 out of 7 norms or 3 out of 5 norms, depending on the version of the scale used in the study.

or conform to traditional norms. We think that there is a common sense explanation for these results. Although most boys are expected to conform to traditional masculinity norms, most adult men come to accept who they are, even if they do not meet all of the masculinity ideals. Masculinity is, after all, a tough standard! That is, they come to terms with the messages from their childhoods and recognize that their unique personalities do not fit or need to fit the ideal in all ways.

What Accounts for Masculinity's Destructive Correlates?

Although we have yet to delve into the roles that masculinity plays in sexual and gun/physical violence and other social problems, we can make a statement based on this analysis of MRNI and CMNI scores. The research that we will review in subsequent chapters will show that one or another masculinity scale is correlated with one or another negative outcome related to sexual and/or physical violence and/or men's health. This occurs in one of two ways: Scores on the masculinity scale are shown to be correlated with either higher scores on a negative outcome, or lower scores on a positive outcome. Thus higher scores on the masculinity scale will be associated with more negative and less positive outcomes. Hence, we make this *very important qualification* about masculinity's harmful effects: Masculinity's destructive outcomes arise from those men in the upper tail of the distribution of the masculinity scale—those who endorse TMI, or conform to masculine norms, or experience gender role conflict or stress to the greatest extent. And, although we have not yet explicitly tested this, extrapolating from another study that examined fathers' expectations for their sons' masculinity (Levant, Gerdes, Alto, Jadaszewski, & McDermott, 2016), we also think that the harmful effects are due to high scorers being quite rigid in regard to their endorsement of TMI and their conformity to masculine norms.

To provide some preliminary confirmation of this hypothesis, we first circle back to the McDermott et al. (2018) study, which found that some attributes identified as both positive and masculine represent moderate expressions of traditional masculine norms, implying that the high scores account for masculinity's problematic aspects. Second, we return to the topic of toxic masculinity. While we have shown that this is a popular/media construct, one without a stable definition, one article (Carley, 2018) suggests that toxic masculinity is defined by high levels of masculinity adhered to rigidly:

> Many things associated with traditional masculinity have great value. If you enjoy sports, play them, follow them, and participate either as a player or a fan. But, if you ridicule those who do not play or who are not good at sports, you just crossed the line into toxic masculinity.

The same is true if you belittle athletes who are female. The same is also true if you associate manhood with engaging in excessive risk in sports or elsewhere, encouraging yourself or others to jeopardize their health and safety in an effort to live up to unhealthy hyper-masculine expectations.

Do Men Who Do Not Endorse Traditional Norms Have Progressive Norms?

What about the men who do not endorse or conform to these traditional norms? Do they have another set of norms, a progressive set based on gender equality? A clever experiment suggests that they *may not*. Calton, Heesacker, and Perrin (2014) randomly assigned male and female college students to describe a time in which they had behaved either traditionally or progressively (i.e., flexible and egalitarian). Over 80% of men and women in the traditional condition provided responses indicative of traditional gender roles specific to their sex (i.e., men responded with traditional ideas of masculinity, and women responded with traditional ideas of femininity). However, something interesting happened in the progressive condition. Women in the progressive condition were able to provide progressive examples of femininity (e.g., childless, career-oriented, opinionated), but only 17% of the men in the progressive condition were able to do the same for masculinity. It would seem that men's only progressive options are to either weakly endorse or reject traditional masculine norms. Unlike femininity, there did not appear to be any options for a more progressive idea of masculinity. Although this study utilized data from college students, who are not representative of the adult population, it nonetheless suggests that we need to help boys and men develop new ways of viewing gender roles more flexibly.

Benefits of the Women's Movement for Girls and the Lack of a Parallel Process for Boys

A half century after the start of the second wave feminist movement, much has changed for girls and women. Women and girls have an extensive history of fighting for equal rights that is still very much alive and well today. Furthermore, girls today benefit from 50 years of conversations about the complexities of womanhood forged out of hardship and solidarity resulting from their status as members of an oppressed group. As a result, some women have become more aware of their traditional socialization to be deferent to and dependent on men and, in fighting against that socialization, have begun rewriting the norms of womanhood to include assertiveness and independence, often altering these norms to better align with their other identities. For example, among Black women who, due to centuries of oppression in the form of slavery and segregation, have had to combine aspects of male and female roles, there is a unique gender ideology known as the strong Black women ideology (Harrington, Crowther, & Shipherd, 2010).

Furthermore, some women have also become aware of the phenomenon of *stereotype threat*—the internalization of denigrating stereotypes, such as the idea that women are not good at math and science (Spencer, Steele, & Quinn, 1999). They have resisted it, and more women now excel in math and science. Many women have come to believe they can be anything they want to be, and overall girls and women now outperform boys and men in many ways, most notably at all levels of schooling (Kohn, 2002).

Unfortunately, no such movement has emerged to help boys navigate or resist their socialization guided by traditional masculinity norms. As discussed in Chapter 1 of this volume, boys and young men need the same kind of culture that feminists created for girls to help boys identify and resist pressures to conform to traditional masculine norms (Valenti, 2018). While some aspects of masculinity appear to have changed, particularly among younger men in regard to their greater participation in parenting and more accepting attitudes toward sexual minorities (Anderson, 2005, 2011), the bedrock issues have not changed. We are referring to many men's inability to remove the shackles of masculinity, or what TED talkers Tony Porter (2010) and Jackson Katz (n.d.) call the "Man Box," and allow themselves to be the unique and fully human beings that they are. They believe they are required to be tough and unemotional guys who do not need anyone. NBA star Kevin Love (2018) has beautifully described the hold that TMI had on him:

> I know it from experience. Growing up, you figure out really quickly how a boy is supposed to act. You learn what it takes to "be a man." It's like a playbook: *Be strong. Don't talk about your feelings. Get through it on your own.* So for 29 years of my life, I followed that playbook. And look, I'm probably not telling you anything new here. These values about men and toughness are so *ordinary* that they're everywhere . . . and invisible at the same time, surrounding us like air or water.

In addition, we have another example,[6] this one from an observation of an actual socialization lesson. A family visited a local office of WIC (the Special Supplemental Nutrition Program for Women, Infants, and Children). The mother

---

[6] We are indebted to Lillian Kuzmik for this anecdote, which she observed as a nutrition and dietetics intern.

was quite pregnant. She was accompanied by the father, a seven- to eight-year-old son, and some other children. A nutrition and dietetics intern greeted them and offered the children some books to read while they waited. The son picked a book about a hospital that happened to have a picture of a girl on the cover. His father, apparently under the influence of traditional gender ideology, said "No, you can't read that; pick another book," which was quickly reinforced by his mother. The intern tried to imagine why the boy would be interested in a book about a hospital and came to the idea that he may have been thinking about hospitals, perhaps even in a worried way, because his mother would soon have to go the hospital for labor and delivery. Yet the parents seemingly felt it was more important to enforce rigid gender norms—"No girl's books for boys"—than to open up a conversation about the son's concerns, which the intern was willing to facilitate.

Clearly we must identify ways for boys and men to escape the outmoded masculinity of the Man Box and develop a more progressive and flexible concept of what it means to be a man today.

Summary and Conclusions

The psychological study of gender began with the view that gender was an inherent reflection of one's biological sex (i.e., in the GRIP: man = masculine, woman = feminine). This perspective brought with it the early gender scales that described gender as dichotomous, and men and women were seen as opposites. Influenced by feminist social scientists, new views of gender emerged, which posited that gender was not rooted in biology, but rather reflected social norms. Based on this new perspective, Pleck (1981) developed the GRSP. As with the paradigm before it, this paradigm brought with it new scales that measured gender in terms of gender ideologies, norm conformity, and strain (which included both conflict and stress), which reflect cultural beliefs of how men and women should think, feel, and behave and with this shift came our current understanding of masculinity. We also discussed the controversial topic of toxic masculinity. As it stands today, most psychological masculinity research is rooted in the GRSP. Even though most men appear to not endorse or conform to many of the norms of traditional masculinity, research has shown many destructive outcomes associated with masculinity, which we hypothesize are accounted for by those who score high on the TMI, conformity, conflict and stress scales, and who are rigid about their endorsement or conformity. We argue that the fundamental problem is that for most boys and men, performing traditional masculinity is construed as obligatory, leaving little to no perceived alternative as far as how they should behave as boys or men. Boys and men need new more flexible ways of thinking about their gender, and we hope that this book helps to move it along.

3

Consequences of Masculinity

I (RL) recall when I first became aware of the effects of such childhood socialization on adult men. I was on the faculty of Boston University where I directed the Boston University Fatherhood Project from 1983 to 1988. The project offered parent education to fathers, who at the time were noticeably taking on a more involved parenting role than had their predecessors. For example, men were now seen in Harvard Square with infants in Snugli packs or pushing strollers. One participant in our Fatherhood Course complained about his son standing him up for a father–son hockey game. Not yet aware of the effects of boyhood emotion socialization on some men's ability to give a good account of their emotions, I asked Tim how he *felt* about being stood up. Tim's response was to point his finger and angrily exclaim: "He shouldn't have done it!" In the Fatherhood Course we used videotaped role-plays to teach fathers parenting skills, in which a father would enact a problematic event with another father playing the role of the child or another family member. The role-play was videotaped and replayed to analyze the interaction and figure out a better way to handle the situation. In this case I asked this father, let's call him Tim, to role-play himself and asked another father to role-play his ex-wife as she delivered the news to him that his son had forgotten the date and gone to a friend's house, while we videotaped the interaction. I played the video back showing Tim's face falling into a frown and his shoulders slumping. I stopped the tape at that point and asked "Tim, what were you feeling right then?" Tim, with his hand on his chin, concentrating intently, said "I guess I must have felt disappointed." " 'I guess I must have felt disappointed' is the best he can do with this much coaching?" I thought to myself. I wondered how a mother in similar circumstance might react, let's say to her daughter standing her up for a shopping date. I imagined her saying

> Well, at first I was surprised. It's not like her to forget a shopping date. Then I felt angry at being stood up. I was also hurt that she acted with so little regard for my feelings. And I was also worried that that she was perhaps upset with me and this was her way of letting me know. And

I was also disappointed and annoyed—I had planned my day around it and now the day was ruined.

The contrast was striking and caused me to wonder why some men could not give an equivalent account of their emotional life.

In this chapter we will discuss theorized—and, to a growing extent, empirically supported—consequences of socializing boys and expecting men to conform to traditional masculinity norms. We will take up, in turn, the socialization of boys; lessons from the Boston University Fatherhood Project; emotion socialization research; the normative male alexithymia hypothesis; masculine depression; obligatory socialization, shame, and the role of fathers; precarious manhood; and privilege.

Boys' Socialization and the Incarceration of Emotions

In general, the socialization of boys to restrict the expression of emotions involves the restriction of emotional expression and even of emotional experience. (However, it should be noted that this process varies somewhat according to the degree to which the boy's family and community endorse traditional gender norms, as well as the particular form masculinity takes in different cultural groups). Specifically, emotions that express vulnerability (such as sadness and fear) are frowned upon. As Feder, Levant, and Dean (2007) put it in an article on boy's violence, "boys learn to shut off their tears and fears" (p. 388). In addition, caring emotions (such as fondness and affection) are also targeted. Boys are expected to not show affection, tenderness, or need for another person. This process often begins in toddlerhood. A recent article called this socialization process "dehumanization" (Ramsey, 2018). Ramsey went on to say:

> Every time we tell a boy that crying is weak, we take a piece of his humanity away. Every time a boy gets teased for showing softness and tenderness, he learns that an essential part of his natural experience is unwelcome and unwanted. And every time we tell mothers that they are wrong for showing love and care to her boy past a certain age, we deprive him of his need for emotional support and consolation.

For another example, Thomas Page McBee (2018) transitioned at age 30. In his male body, he experienced masculinity socialization as an adult. He "started to experience the world differently immediately," he says in a video filmed at the June 2018 Aspen Ideas Festival. "I gained a lot of privileges and also lost a lot of connection." He also said that men are socialized to "act inhumanely."

Lessons from the Boston University Fatherhood Project

Emotion Socialization Research

I (RL) mentioned at the beginning of this chapter an experience in the Boston University Fatherhood Project.

I had similar experiences with other men who were clients in my part-time psychology practice. Curiosity about these men's difficulties with identifying and describing their emotions drove me to review the research literature in developmental psychology on gender differences in the socialization of emotional expression. I found that boys start out life more emotionally expressive than girls. Studies of neonates, hours after birth, generally find that boys are more emotionally expressive than girls—they cry louder and more often. In addition, studies of older infants and toddlers indicated that boys retain this advantage throughout their first year, exhibiting a broader range of emotions than the neonates, such gurgling and cooing at their mothers. This starts to change during the second year of life, at which time boys become less verbally expressive of emotions than girls.

An even larger change happens a few years later. Between the ages of four and six boys became much less facially expressive of emotions, as compared to girls. One ingenious experiment (Buck, 1977) showed 4- to 6-year-old boys and girls emotionally stimulating slides and videotaped their faces. The child's mother was in an adjacent room watching her child's face on a television monitor. The researcher's question was, Are there differences in mothers' ability to accurately identify the slide shown to her child, based on the child's age and gender? At 4 years of age, there were no differences in the accuracy of mothers of sons versus those of daughters. But the older the child the greater the differences, so that by the age of six there were significant differences. Mothers of older sons were much less accurate than those of older daughters, indicating that the boys had become much less facially expressive of emotions. So what is happening to children between the ages of four and six? They are in preschool and school, interacting with their peers, who act as gender police for the boys, enforcing the masculinity norm of restrictive emotionality.

The Normative Male Alexithymia Hypothesis

Based on this review of the emotion socialization literature, I put forth the normative male alexithymia hypothesis (Levant, 1992; Levant & Williams, 2009), which stated that boys reared to conform to the masculinity *norm*[1] of restrictive

---

[1] And thus the word "normative" in the title of the hypothesis.

emotionality will likely become at least mildly alexithymic. Alexithymia is a clinical term that refers to an individual's difficulty identifying and describing their emotional experiences. As previously noted, the term literally means "without words for emotions." Scales have been developed to assess this trait in both clinical and nonclinical populations; the one used most often is the Toronto Alexithymia Scale-20 (Bagby, Parker, & Taylor, 1994). I subsequently did a narrative review (Levant et al., 2006) and then a meta-analysis (in which the results of numerous studies are statistically aggregated; Levant, Hall, Williams, & Hasan, 2009) of the literature on gender differences in alexithymia and found that men are more likely than women to meet the criteria for this trait. The normative nature of alexithymia for boys and men has been observed by others. For example, one of Niobe Way and colleague's (2014) teenage research participants put it this way: "It might be nice to be a girl . . .` then you wouldn't have to be emotionless." The educator Jackson Katz has advocated systematically exposing boys to language for talking about feelings—to help make them "relationally and emotionally literate" (Katz, n.d.).

Not All Emotions Are Prohibited

Boys are allowed, even encouraged, to express anger aggressively. And older boys are encouraged by their peers to express lust. In regard to the latter, I can remember as a teenager that a group of boys in our "clubhouse" (which was usually someone's garage) would gather around a copy of a magazine like *Playboy* or *Penthouse* and ogle the naked women depicted therein. However, as we previously stated, boys reared in homes and neighborhoods that endorse traditional masculinity norms are not allowed to cry nor show fear. That is, they are not allowed to show any kind of emotional vulnerability, which is a rock-bottom requirement of traditional masculinity ideology. To add insult to injury, boys are also restricted from expressing affection or attachment to another person. They cannot be affectionate with another boy lest they be accused of being gay. They cannot express affection to a girl, because children play in sex-segregated groups, and boys demonize girls (remember "cooties"?). They cannot express affection to their mother, lest they be denounced as a "mama's boy." Finally, fathers who subscribe to traditional masculinity norms stop expressing physical affection to their sons around the time they enter school, out of a fear that they will emasculate them. A magazine story titled "Daddy's Home" illustrated this process:

> Daddy drove into the driveway, parked and got out of the car. His three children were waiting to greet him. He first hugged and kissed one daughter and then another, while his 5 year old son stood waiting. Daddy said: "No Timmy, men don't do that." Slowly Timmy got reorganized and extended a stiff little manly hand for a handshake.

Transforming Vulnerable Emotions into Anger

Gender role socialization thus teaches boys to lock up their vulnerable and caring emotions and throw the key away. They do this because they have been made to feel enormous shame about even having these emotions. For example, McBee (2018), the man who transitioned at age 30, stated that after transitioning he got the sense that being vulnerable was something of which he should feel ashamed. Fueled by this shame, which is really self-directed hatred, boys learn to transform their vulnerable emotions into anger, aggression, and even rage. Imagine a boy pushed down on the playground by another boy. At some level he probably feels hurt, sad, maybe also afraid. But he knows he must come back up with his fists flying and certainly not with a face full of tears. Men who have been socialized in this manner have been known to fly into a rage, igniting, much like a match struck to magnesium, when someone hurts their feelings.

One important consequence is that boys learn that close friendships are generally a gay thing and not a guy thing, and thus they become isolated and very lonely, as if they were in solitary confinement, as Shankar Vedantam has documented on his NPR podcast "Hidden Brain" (Cohen & Vedantam, 2018). In support of this, in a recent survey of more than 1,000 10- to 19-year-olds (Plan International USA, 2018), two thirds of boys reported that society expects them to "hide or suppress their feelings when they feel sad or scared" and that they are supposed to "be strong, tough, 'be a man' and 'suck it up.'" As boys reach late adolescence, they tend to disconnect from their emotions and their peers, and become very lonely.

Consequences of Normative Male Alexithymia

The inability that some traditionally reared men have to identify their emotions and put them into words blocks them from utilizing life's most effective means known for dealing with personal problems, ranging from minor hassles to major traumas. We are course referring to the process of identifying, thinking about, and discussing one's emotional response to a hurtful remark or action with the person who delivered it, or with a third party (friend, family member, religious counselor, or therapist). Having an emotionally honest conversation about a stressful or hurtful situation with another person provides empathy and emotional support and allows the person to put the incident into perspective and figure out a way to handle it. It also provides an opportunity for emotional relief though crying, which is—in and of itself—another one of life's effective means for reducing stress. In this light, punishing boys for crying and instilling in them a deep sense of shame (and self-hatred) for even wanting to cry must be seen as an incredibly cruel act. After all, we all have tear ducts, irrespective of our gender. Why would males have them if it were unnatural for boys and men to cry?

Consequently alexithymia predisposes men to deal with personal problems in less constructive ways, which may involve externalizing their problems, as in aggressive and even violent behavior. Other possible harmful responses include sexual compulsions, substance use, porn addiction, gambling addiction, stress-related illnesses, and early death. Furthermore, men who learned as boys to transform vulnerable emotions into aggression will be more prone to act violently when faced with personal problems and hurt feelings.

Masculine Depression

There is yet another aspect of men's emotional life to be considered, and that concerns the mental health disorder of depression. We will discuss this in more depth in Chapter 7 of this volume, but for now we wish to point out that the sex differences in lifetime prevalence for serious depression (i.e., major depressive disorder) of approximately two cases in women for every case in men have been found to be quite robust across large-scale epidemiological studies. However, according to a 2016 report from the Centers for Disease Control and Prevention, 7 out of 10 of all completed suicides were by White males, and suicide is linked with depression. Why are men not diagnosed with depression more frequently? Theorists in the psychology of men and masculinities have proposed that the prototypical symptoms of depression violate traditional masculine role norms, particularly the requirement to never show vulnerability (Addis & Hoffman, 2017). These symptoms include sadness, depressed mood, feelings of worthlessness and guilt, loss of energy, and recurrent thoughts of death. As a result, these theorists suggest that men who subscribe to traditional masculinity ideology who are depressed either mask their symptoms through substance use and/or isolation or express them differently, by externalizing their distress through irritation, anger, and violence. Such men are often argumentative, and some get into physical fights. And as we shall see in Chapter 5, there is evidence that some school shooters were depressed and externalized it as horrific violence.

Obligatory Socialization, Shame, and the Role of Fathers

As we have noted, the masculinity socialization process is for most boys so all-encompassing that they grow up believing that they have no other choice but to conform to masculinity norms. Think back to Kevin Love's comment about the masculine "playbook." For another example, a recent article in *The Atlantic* noted:

> There are so few positive variations on what a "real man" can look like, that when the youngest generations show signs of reshaping masculinity, the only word that exists for them is nonconforming. The term highlights that nobody knows what to call these variations on maleness. Instead of understanding that children can resist or challenge traditional masculinity from within the bounds of boyhood, it's assumed that they're in a phase, that they need guidance, or that they don't want to be boys. (Rich, 2018)

To be socialized in this way is, in effect, to be in banished to a psychological dungeon. That is, for most boys, masculinity is obligatory, policed by fathers, male teachers, coaches, and other boys through shaming or worse. Worse includes beatings and bullying by other boys. Boys are made to feel deeply ashamed of themselves for violating masculinity norms, particularly the expression of vulnerable and caring emotions, as we have discussed. The net result is that boys socialized in this manner feel immense shame and wind up hating themselves— and we mean that quite literally—for experiencing normal human emotions. They also experience loneliness and limitations in expressing empathy.

It is really interesting to observe that men experience this shame in relationship to other men (and in particular to their fathers) and are concerned about what these men will think of them—they might wonder "Will they confiscate my 'man card?'" This reflects a central feature of masculinity—namely, its homosociality. This holds true even if the incident that they are ashamed of had hurt other people. A recent episode of the NPR show "On Being" hosted by Christa Tippett with psychotherapist Avi Klein made this point very well:

> Ms. Tippett: I want to ask you about something you wrote. I want to ask you to explain this: "Shame is the emotional weapon that allows patriarchal behaviors to flourish."
> Mr. Klein: [laughs] I guess what I was trying to say there is that— and I would imagine there are other people who could say this more eloquently than I can—but there's a sense that I have with men, working through some of the behaviors that they've engaged in and some of the attitudes that they've had, where the shame that they're really feeling, sadly, is not about how they're treating women. It's about how they appear in the eyes of other men. So much of it is motivated by that: about saving face in front of your peers, your friends, your father. One of

the quotes of someone I worked with who, in that piece, talks about having a notch in his belt when he thinks about serial cheating on his partner. That's really about what his friends think of him. It's not about impressing women. In that way, I think that there's the shame of not being a man. It's about where you stand in patriarchy.

Loneliness

To add insult to injury, boys socialized in this manner are also emotionally isolated, and grow up to be very lonely men, as observed in Vedantam's NPR podcast as previously discussed, even those who are married and have families. That may seem strange, but consider this: They are emotionally isolated from their families due to their inability to express their own vulnerability and caring or to respond to the vulnerability of family members with a caring empathic response. Consider for a moment how similar alexithymic men's experience of emotional isolation from their families is to the forced separation of prisoners from their families in imprisonment. A recent article on Nelson Mandela's prison letters is illustrative (Jones, 2018). The article focused on his isolation from his family during his 28-year imprisonment to the point of not being able to see his daughters until they were 16 years old and not being able to attend his son's funeral. This article also discussed how he coped through writing letters to them and reading and rereading their letters.

Impaired Empathy

Not intending to pile on here, but we should also add that boys' socialization to restrict their emotional expression likely accounts for the observed gender differences in empathy. Eisenberg and Lennon (1983) reported that while men and women are equally good at the cognitive aspect of empathy—taking another person's perspective and understanding what they think—women are better at the emotional aspect—knowing how that person feels. To do this requires the vicarious experiencing of that person's emotion. Men who have difficulty experiencing their own emotions and putting them into words would likely also have difficulty experiencing another person's emotions.

Fathers' Role

Studies have shown that fathers play a key role in the gender socialization of their sons (Hess, 2014). For example, Fagot and Hagan (1991) observed that fathers gave less praise to their sons when they engaged in behaviors typically construed as "feminine." So too, Epstein and Ward (2011) found that college men, more than college women, recalled numerous incidents in which their fathers impressed upon them the importance of being tough. In addition, Endendijk et al. (2014) examined mothers' and fathers' gender talk with their 2- to 4-year-old children and found that fathers made more comments confirming gender stereotypes than mothers. This type of paternal behavior is based on the belief that the father's *essential* role in the family is to be a role model for his son's masculinity and heterosexuality, which is known as the essential father hypothesis (Silverstein & Auerbach, 1999). A critical review of the literature concluded that this hypothesis has received highly qualified or, at most, modest support (Pleck, 2010). Furthermore, a recent study found that adult sons' recollections of their fathers' expectations that they conform to masculine norms was related to their lower self-esteem and poorer psychological health (Levant et al., 2016).

On the other hand, involved nurturing fathers have a beneficial effect. Finley and colleagues have focused on adult sons' recollections of their fathers' involvement as parents and their nurturing behavior, finding that both were positively associated with the adult son's psychosocial functioning (Finley & Schwartz, 2004, 2007). Furthermore, fathers who are emotionally available can positively impact their sons' attitudes regarding how women should be treated. Among Black youth, for example, having a perceived closeness with their fathers significantly reduced the chance of dating violence such as date rape or assault (Alleyne-Green, Grinnell-Davis, Clark, & Cryer-Coupet, 2015).

Precarious Manhood

As a result of the shame- and fear-based gender socialization process that we have been describing, boys' and men's hold on their sense that they have met the tough standard of the traditional masculinity norms is extraordinarily precarious. Vandello and Bosson (2013) have focused on the precarious structure rather than the content of masculinity (i.e., the norms). They view masculinity as having three characteristics. It is *hard won*, requiring the passing of difficult tests. It is *easily lost:* "A single feminine or unmanly act can temporarily reverse a man's gender status regardless of how many times he has proven it" (p. 103). And it requires *continual public proof*, which must be confirmed by others, particularly other men. Compare this to femininity, which is permanently ascribed to women as matter of biological maturation. Theorizing that the most fundamental masculinity norm is to avoid femininity,[2] they have conducted experiments designed

---

[2] They are not the only ones to so theorize. O'Neil (2008, Figure 1) put fear of femininity at the very center of his gender role conflict model.

to make men feel that they have violated that norm and thus undermine their sense that have met the masculinity standard. They have done this either by inducing men to perform stereotypical feminine tasks (i.e., braiding the hair of a mannequin and putting on pink ribbons) or by giving men personality tests and then telling them that their responses were typical of women. The gender-threatened men were (in one study) more physically aggressive or (in another) took greater financial risks, showing just how fragile men's sense that they have met the masculinity standard is. We theorize that this is the result of the shaming and threatening that goes into socializing boys to conform to masculinity norms. It produces men with a brittle belief that they have met the standard. This masculinity socialization is also invisible and assumed to be "just the way things are," "the way men are," as if it came with the Y chromosome, as Kevin Love previously noted.

Finally, we wish to point out that precarious manhood can be considered a form of discrepancy strain, which we discussed in Chapter 2 of this volume, when covering the gender role strain paradigm. As the reader will recall, this type of gender role strain occurs when one fails to live up to one's internalized masculinity ideal. Threatening a man's sense that he has met the masculinity standard through an experimental manipulation, such as braiding a mannequin's hair and putting pink ribbons on it, induces the man's perception that he is not living up to his masculinity ideal.

Top Secret Task

To illustrate, I (RL) led men's growth groups in the mid-1990s, in which a group of 10 or so men gather for several hours. One of the exercises is the "Top Secret" task. I passed out 3×5 index cards and pencils and asked the men to write down their top secret, that they have never told anyone and would never tell anyone. I then collected the cards and made an elaborate show of shuffling them, while gasps go up—"He's going to read them!" And read them I did. What is amazing and also healing to the men is the similarity of the secrets, which is healing because many men believe that they are the only man to have ever violated masculinity norms, and they experience immeasurable relief to discover that other men feel the same way. The secrets themselves are usually utterly banal violations of the masculinity standard, some of which have occurred in childhood: Fears of being too close to one's mother, unresolved anger (with underlying grief) about the lack of emotional connection to one's father, hidden dependency on other people, and cowardice (e.g., backing down from a fight in high school)

Privilege

This word has been used quite a lot lately by social justice activists and educators alike. Many people have a negative reaction when faced with the idea of privilege and what it means for them. While it is indeed a difficult thing to talk about, we would be remiss to keep it out of this book. While we will be talking about privilege from primarily a gender standpoint, privilege encompasses several different identities such as race, religion, disability status, educational attainment, economic status, sexual orientation, gender identity and even being married or single. Consider these statistics on race/ethnicity and poverty in children under the age of 18. As of 2016, 34% of Black children are living in families who are in poverty. Additionally 34% of American Indian/Alaska Native children, 28% of Latinx children, and 23% of Pacific Islander children are also living in poverty. Only 11% of White children are living in poverty; they are also joined by Asian children with 11% in poverty and 19% of children with two or more races being in poverty (U.S. Department of Commerce, 2016). To gain perspective on this, please take a moment and consider your own privilege (or lack thereof). What privileges are you aware of having (or not having)? How do you feel about the idea of having (or not having) privilege? What does privilege mean to you?

We will next discuss masculinity's role in undergirding men's privilege. The sociologists Connell and Messerschmidt (2005) have shown that masculinity practices (behaviors that demonstrate one's conformity to a masculinity ideology) serve to keep men in a dominant position over women. A *Time* magazine article illustrates men's long-term dominance of women: "Women make up more than half the U.S. population, but 240 years after the nation's founding they are still not equally represented in government" (Abrams, 2016). Indeed, in 2018 only 25% of state legislators are women, 22% of U.S. senators are women, and 26% of U.S. representatives are women (Center for American Women and Politics, 2018). Although masculinity practices also divide men, making White cisgender heterosexual men superior to men of color and gender and sexual minority men, all men receive a "patriarchal dividend" in the form of superior status over women. A patriarchal society provides many more opportunities for men than for women (e.g., higher paying jobs, status, power over political systems and businesses). It also enables some men to think of women as existing for their sexual pleasure. We will discuss this in much more detail when we discuss masculinity's role in sexual and gun violence, but it is important to state here that that the "aggrieved entitlement" that Kimmel (2013, p. 21) identifies as the core characteristic of today's angry White men is based on this sense of privilege. In the case of White men, privilege is doubled: White men are privileged both as men and White people. Whereas, men of color are privileged in being men but hold less privilege than white men because they have an oppressed identity, their race. Endorsing and conforming to traditional masculinity norms comes with its benefits. It maximizes privilege, status, and opportunity within a patriarchal society; however, as should be obvious to the reader by now, it also comes at a price—a steep price.

Summary and Conclusions

In this chapter we discussed gender role socialization and showed how young boys are encouraged or bullied to inhibit and restrict their emotions. We supported this narrative with research on emotion socialization and on the father's role in the socialization process. The socialization process (for which the intended endpoint is boys adhering to masculinity norms, a hard-won status) is too often associated with shame, loneliness, difficulty expressing emotional empathy, and an inability to identify or describe their emotions or that of others (i.e., normative male alexithymia). For many men, to feel vulnerable emotions like sadness, fear, disappointment, hurt, fondness, dependence, and neediness is tantamount to unmanliness and therefore shameful, which precipitates a bout of self-hatred, which for some is transformed into anger, aggression, and rage. This process and its results limits those men who suffer from normative male alexithymia from having strong, healthy, and emotionally intimate relationships with others. Research strongly suggests that men who spend much of their lives striving to attain the ideals of masculinity will be faced repeatedly with feelings of inferiority, something we have discussed in this chapter as precarious manhood and discrepancy strain. Finally, masculinity performances that may or may not be hard-won bring with them the gift of privilege, which ultimately reinforces this behavior, and around and around we go.

There is a popular saying that if you block out undesirable emotions, you block out the desirable emotions too. If boys and men are expected to block out sadness and fear, then happiness will be blocked out as well. If the only emotions that men are permitted to have are anger and lust, then it is no wonder that we see some of the destructive correlates that we mentioned earlier (and will discuss in detail in subsequent chapters). From at least 12 months of age, the behavior of fathers has a huge impact on how their sons feel about themselves as boys becoming men. Yet many fathers may still be imprisoned in masculinity themselves and might be unable to offer their sons the guidance that they need to find healthy ways of being a man. Looking at all of this together, we can see how large the price we pay to raise our sons to conform to traditional norms. Is it worth it? On this point, we are in agreement with and inspired by van Mulligen's (2018) comment, which advocates a more flexible approach to masculinity socialization:

> There are stereotypes and expectations about how men should behave and be. Google "How to be a Man" and the world and his dog has advice on the topic. What if we teach our sons instead that there is no right way to be a man?

|| 4 ||

Summaries of Research
on Masculinity's Harmful Linkages

Over four decades of research in the psychology of men and masculinities shows that masculinity, measured using well-developed scales with good psychometric properties, is overwhelmingly associated with harmful outcomes, for the man himself, for those close to him and for society at large.

We are fortunate to have readily available resources to summarize the research on the correlates of masculinity. We have compiled results from several reviews, including a narrative review, a meta-analysis and two content analyses, completed on the big three masculinity measures (i.e., Male Role Norms Inventory [MRNI], Conformity to Masculine Norms Inventory [CMNI], and Gender Role Conflict Scale [GRCS]) to explain these consequences. In Chapter 2 of this volume we defined these scales and explained their similarities and differences, but to briefly reprise, the MRNI measures an individual's beliefs about how boys and men should think feel and behave (i.e., traditional masculinity ideology), the CMNI measures an individual's self-concept about the extent to which they conform to traditional masculinity norms, and the GRCS measures the conflict that an individual reports experiencing as a result of conforming to those norms.

Before we continue, we should take a moment to briefly explain what narrative review, meta-analysis, and content analysis are. All involve assembling the existing body of research literature on a particular topic, such as the correlates of the MRNI, through an exhaustive search of the scientific literature. A narrative review then writes a narrative discussing what the studies have found. Meta-analysis and content analysis are generally more systematic than narrative reviews. They involve the construction of a coding manual, which is used to tally the various features of the individual studies, such as the demographic characteristics of the sample, the measures used, the analyses conducted, and the results found. A meta-analysis is a quantitative technique, in which the investigator calculates an effect size for every study. An effect size measures the strength of either group mean score differences on scales or of associations between scales. A content analysis, on the other hand, is qualitative. It involves coding raw data and constructing categories that capture relevant characteristics of the content. It is typically an inductive process that proceeds from the data to themes arising from the data and then on to connect to the larger literature. In this chapter, we will be discussing reviews completed on each of three major masculinity measures (i.e., MRNI, CMNI, and GRCS). We will discuss, in turn, (a) a content analysis of 91 studies that used various version of the MRNI (Gerdes, Alto, Jadaszewski, D'Auria, & Levant, 2017); (b) a meta-analysis of 78 studies that examined various versions of the CMNI in relationship to men's mental health (Wong, Ho, Wang, & Keino Miller, 2017) and a content analysis of 17 studies correlating the 11 subscales of the CMNI-94 with 63 criterion variables (Gerdes & Levant, 2018); and (c) a review of the literature of 232 studies that used the GRCS from 1982 to 2007 (O'Neil, 2008).

In general, over the past 40 years, research in psychological science on men and masculinities has largely concluded that various masculinity constructs, measured in various ways, have been associated with a myriad of harmful outcomes. These include: anxiety, depression, low self-esteem, alexithymia, psychological stress and strain, higher blood pressure levels, substance use and abuse, negative attitudes toward help-seeking for both mental and physical health problems, negative attitudes toward women and sexual minorities, negative attitudes about father involvement, dangerous risk-taking behavior and attitudes, delinquent behavior, hostility and aggression, sexual aggression, violence, and marital and family problems.

As final prefatory note, we wish to discuss some limitations in this body of research. The bulk of the research is cross-sectional research, taking a snapshot (as it were) at a particular moment in time. There is small amount of longitudinal research that studies the participants over a period of time, which we do report. Second, many of these studies rely on convenience samples of college students derived from university department voluntary research participation pools. There are studies, growing in frequency, that draw community samples, particularly by using the Internet, and we report those. Third, most studies are correlational in nature and thus unable to determine causation, but there are a few experimental studies, which can determine causation, and we report those. Finally, most studies rely on self-reports using scales, which introduces the possibility of a social desirability bias. These limitations, which are also found in other subdisciplines of psychology, suggest that the findings we report should be viewed with some caution.

Scale Development

This chapter is focused on research using psychological scales, so a brief overview of this topic may be helpful for readers unfamiliar with this topic. For readers desiring more detailed information on scale construction we would refer you to Worthington and Whitaker (2006). Readers who are not comfortable with statistics may wish to skip to the next section. For simplicity, and because we have access to all the materials, we will only be describing the process of creating and revising the MRNI, which is very similar to the process for creating the other masculinity scales.[1] It was first developed in the late 1980s by a doctoral class in research methods at Rutgers University's counseling psychology program taught by Levant. At the time the most prominent scale was the Brannon Masculinity Scale (BMS; Brannon & Juni, 1984), which posited 7 subscales, reflecting the authors' view of the norms of the male role. It had 110 items (in this case in the form of statements about what men should and should not think, feel and do), to which participants responded using 7-point Likert-type scales, in which the scale score labels ranged from 1 (*strongly disagree*) to 7 (*strongly agree*). A big problem with the BMS was that a necessary early step for multidimensional scales (exploratory factor analysis) had not been successfully completed. Hence, its dimensionality was uncertain.

The Development of the MRNI

Levant's class took the BMS as a starting point and did a thorough literature review to ascertain the consensus among scholars on the norms for the male role in the United States. Like the BMS the class posited seven traditional subscales, but also included one nontraditional subscale, used the same 7-point Likert-type scale used in the BMS, and began writing items. Other ways to generate items include conducting focus groups or qualitative interviews. In both of these cases, the interviewer proceeds from the general (e.g., "What does it mean to be a man?") to the specific (e.g., "Should men avoid the expression of sadness?"). After pilot testing the items with a small sample to weed out or revise ambiguous or poorly worded items, the next step is to collect a sample. We administered the new set of items, plus a demographic questionnaire that inquired about age, family/household income, level of education, race/ethnicity, gender identity, and sexual orientation. In addition, it is common practice to include several

[1] For information on the development of the CMNI and GRCS, consult Mahalik et al. (2003) and O'Neil (2008), respectively.

other scales to assess the scale's validity. These include scales that measure the same construct as the scale, to assess convergent evidence for validity; measure something very different, to assess discriminant evidence for validity; or measure a theorized outcome associated with the scale, to assess criterion-related evidence for validity. Reliability is usually assessed in two ways: internal consistency, which can be assessed with the data set that was collected, and temporal stability, which requires retesting some participants at a later time (e.g., 2–3 months later).

Factor Analysis

Once the data are collected, they are screened and cleaned to remove participants who did not meet the inclusion criteria or who did not complete most of the survey and to assess and treat departures from normality and outlier scores. The next step is factor analysis, which includes two parts, using a separate part of the data set for each—exploratory factor analysis (EFA) and confirmatory factor analysis (CFA). In general, factor analysis is a method for modeling observed or manifest variables (i.e., the questions, termed "items") and the matrix of their co-variation, in relationship to a smaller number of underlying unobserved (latent) factors. The relationship of each item to its underlying factor is expressed by a factor loading, a number that ranges from zero to 1 and should meet criteria for strength of loading on the primary factor and for not loading on other factors (cross loading). If either of these criteria are not met, the item is deleted. The EFA does require the specification of the number of factors expected. There are several ways for doing this, but in the case of the MRNI we specified eight, since we had theorized that the scale consists of eight factors. The major difference between EFA and CFA is that EFA allows the rotation of the factors in relation to each other to attain an optimal fit.

For the CFA, we had a smaller pool of items, as some items were deleted for low primary loadings or high cross loadings. While the EFA is conducted using conventional statistical software (e.g., Statistical Package for the Social Sciences [SPSS]) the CFA requires the use of structural equation modeling software, such as MPlus (Muthén & Muthén, 1998–2008) and requires that one specify exactly on which factor you expect the items to load. After running the analysis, the researcher applies to the result a set of fit statistics, each with recommended cut-offs for reasonable or good fit and also inspects the factor loadings to assess the resultant factor structure.

Multidimensional scales in which a total scale score is used are then required to go through several additional analyses, all using CFA. This involves testing different ways of modeling a general factor along with the specific factors

(corresponding to the subscales). A later version of the MRNI, The MRNI–
Short Form (MRNI-SF; which no longer had the nontraditional subscale and
therefore had only seven factors) was best modeled with a bifactor structure
(Levant, Hall & Rankin, 2013). In this model, each of the items was specified
as having factor loadings on both a general traditional masculinity ideology latent factor and a specific latent factor corresponding to one of the subscales in
the original seven-factor model. The results of the CFA for the MRNI-SF with a
bifactor structure are shown in Table 4.1, and the bifactor structure is depicted
in Figure 4.1, both of which are in the Appendix. Both the table and figure show
that each item has factor loadings on both the general traditional masculinity
ideology factor and their respective specific factor.

Linkages of the Male Role Norms Inventory

The MRNI (Levant et al., 1992), its successors (the MRNI-49, MRNI–Revised
[MRNI-R], MRNI-SF, and the MRNI–Very Brief [MRNI-VB]), and adolescent versions (MRNI–Adolescent, MRNI–Adolescent–Revised [MRNI-A-r])
have been used in 91 studies reported in 84 manuscripts as of April 2015 with
over 30,000 participants, including investigations in the United States and in at
least 13 other countries. Levant and Richmond's (2007) review noted over 15
categories of constructs related to the MRNI. The MRNI has been cited as one
of the most commonly used measures of masculinity ideologies from 1995 to
2004 (Whorley & Addis, 2006), and more recent work suggests this is still the
case (O'Neil, 2012).

Sample Characteristics

While the MRNI[2] has been completed by diverse samples in regard to race/
ethnicity, gender and age, the most common participant tended to be a White
male in his 20s. The majority of studies ($n = 76$, 83.5%) reported the racial and
ethnic identities of the participants. Studies that reported more than one race/
ethnicity included, overall, 73.3% European American participants or White
($n = 61$ studies), 13.3% African American participants or Black ($n = 42$), 9.4%
Latinx participants ($n = 33$), and 7.40% Asian or Asian American participants
($n = 30$). Eleven studies included only African American or Black participants,
one study had exclusively Latinx participants, and one study was made up of

---

[2] From here on we use MRNI to refer to any version of the MRNI.

Asian participants only. Native American, Pacific Islander, Middle Eastern, and multiracial participants were often not reported. The sexual orientation of participants went largely unreported; the studies that did report this identity had samples that were predominantly heterosexual. Most studies (n = 59, 64.8%) only looked at male participants, even though the MRNI has been found to be valid with participants of any sex or gender identity. Only two studies included transgender participants, which constituted less than 1% of each sample. One study used a female exclusive sample. Of the studies that reported a mean age (n = 77), the average mean age of all samples was 27.6 (SD = 9.8, median = 25.6). Four studies reported having an adolescent-only sample; only a single study had a sample of older adults over age 70, with an additional study having examined men over the age of 45.

Study Topics and Outcomes

The MRNI has been used in studies that hosted a variety of topics, and many of these topics were studied several times. Topics included mental health (e.g., psychological help seeking, depressive symptoms), help-seeking (e.g., academic help-seeking), emotions (e.g., alexithymia, emotionality), physical health (e.g., eating habits, attitudes about doctors), sexual health, health risk behaviors (e.g., energy drink consumption), attitudes toward marginalized groups, aggression and violence, body awareness, athletic identity, romantic and friend relationships (e.g., social support, relationship satisfaction), vocational decisions, psychometrics (e.g., scale validation, factor analysis), and racial/ethnic/nationality group differences (e.g., observing differences and similarities in MRNI scores of different racial/ethnic/nationality groups).

Of the 91 studies that were reviewed, 70 significant correlations were found with the MRNI and other measures. However, the content analysis did not differentiate whether the reported results were due to the subscales or total scale score. Effect sizes were classified using criteria for correlational analyses, where a correlation coefficient of <0.5 is considered small, one ≥0.5 is moderate, and ≥0.8 is large.

Correlations with medium effect sizes were found with other masculinity constructs, help-seeking, alexithymia, and attitudes toward marginalized groups (i.e., racial or ethnic minorities, sexual minorities, and women), including attitudes conducive to sexual harassment, sexism, fundamentalist religious beliefs, and homonegativity. Further, MRNI scores were related to negative attitudes toward mental health service seeking and to alexithymia. Positive correlations with moderate effect sizes included correlations with other masculinity-related measures, which support the notion that traditional masculinity ideology is closely related to conformity to masculine norms, gender role conflict, male role attitudes and hypermasculinity.

Correlations with small effect sizes were also found. For example, the MRNI was negatively associated with gay social support and positively related to stigmatizing "emo"[3] culture. Additional results included correlations with barriers to help-seeking, self-stigma of seeking help and negative attitudes toward seeking psychological help. Various studies found the MRNI to be associated with alcohol and other substance use, exposure to violent videogames, and aggression. Several other studies found that MRNI scores were associated with less responsible paternal engagement and decreased time spent with children.

Thus, the results indicate that the MRNI is overwhelmingly associated with unfavorable outcomes; however, a few studies have found the opposite. Levant, Wimer, and Williams (2011) found that the MRNI was inversely related to the health risk behavior of responding to stress with anger, and Levant et al. (2019) found that MRNI scores were associated with positive general health status (health-related quality of life) for self-identified men, regardless of their sex assigned at birth (and thus included transgender men). Thus, the MRNI is not always associated with unfavorable outcomes, and it will be important in the future to identify what accounts for the difference between unfavorable and favorable associations. A possible clue comes from the recent study by McDermott et al. (2018) discussed earlier that investigated the Positive Psychology Positive Masculinity perspective (discussed in Chapter 2 of this volume). The investigators found that many definitions of positive masculinity in the literature correctly represented positive social expectations of men, such as male service, bravery, provider, protector, generative fathering, and the like. Perhaps these results shed light on previous findings that the MRNI and the CMNI, which are generally associated with negative outcomes, sometimes (although much less frequently) show a few relationships with positive constructs.

Linkages of the Conformity to Masculine Norms Inventory

Wong et al. (2017) conducted a meta-analysis on the relationship between conformity to masculine norms (as measured by the CMNI-94 and other versions of this scale, including the CMNI-55, CMNI-46, and CMNI-22) and mental

---

[3] Emo is a style of punk rock music that emerged in the 1980s characterized by an emphasis on emotional expression, sometimes through confessional lyrics.

health-related outcomes in a variety of contexts, using 78 samples in 74 reports with a total of 19,453 participants.

Sample Characteristics

Wong et al. (2017) reported the sample characteristics for the CMNI[4] a bit differently than did Gerdes et al. (2017) for the MRNI, providing the number of samples with various sample characteristics, rather than calculating the percentage in various categories over all studies. In regard to race and ethnicity, 45 studies were predominantly White/European American, 9 were predominantly Black/African American, 5 did not report race, and 3 were predominantly Asian American or multiracial. With regard to sexual orientation, 52 did not report on this, 23 were predominantly heterosexual, and 3 were predominantly gay. With regard to gender, 71 studies were men only, 4 were female only, and 3 were mixed gender (male and female). Finally with regard to age/developmental stage, 27 studies used noncollege adults with men age <65, 25 studies used college students, 19 studies had a mixed college and noncollege sample, 6 studies used an adolescent sample (mean age <18 and $\geq$12), and one study used older adults (>65).

Study Topics and Outcomes

Effect sizes were classified a bit differently than was done with the MRNI with correlation coefficients of ≤ 0.1 classified as small, ≤ 0.3 as medium and ≤ 0.5 as large. Conformity to masculine norms was modestly and unfavorably associated with both mental health status as well as psychological help-seeking. The CMNI was more strongly correlated with negative social functioning than with indicators of negative mental health, which makes sense because most of the subscales of the CMNI address interpersonal rather than intrapersonal concerns (e.g., dominance, playboy, winning, power over women, risk-tasking, violence, and disdain for gay men). Conformity to the masculine norms of self-reliance, power over women, and playboy were consistently, robustly, and unfavorably related to mental health outcomes, whereas conformity to the masculine norm of primacy of work was not significantly related to any mental health outcome. Finally, conformity to the masculine norm of risk-taking was correlated with both positive and negative mental health. Wong et al. (2017) did not go into detail on the negative social functioning, but Gerdes and Levant (2017) did,

---

[4] Henceforth we use CMNI to refer to any version of this scale.

and they reported that CMNI subscales were associated with sexually aggressive behavior and prison inmate violence; regressive views of gender, sex, and sexual orientation; and rape myth acceptance. They also noted that subscales differed in terms of their outcomes:

> While one subscale (Primacy of Work) was predominantly associated with positive outcomes, four others had a fairly equal balance of positive and negative outcomes (Winning, Risk-Taking, Pursuit of Status, and Disdain for Homosexuals). However, six subscales were mostly associated with negative outcomes (Violence, Emotional Control, Dominance, Power over Women, Playboy, Self-Reliance). (p. 237)

These findings strongly suggest that more information can be gleaned by focusing on the specific subscales rather than the CMNI total scale score, which Hammer, Heath, and Vogel (2018) actually advised against because they could not find CFA evidence to support the use of the total scale score.

Linkages of the Gender Role Conflict Scale

O'Neil (2008) narratively reviewed 232 studies that used the GRCS over the 25 years period of 1982 to 2007. O'Neil found that gender role conflict was associated with many problems that men experience, specifically of the psychological and interpersonal variety. Unlike Gerdes et al. (2017) and Wong et al. (2017), effect sizes are not reported.

Sample Characteristics

O'Neil (2008) reported the sample characteristics for the GRCS a bit differently than did Gerdes et al. (2017) for the MRNI, providing the number of samples with various sample characteristics, rather than calculating the percentage in various categories over all studies. The majority of the studies have used samples of White, heterosexual college students. In all, 8 studies have been completed on older gay men, 23 studies on non-White minority men, and 31 studies on adult men older than 30. There have been 17 studies that examined how gender role conflict (GRC) might be different across the lifespan. Also three studies have been completed on retired men's GRC, and five studies have studied adolescent boys' GRC using the Gender Role Conflict Scale for Adolescents. The GRCS has been translated into 14 languages, with 41 studies having been completed in 19 foreign countries.

Study Topics and Outcomes

GRC and Intrapsychic Outcomes

Significant relationship have been found between all four patterns of GRC and depression, but restrictive emotionality has been the most consistent predictor. GRC is significantly related to men's anxieties, global levels of psychological stress, physical and psychological strain, competition/comparison strain, performance failure, and physical inadequacy. GRC is also significantly correlated with low self-esteem, alexithymia, shame, and alcohol/substance use and abuse. Low- and high-risk health groups have been significantly differentiated by GRC GRC has also been significantly related to suicidality.

GRC and Interpersonal Outcomes

Men's GRC has been found to negatively impact others and contribute to problems such as rigid and dominant interpersonal functioning, dysfunctional attachment, problems with one's father, low marital satisfaction, poor family dynamics, low intimacy, low self-disclosure, few friendships, stereotypic and negative attitudes toward women, homophobia and antigay attitudes, racial bias toward African Americans, and interpersonal and sexual violence toward women. Specifically, GRC has been significantly correlated with abusive behaviors and coercion, hostile sexism, dating violence, sexually aggressive behaviors and likelihood of forcing sex, hostility toward women, positive attitudes toward and tolerance for sexual harassment, rape myth acceptance, and self-reported violence and aggression. Further, GRC significantly predicted entitlement in men, which in turn predicted sexual entitlement, which finally predicted rape-related criterion variables. Finally, studies have shown that high levels of GRC tend to be associated with sexually coercive behaviors in men. In contrast, men who exhibit lower levels of GRC are more likely to be noncoercive. The same relationships with GRC has been found for sexually aggressive college men vs. nonaggressive men, as well as in domestic abusers vs. nonviolent men. Men who go on to be sexually aggressive and violent tend to be much higher on GRC than men who do not exhibit these behaviors. Taken together the studies indicate that GRC is significantly related to abusive and violent thoughts, attitudes, and behaviors that are directed toward women.

Summary and Conclusions

It may be hard for nonpsychologist readers to imagine that something like gender (in this case, masculinity) could be objectively measured. To some, gender may seem to be a mysterious phenomenon that just is what it is, but as we have seen, we have measured masculinity. We discussed three major scales for measuring aspects of masculinity (i.e., MRNI, CMNI, and GRCS). These scales have been empirically supported for their intended use of measuring masculinity constructs. Reviewing the research that used these scales showed that endorsing and/or conforming to traditional masculine norms or experiencing gender role conflict is linked with many negative outcomes. These outcomes not only negatively affect individual men, but also those with whom they have their closest relationships, those with whom they work, and even society at large. The negative effects of masculinity visit us every day in the news with reports of physical and sexual violence. Some of us can see the negative effects of masculinity in those of our fathers, husbands, sons, boyfriends, brothers, friends, and extended family members who are caught up in substance use and abuse, depression, and violent expressions of anger. Men struggling through this sometimes struggle alone and often do not even recognize that they are struggling at all. Furthermore, as we read about a seemingly endless series of acts of violence we may become desensitized. Some may accept these negative outcomes as something that just is and cannot be changed. If so, these negative outcomes become the norm.

However, there is always another way, if we put our minds to it and work together. We have been analyzing the embodiment of gender as a result of the process of socialization. The beautiful thing about socialization is that we can change it. To the reader, we ask, What would you want to change about how we socialize boys?

Masculinity's Role in Gun and Other Physical Violence

We had earlier noted that 87% of violent crime in the US is committed by boys and men. Yet we also noted that the overwhelming majority of males are not violent. And we have indicated that the way to explain this apparent paradox is by way of masculinity constructs—multidimensional constructs which vary a great deal in the male population. In particular, we proposed that masculinity's harmful outcomes (including violence) can be accounted for by boys and men who strongly endorse or conform to masculine norms or experience high levels of gender role conflict or stress.

In this chapter we focus in on masculinity's role in gun and other physical violence. Violence is an extreme form of aggression in which the purpose is to harm another person or persons. The forms of violence to be discussed in this chapter includes school and other mass shootings, the killing of unarmed Black men by White police officers, hate crimes like the attacks on Jewish synagogues, LGBTQ persons, and Black churches, and domestic/intimate partner violence (IPV). Not discussed in the chapter are the other forms of gun and physical violence ranging from individual acts such as homicide to societal acts such as war. In addition, we take up suicide using guns in Chapter 7 of this volume.

Aggression in general is a complex subject and well beyond our scope for this book, but it is worth noting for the sake of perspective that when I (RL) have taught social psychology, I covered nine different theories of human aggression. These range from theories that have been largely discredited, such as the psychoanalytic theory of catharsis, to those that have empirical support, such as social learning theory. We will briefly describe these two theories of aggression to give the reader a sense of the range of theories of human aggression.

Catharsis theory posits that venting anger to not let it build up inside reduces the likelihood of additional aggression. For example, in the film *Analyze This,* Billy Crystal plays a psychotherapist who tells Robert DeNiro, playing a gangster patient, to "hit" a pillow. At one time psychotherapist's offices were equipped with foam bats for just this purpose. However, in "gangster-ese," hit equals kill, so the patient pulls out a gun and shoots the couch. After regaining his composure, the therapist asks him if he feels better, to which he replies "Yeah, I do." Overall, this theory has not been supported by research. For example, in a study conducted by Bushman (2002), college student participants were angered by an insult from a fellow student and then randomly assigned to one of three experimental conditions: (a) Hit a punching bag while thinking about the person who insulted them; (b) hit a punching bag while thinking about getting physical exercise; or (c) sit quietly. The insulted student was then given a chance to aggress by administering a loud horn blast to the offender. The most aggression occurred in the hitting/ angry condition, whereas the least was sitting quietly. Bottom line: Catharsis does not dissipate aggression.

On the other hand, social learning theory proposes that aggression is learned by imitating the behavior of role models. Bandura, Ross and Ross (1961) demonstrated this in the famous Bobo doll studies. An adult knocked around a rubber air-filled Bobo doll (that bounces back up after being knocked down). Children who watched the adult were then allowed to play with the doll. They not only imitated the model by hitting the doll, but also improvised new forms of aggression. No gender differences were reported. Bottom line: Children learned aggressive acts against the doll by imitating the behavior of an adult model.[1]

Gun Violence

Gun violence is a very urgent and highly complex problem. Gun fatalities are on the rise in the United States. There were nearly 40,000 deaths due to firearms in 2017, the largest annual total recorded in the database of the Centers for Disease Control and Prevention (CDC), which goes back 50 years (Mervosh, 2018). Two thirds of these fatalities were suicides. Every day in the United States, approximately 30 persons die of homicides committed by someone using a gun (CDC, 2013). More than 90% of the perpetrators of homicide in the United States, in which the sex of the murderer is known, are male, as are 78% the victims (Bureau of Justice Statistics, 2008; Federal Bureau of Investigation, 2007). In addition, approximately four times as many youths visit hospitals for

---

[1] Of necessity, our discussion of general aggression theories was brief. For a fuller treatment of aggression theories, including the challenge hypothesis, recalibration theory, the general aggression model, and 1[3] (I-cubed) theory, see Kilmartin and McDermott (2016).

gun-induced wounds as are killed each year (CDC, 2013). Clearly gun violence is a men's issue.

What about the role of gender (i.e., masculinity)? According to a seminal report by the American Psychological Association (2013),

> gender remains largely invisible in research and media accounts of gun violence. In particular, gender is not used to explain the problem of "school shootings," despite the fact that almost every shooting is perpetrated by a young male. Newspaper headlines and articles describe "school shooters," "violent adolescents," and so forth, but rarely call attention to the fact that nearly all such incidents are perpetrated by boys and young men. (p. 14)

Recently, however, there have been a spate of popular articles relating gun violence to "toxic masculinity" (e.g., Epps, 2018; Kiesel, 2018; Vagianos, 2018), a controversial topic that we discussed in Chapter 2 of this volume. Many articles in the popular media assert links between toxic masculinity, guns, and violence, pointing out that boys are raised playing with toy guns and learn to fight early. Many of them also strongly disagree with the idea that mental illness[2] causes mass shootings in favor of toxic masculinity being the cause. While we hail the fact that attention has—at long last—been drawn to the role of masculinity in gun violence, these popular accounts tend to be overly broad and imprecise and thus do not provide meaningful insight into the problem.

It is therefore important to be precise, so we will first clarify what we are *not* saying. We are not saying that masculinity is the sole or even most important cause of gun violence. To understand this all one has to do is consider the numbers involved. A very small percentage of men commits gun violence. For example, between 1982 and 2018, there were 100 mass shootings carried out by male shooters (Statista, n.d). As we discussed in Chapter 2, a much larger part of the population of men either endorses traditional masculinity ideology or conforms to masculine norms (slightly less than or slightly more than half of men, respectively, which is approximately 57 million men). Therefore an infinitesimally small percentage of men commits gun violence (100 out of 57,000,000 men over a 36-year period, or 0.000049% per year). Furthermore, gun violence

---

[2] In fact there is no evidence that mental illness causes mass shootings (APA, 2013), but this theme has often been raised by politicians who wish to steer the discourse away from gun control. The U.S. Congress has long been stymied on gun safety legislation, However, stimulated by the mass shooting in Parkland, Florida, state legislatures passed 69 gun control measures in 2018, more than any other year since the Newtown, Connecticut massacre in 2012, and three times as many as in 2017 (Astor & Russel, 2018).

likely has many determinants and pathways. According to the previously mentioned APA (2013) report,

> a complex and variable constellation of risk and protective factors makes persons more or less likely to use a firearm against themselves or others. For this reason, there is no single profile that can reliably predict who will use a gun in a violent act. Instead, gun violence is associated with a confluence of individual, family, school, peer, community, and sociocultural risk factors that interact over time during childhood and adolescence. . . . *The most consistent and powerful predictor of future violence is a history of violent behavior.* (p. 1; emphasis added)

For example, the psychologist Peter Langman (2009) examined the psychological and psychiatric evaluations as well as other available records of 10 school shooters and showed how each fit one of three patterns of psychopathology: (a) traumatized (i.e., having suffered a trauma and exhibiting posttraumatic stress symptoms); (b) psychotic (i.e., suffering from a serious mental illness such as schizophrenia); and (c) psychopathic (i.e., meeting criteria for oppositional defiant disorder for an adolescent or antisocial personality disorder for an adult). He also examined the role of three other factors: family structure, role models, and peer influence. However, he did not even mention the role of masculinity, which makes our point—namely, that masculinity's role in violence has largely been unexamined in *serious* investigations of gun violence.

Masculinity's Role in Violence and Aggression: A Review of Research

According to the APA report (2013), "any account of gun violence in the United States must consider both why males are the perpetrators of the vast majority of gun violence and why the vast majority of males never perpetrate gun violence" (p. 13). This is indeed the double-edged sword question, and both edges should be addressed. Referring back to our discussion in Chapter 2 of this volume, we would suggest that the answer to the first side—why males are perpetrators—lies, in part, in the upper tail of the distribution of men's endorsement of and conformity to traditional masculine norms and of experiencing gender role conflict. Men with a very high degree of endorsement/conformity/conflict likely account for masculinity's linkage with destructive outcomes, and those are a small percentage of all men. While women can and do commit violent acts, those who do so are an even smaller minority of women.

Masculinity's Linkages with Aggression and Negativity Toward Marginalized Groups

Furthermore, as we have seen in Chapter 4, the endorsement of traditional masculinity ideology, as measured by Male Role Norms Inventory (MRNI) scores, is correlated with both aggression and with negative attitudes toward marginalized groups (i.e., women, racial or ethnic minorities, and sexual minorities). Conformity to masculine norms, as measured by Conformity to Masculine Norms Inventory (CMNI) scores, is associated with prison inmate violence, as well as regressive views of gender, sex, and sexual orientation. Finally, gender role conflict, as measured by Gender Role Conflict Scale (GRCS) scores, is correlated with self-reported violence and aggression, as well as rigid and dominant interpersonal functioning, stereotypic and negative attitudes toward women, homophobia and antigay attitudes, racial bias toward African Americans, and interpersonal violence toward women. This set of correlates might help us understand masculinity's role in aggression in general and in intimate partner violence and hate crimes.

A recent study tried to isolate the gendered part of men's physical aggression (Berke, Wilson, Mouilso, Speir, & Zeichner, 2015). The investigators analyzed the extent to which CMNI and GRCS scores uniquely predicted self-reported physical aggression, over and above low scores on the personality trait of agreeableness (in which low scores signify disagreeableness). They estimated the direct effects of conformity to masculine norms and gender role conflict on aggression and their indirect effects as mediated though trait agreeableness. Mediation is a statistical phenomenon in which a third, intervening variable transmits the effect of the one variable on another. Their results indicated that both CMNI and GRCS total scale scores were directly linked to men's aggression, in line with prior research. However, when GRCS scores were considered in tandem with using only the subscale of the CMNI most salient to physical aggression (e.g., violence), the direct effect of the GRCS on aggression became insignificant, leaving only an indirect effect mediated through agreeableness. This might be explained by the fact that the GRCS taps the state of a person being in conflict, and low agreeableness likely taps a similar state. Of note, the violence norm retained its direct effect when agreeableness was in the model.

Masculinity's Indirect Role in Violence

There is a more dramatic demonstration of masculinity's indirect role in violence, coming from a study of the relationship between exposure to violent video games (also identified as a potential factor in gun violence, which is likely facilitated by social learning) and aggression by Thomas and Levant (2011). This study included masculinity as a factor—specifically as a moderating variable. Moderation is another statistical phenomenon in which a third variable can change the strength and/or direction of the relationship between two variables—in this case, exposure to video games and aggression. The investigators found that there was a linear positive relationship between video game exposure and aggression (both measured with self-report scales), in which the greater the exposure, the greater the aggression. Further, for young men, the endorsement of traditional masculinity ideology moderated that relationship, changing its strength, so that the greater the endorsement, the steeper the slope of the relationship between exposure and aggression (see Figure 5.1 in the Appendix). This means that for men who strongly endorse masculine norms, there is a greater increase in aggression for every unit increase in exposure, as compared to men who weakly endorse these norms. This finding also lends support to our hypothesis that the destructive effects of masculinity are due to those who have high scores on the masculinity scale. In a companion study of young women, this moderation effect was not found, indicating the different role that traditional masculinity ideology plays in men's and women's lives.

Behavioral Measures of Aggression

Most of the research linking masculinity to aggression has used self-report measures of aggression, in which participants were asked if they would be aggressive or have been aggressive. Since being aggressive is not considered socially desirable, participants may underreport their aggression, which is a limitation in this research. These self-report measures are used frequently due to the difficult ethical problems in using behavioral measures of aggression—that is, inducing participants to aggress against another person or persons. However, several studies have devised such behavioral measures. One study (Berke, Sloan, Parrott, & Zeichner, 2012) led participants to believe that they were giving shocks to their fictional opponents, similar to the infamous obedience experiment conducted by Stanley Milgram.[3] This particular study used women as the target,

---

[3] In Milgram's study participants were induced to give fictitious shocks to a confederate of the experimenter using a fake shock machine that had switches labeled from slight shocks (15–60 volts) to XXX (435–450 volts), and 67% went to the maximum voltage.

manipulating the woman's gender expression as either gender-conforming (feminine) or nonconforming (masculine), as denoted by her hairstyle and manner of dress. Aggression was measured in terms of frequency, intensity, and duration of electric shocks ostensibly administered by the participant to his fictional opponent. Results indicated first that CMNI scores moderated (i.e., changed the strength or direction) of the relationship between men's physical aggression and women's gender expression. Men with high CMNI scores were equally aggressive to the masculine and feminine woman opponent. This finding also lends support to our hypothesis that the destructive effects of masculinity are due to those who have high scores on the masculinity scale. However, low masculinity-conforming men behaved more aggressively against the feminine opponent than they did against a masculine opponent. These results may be explained by noting, first, that it is easier to aggress against a person perceived as member of an outgroup and, second, that to high-conforming men, all women are in the outgroup, due to the avoidance of femininity norm and the otherizing of women as discussed earlier. Whereas low-conforming men may perceive only the nonconforming woman as a member of an outgroup.

Furthermore, research has found that threatening a man's masculinity is linked to aggression, measured behaviorally. Bosson and Vandello (2011) randomly assigned men to complete one of two tasks, braiding the hair of a mannequin and putting on pink ribbons (experimental group) or braiding a rope (control group). The experimental task was selected to activate the avoidance of femininity masculine norm—the task of braiding hair is seen as a feminine act, and to a man who endorses masculinity norms, what could be more emasculating? After the task, the men were given the choice to punch a punching bag or solve a puzzle. Men who braided hair chose to punch the punching bag significantly more frequently than men who braided rope. Additionally, men who braided hair punched the punching bag harder than men who chose to punch the punching bag after braiding rope. At the end of the study, anxiety levels were measured, and they found that men who punched the punching bag after braiding hair had significantly less anxiety than men who did not punch the punching bag. While this example of threatened masculinity may seem somewhat facetious, it does show that completing a small task that is seen as emasculating is enough to result in aggression and, further, that aggression restores threatened men's sense of masculinity, as reflected in their lowers levels of anxiety.

We have earlier theorized that the underlying dynamic is that threatening a man's masculinity results in feelings of shame, which requires a masculine display to dispel. A recent study provides further support for this hypothesis (Gebhard, Cattaneo, Tangney, Hargrove, & Shor, 2019). The investigators created a new measure of threatened-masculinity shame-related responses. The Masculinity and Shame Questionnaire provides descriptions of situations that threaten a man's masculinity, using scenarios similar to those used by Bosson, Vandello, and colleagues in their precarious manhood research and asking participants to indicate how likely four different responses would be for them. The four responses each reflect a different subscale, which are Feel Shame, Escape, Prevent Exposure, and Externalize Blame. They then explored how these experiences related to aggression, finding a clear connection between threatened-masculinity shame-related responses and self-reports of a tendency to be physically aggressive. In addition, they found that threatened-masculinity shame-related responses accounted for variance in self-reported physically aggressive behaviors above and beyond the variance accounted for by general shame.

Analysis of School Shooters

We turn now to an analysis of school shooters. We reviewed a database of available information (such as school and medical records, police reports, and the shooters' own writings, including journals and manifestos) on school shooters compiled by Peter Langman.[4] Although Langman (2009) never mentioned masculinity and presumably did not assemble his database with masculinity in mind, we were able to make some connections to masculinity. Our analysis revealed that school shooters appear to have a strong need to keep their emotions under control, which reflects the restrictive emotionality/emotional control of four popular masculinity measures—the MRNI, CMNI, GRCS, and Masculine Gender Role Stress Scale (MGRSS). In addition, the shooters seem to have experienced an emotional deficit—by which we mean that, first, they have a restricted range of emotions (mostly feeling only negative emotions), and second, they lack capability to deal with those negative emotions in healthy ways. As a result, these negative emotions were often expressed through unhealthy externalizing behaviors (disturbing writings/pictures, socially isolating themselves, making threats, physical aggression). These writings are now being talked about as "red flags" that might be used to intervene to prevent shootings.

The behaviors exhibited by many of these shooters reflected their adherence to several masculine norms such as aggression and toughness, with stereotypically "feminine" emotions such as sadness being discussed only within the privacy of their personal journals. Feelings of sadness felt by these shooters who experienced rejection, bullying, and loneliness were transformed into anger and aggression, including violence. This illustrates the difficulties that boys and men who were reared to conform to traditional masculinity norms have in dealing with

---

[4] https://schoolshooters.info/

vulnerable emotions such as sadness, loneliness, and hurt feelings and speaks to the lack of options that boys and men imprisoned within masculinity have when faced with the everyday ups and downs of life. Additionally, many of the shooters talked about struggles commonly experienced by teenagers (i.e., difficulties with relationships, grades, driving, family), yet somehow they lacked the ability to cope with those everyday struggles in a healthy way. They also lacked a sense of personal accountability and had an enormous sense of privilege and entitlement. This, mixed in with the turbulence of adolescence, created an explosive cocktail.

In the following discussion, we offer a detailed report on the most well-known shooters, for whom there is lot of information. We have organized our report to systematically cover the consequences of socializing boys and requiring men to conform to traditional masculine norms that we discussed in Chapter 3 of this volume: emotion socialization to restrict the expression of vulnerable emotions, transforming vulnerable emotions into anger, masculine depression, precarious manhood, the role of the father, loneliness, alexithymia, and privilege. Not every shooter exhibited behavior in all of these categories, and some will display more than others.

Elliott Rodger

Shooting. Isla Vista Massacre (2014). His motivation was revenge for perceived sexual and social rejection. He termed his shooting "The Day of Retribution." He stabbed three men in his apartment, shot three women (killing two) at a sorority house, shot a man in a deli, and ran over people in his car. He killed 6 people in total and injured 14. He shot himself in the head after having a shootout with police.

Emotional socialization. Rodger described crying many times. He did not say whether other people might have reacted negatively to it, but rather he described the people around him as being responsive to this behavior, and he used it manipulatively several times to get what he wanted. Thus, Rodger did not restrict the expression of vulnerable emotions, but rather he used such expression to manipulate others.

Transforming vulnerable emotions into anger. Rodger talked about how his feelings of sadness and jealousy began to transform into intense anger toward his peers after he was repeatedly bullied and rejected. Rodgers stated that the more lonely he felt, the more angry he became. After losing interest in the game World of Warcraft, which he had used as a coping mechanism, Rodger began to reinforce his feelings of anger by seeking out information online that validated his feelings about the world being an awful place. His father lost his assets in a movie scheme that went bad, and Rodger reported having less support financially and emotionally as his father was dealing with his own hardships resulting from the financial crisis. Rodger continued to have fantasies about exacting revenge on people who hurt him and whom he envied. Rodger appeared to compare himself to others constantly, which caused him to feel envious and then angry and vengeful. Rodger began to feel extremely hostile toward couples, especially biracial couples composed of a dark-skinned man and a blonde White woman. He went so far as to pour a drink on the heads of such a couple at a restaurant. A few girls that Rodger drove past did not smile back at him, and he became enraged and made a U-turn and stopped, got out of his car, and splashed his latte on them. Rodger described his reasoning as his need to have sex and not being allowed to which resulted in him wanting to take it away from everyone else (i.e., "If I can't have it, no one can").

Masculine depression. Rodger described feeling angry as a result of repeated bullying, thereby externalizing his vulnerable feelings as anger and aggression. Rodger developed fewer friendships as he got older (he moved a few times). He describes how he spent most of his time alone playing World of Warcraft.

Precarious manhood. Rodger seemed to feel that he didn't measure up as a male. As young as 9 years old Rodger talked about how he envied the athletic ability of the other boys and stated that he felt "vexed" about the fact that he was shorter than most of the boys in his class. He believed that he was physically weak because of his short status. Rodger described feeling inferior to other boys who were able to have sex with girls and feeling distressed when other boys would brag about their sexual exploits. Sex appeared to be very important to Rodger. He described feeling that his right to sex was being denied and this caused him a lot of distress. He used the word "failure" to describe himself many times. He wrote: "What I truly wanted . . . what I truly NEEDED, was a girlfriend. I needed a girl's love. I needed to feel worthy as a male. For so long I have felt worthless, and it's all girls' fault. No girl wanted to be my girlfriend."

The role of the father. Rodger's did not describe his father in any detail. His parents appeared to be well-off, and they catered to him often. His parents saw how radical he was becoming toward the end and attempted to send him to Morocco to live with his step-mother. Rodger reported throwing a tantrum to get them to stop, but they sent him away anyway. He spent a week in Morocco before he was able to get his mother to take him home by emailing her how horrible it was and how much he was crying.

Loneliness. Rodger played World of Warcraft up to 14 hours a day to combat his feelings of loneliness. At around 17 years old, playing World of Warcraft no longer ameliorated his loneliness. It was around this time that he reported feeling "extreme feelings of envy, hatred, and anger towards anyone who has a sex life." He described them as the "enemy." Also, around this time, he decided that he no longer wanted to sit passively and hide his feelings about this anymore.

Alexithymia. Rodger was very clear in explaining his feelings and had no problem using emotion words. He seemed to be able to describe why he was feeling what he was feeling. No evidence of alexithymia was found.

Privilege. Rodger was very clear about feeling that he was entitled to the affection and sexuality of women. Rodger appeared to get everything that he needed/wanted from his parents, who appeared to be financially well-off.

Other observations. Rodger appeared to think in black-and-white terms. For example, he described the early years of his life as extremely happy and wonderful and the final years of his life as horrible. While that may have seemed to be true to him, he lacked the ability to understand that there are good and bad aspects to every situation. He showed signs of insecurity and jealousy in his early relationships with other boys. His growing disinterest in playing World of Warcraft as a coping mechanism to buffer against his loneliness appeared to be the tipping point, after which he began exhibiting signs of shooter mentality (i.e., having fantasies of being powerful and stopping others from having sex). There was a short period of time when he was 17 to 18 years old when Rodger rekindled some feelings of hope and attempted to work on himself to get a girlfriend. His parents paid for him to get a new haircut and new clothes, but therapy was never an option.

Seung Hui Cho

Shooting. Virginia Tech Massacre (2007). He killed 32 people before killing himself.

Emotional socialization. Not identified.

Transforming vulnerable emotions into anger. Cho wrote in his manifesto: "Congratulations. You have succeeded in extinguishing my life. Vandalizing my heart wasn't enough for you. Raping my soul wasn't enough for you. Committing emotional sodomy on me wasn't enough for you." Additionally, Cho exhibited immense anger in his manifesto, condemning false Christians, the wealthy, Satanists, and terrorists.

Masculine depression. Cho was diagnosed with major depressive disorder and appeared to express it as masculine depression, in which vulnerable feelings such as sadness were externalized and expressed as anger. He was an English major and often wrote stories with strong depictions of violence. Teachers regarded his writings as disturbing.

Precarious manhood. Not identified.

The role of the father. Not identified.

Loneliness. Cho wrote a long poem called "A Boy named LOSER," the meanings of which can only be speculated on. The poem appeared to tell the story of a boy facing immense loneliness and isolation from the world around him. It is not clear whether Cho wrote this poem with himself in mind.

Alexithymia. Not identified.

Privilege. Cho had less privilege as being both a person of color and an immigrant from South Korea.

Other observations: In 2005 Cho was diagnosed as mentally ill and an "imminent danger to himself. Cho referenced the Columbine Massacre in his writings and appeared to idealize its shooters.

Eric Harris

Shooting. Columbine Massacre, killed 13, injured 27, committed suicide.

Emotional socialization. Not identified.

Transforming vulnerable emotions into anger. Harris's journals and other writings were dripping with anger and distain for most of humankind. It is not clear where these strong feelings came from. Harris was driven to school by his friend Brooks Brown, who was late one day to pick him up. After Harris "chewed him out" about it, Brown told him to find another ride to school. Harris broke Brooks' windshield with a rock and vandalized the Brown residence by placing firecrackers on the windowsill. Harris likely felt vulnerable emotions, but it appears that he transformed them into aggression and violence.

Masculine depression. It is likely that he suffered from depression as his final act of violence ultimately ended in his death, which, like the shooting, was premeditated.

Precarious manhood. He seemed to react aggressively to rejection, something that has been reflected in the literature as a side effect of insecure masculinity.

The role of the father. Harris's father was an Air Force transport pilot and kept a diary with information about the negative behavior that he observed from his son.

Loneliness. Not identified.

Alexithymia. Not identified.

Privilege. Harris appeared to be from a White middle-class family.

Other observations: Harris seems to be a boy who harbored a lot of rage and appeared to be the more dominant of the two shooters. Harris's solution to problems was violence; he exhibited this in a few other minor instances in his life before the shooting.

Dylan Klebold

Shooting. Columbine Massacre, killed 13, injured 27, committed suicide

  Emotional socialization. Not identified.

  Transforming vulnerable emotions into anger. Klebold talked about experiencing heartbreak and feeling like an outcast. His feelings of rejection and sadness eventually evolved into intense anger toward "jocks" and others who he felt had abandoned and scorned him.

  Masculine depression. Klebold was known to drink and referenced it a few times in his journal; he may have practiced some self-mutilation (cutting), and he mentioned suicide often in his journal. Like Harris, he also committed suicide.

  Precarious manhood. Klebold talked about being intimidated by sports and appeared to largely dislike his shyness. He believed that acting shy was a BIG (he used all caps in his journal) problem. The emphasis on "big" is telling about how he wanted to be perceived and how he might have felt inferior by not being able to measure up to his own expectations on how a teenaged boy should behave.

  The Role of the father. Not identified.

  Loneliness. Klebold spoke of having a falling out with his first best friend, and he described himself as feeling very lonely without him. He also spoke of feeling incredibly lonely after he was rejected by a girl with whom he was in love. He stated that he wanted to find love. "People eventually find happiness, I never will. Does that make me non-human? YES" (This depersonalization from feeling human might have contributed to his ability to shoot innocent people)

  Alexithymia. Not identified.

  Privilege. Appeared to come from a White, middle-class family.

  Other observations. Klebold and Harris committed several petty crimes together before they became shooters. These crimes consisted of break-ins, stealing, vandalism, drinking, smoking, and making pipe bombs. Hong, Cho, Allen-Meares, and Espelage (2011) analyzed the social ecology of Columbine High School, using Connell and Messerschmidt's (2005) theory of hegemonic masculinity. They described the school as a jock culture, where athletes were the dominant force in the school, representing the ideal version of masculinity as dominant and aggressive. They noted that both Klebold and Harris were consistently bullied and harassed by athletes, relegating them to subordinated masculinity status. Hence, it is likely that their attack was an attempt to restore their lost sense of masculinity, as in the precarious manhood paradigm. As Hong et al. (2011) wrote "hegemonic masculinity does not cause violence, but rather violence . . . [is a resource] for 'doing' masculinity" (p. 863).

Murder–Suicides

Finally, since most of the school shooters were murder–suicides (M-S), the findings of a recent study on M-S are relevant and offered here as a coda to the foregoing. Oliffe et al. (2015) investigated M-S by analyzing 296 newspaper articles describing 45 North American M-S cases. A qualitative analysis revealed three themes that ran though the reports: (a) domestic desperation, (b) workplace justice, and (c) school retaliation. To quote from the authors,

> cases in the domestic desperation theme were characterized by the murder of a family member(s) and were often underpinned by men's self-perceptions of failing to provide economic security. Workplace justice cases emerged from men's grievances around paid-work, job insecurity, and perceptions of being bullied and/or marginalized by coworkers or supervisors. The school retaliation cases were strongly linked to "pay back" against individuals and/or society for the hardships endured by M-S perpetrators. Prevailing across the three themes was men's loss of control in their lives, hopelessness, and marginalized masculine identities. Also evident were men's alignments to hegemonic masculinities in reasserting one's masculine self by protesting the perceived marginalization invoked on them. (p. 473)

Observe how Oliffe et al. emphasize self-perceptions and marginalized masculine identities. Implied in their use of "marginalized identities" is men who have internalized traditional masculinity ideology but who do not find themselves capable of living up to these standards.

Police Brutality and #BlackLivesMatter

For decades there have been numerous shootings of unarmed Black boys and men[5] by mostly White policemen, which in recent years has been exposed and protested by the #BlackLivesMatter movement. Although the #BlackLivesMatter movement has focused on the roles of race and racism in police brutality, some attention is beginning to be paid to the role of gender. Using data from the Riverside County Sheriff's Department in California, a study by McElvain and Kposowa (2008) found that male officers were three times more likely to commit unwarranted shootings than their IPV counterparts. Additionally,

[5] Shooting also include Black women and transgender persons, although less frequently than Black boys and men.

White male police officers were 57% more likely than Latino male officers to commit such a shooting. These statistics refer to the group that constitutes the majority of police officers in America (i.e., White men). However, there are only a few studies investigating why White male police officers are more likely to be involved in such shootings.

One study found that police violence is likely rooted in negative stereotypes of Black men held by many in law enforcement (Najdowski, Bottoms, & Goff, 2015). These stereotypes consist of seeing Black men as hyperaggressive and violent. In this context, it is interesting to note that a Black male hashtag has emerged, encouraged by Chance The Rapper, as #BlackBoyJoy. This hashtag aims to erase the negative stereotypes of the "angry Black man" and replace it with a notion that not only is there nothing wrong with being a Black man who is lighthearted and happy but also that Black men have the same capacity for happiness as everyone else (Santana, n.d.). Perhaps this will push back against the negative stereotype of the angry Black man and reduce the negative views that White police officers harbor toward them, which may facilitate safer interactions between police and Black men.

Second, a recent article discussed the *fear* that White police officers feel toward Black men. Fear is unmanly and therefore unacceptable and seems to play a role in police brutality (Cooper, 2016). In other words, this unrealistic fear may threaten officers' masculinity, requiring a forceful demonstration of their masculinity by dominating the Black man. And dominance is one of the masculine norms.

In the absence of much research, we turn to theory to identify other masculinity factors that may potentially be at work in police violence against Black boys and men. For one thing, the culture of police departments tends to be macho and hypermasculine—a culture which glorifies violence. This has always been the case but has intensified as police departments across the county have moved from the community policing approach to militarization, aided by federal grants. Second, one of the principal functions of masculinity is to establish several hierarchies—of men over women, of White men over men of color, and of cisgender heterosexual men over gay, bisexual, and transgender men (Connell & Messerschmidt, 2005). We believe that this power hierarchy coupled with pervasive negative stereotypes of Black men in our society plays a significant role in police shootings of Black men.

Finally, Huisman, Martinez, and Wilson (2005) suggested that the lack of diversity in police forces might contribute to violence against minorities. They noted that it is likely that the only kind of interaction that White police officers have with a person of color is when that person is associated with a crime. This repetitive association makes negative racial stereotypes more salient in the minds of police officers. More diverse police forces would likely weaken that association and counteract the negative stereotypes. This is supported by a finding from Schaefer (2001) that prejudice was associated with lack of social contact, reflecting Gordon Allport's (1954) famous contact hypothesis, which was published in 1954.[6] Furthermore, police officers are not routinely trained to understand diversity, privilege, and oppression. This can make for some dangerous situations when out in the field.

Intimate Partner/Domestic Violence

In the United States, one in four women and one in nine men will experience some form of IPV/domestic violence in their lifetime (Smith et al., 2017). IPV is defined as punching, hitting, shoving, choking, and otherwise physically harming an intimate partner. While masculinity is not the main focus of the IPV/domestic violence research literature, it has emerged as a contributing factor. Traditional masculinity ideology, hegemonic masculinity and masculine gender role stress (MGRS) have been linked with IPV in the research literature.

Moore and Stuart (2005) critically examined a broad range of literature on the relationship between masculinity conceptualized in three different ways and IPV. The trait approach, in which masculinity is conceptualized as set of stereotypical personality traits, using scales such as the Bem Sex Role Inventory (which we discussed in Chapter 2 of this volume), did not show a relationship between masculinity so defined and IPV. The traditional masculinity ideology approach revealed mixed findings, with Male Role Norms Scale (MRNS) most consistently linked with IPV.[7] The MGRS approach showed a moderate association with IPV. According to the authors,

> the consistent and positive relationship between gender role stress and the use of verbal and physical conflict tactics in relationships suggests that the level of men's appraisal of stress and threat to situations that challenge masculine norms may be a critical component in understanding why some men behave violently. (p. 52)

IPV and Traditional Masculinity Ideology

Willie, Khondkaryan, Callands, and Kershaw (2018) found that traditional masculinity ideology predicted IPV. IPV was measured at three time points

---

[6] The contact hypothesis predicts that prejudice against members of a minority group is reduced by meaningful contact between majority and minority groups.

[7] The MRNI was not included because there was only 1 study of its link with IPV at the time of the review.

(baseline, 3 months, and 6 months) using interviews. Emotional and psychological abuse was measured using five items from the physical assault and psychological aggression subscales from the Conflict Tactics Scale (CTS-2, Strauss, Hamby, & Warren, 2003). Traditional masculinity ideology was assessed using the MRNS (Thompson & Pleck, 1986).

Gage and Lease (2018) investigated men's fear of intimacy, hostile and benevolent sexism, and relationship dominance as potential mediating factors of the linear positive relationship between endorsement of traditional masculinity ideology using the MRNI and the acceptance of myths about male-to-female IPV. As noted earlier, mediation is where a third variable transmits the effect of the one variable on another. The IPV myths minimized the impact of male-to-female IPV or shifted the perceived responsibility for the offenses from the male perpetrators to the female victims. Analyses indicated that while men's fear of intimacy did not mediate this relationship, hostile sexism and a domineering orientation toward relationships did partially mediate it.

IPV and Hegemonic Masculinity

Some men who adhere to traditional gender roles believe that they should be in control of their wives. This comes straight out of the definition of hegemonic masculinity (Connell & Messerschmidt, 2005) as establishing a dominance hierarchy of men over women. To illustrate, the Promise Keepers, which packed football stadiums with programs for men during the masculinity crisis of the 1990s (Levant, 1997a), proposed to return the man to his "rightful place" as the "leader of his family." Evans (1994) wrote, in a section in the book *Seven Promises of a Promise Keeper* titled "Reclaiming Your Manhood:"

> The first thing you do is sit down with your wife and say something like this: "Honey I've made a terrible mistake. I've given you my role. I gave up leading the family, and I forced you to take my place. Now I must reclaim that role." Don't misunderstand what I am saying here. I'm not suggesting that *ask* for your role back. I'm urging you to *take it back*. (p. 79)

This need to control wives plays a significant role in men who perpetrate IPV. Controlling a partner (e.g., determining where they can go, what they can wear, and whether they can work) allows some men to feel as if they are rightly acting in accordance with the prerogatives of their gender and therefore secures their identity as men. In a study that interviewed male perpetrators of IPV, Peralta and Tuttle (2013) found that men who were the breadwinners in their household felt as if that role demanded deference from their wives. Several participants regarded it as disrespectful when their partner told them what to do. Consider this short passage from an interview where the participant discusses his conflicts with his girlfriend:

> Participant: As long as I'm going to work and paying these bills and you sitting at home you can ask me to do something but you don't tell me. You know, there's a big difference.
> Interviewer: Because you're supporting the family.
> Participant: Ah hah, you can ask me but don't tell me don't do this and don't do that like I'm a child. I ain't no child. (p. 268)

The notion that providing for a female partner is a requirement of manhood and that fulfilling it allows the man to control her is seen in another participant who says "a man's natural instinct is to provide and to be the man. To be in control" (Peralta & Tuttle, 2013, p. 269). Notice the usage of "natural instinct." He appears to be saying that providing and being in control are synonymous with being a man. This participant suggests that this instinct is normal and unchanging, something that is as biologically male as having an X and a Y chromosome.

The Duluth model of domestic violence, which has been influential in the treatment of men who commit IPV, suggests that men are socialized to believe that violence is an acceptable way to maintain control and dominance in a relationship (Pence & Paymar, 1993).

IPV and Masculine Gender Role Stress

Other research indicates that MGRS moderates and mediates the relationship between traditional masculinity ideology and IPV perpetrated by men on women. Jacupcak, Lisak, and Roemer (2002) investigated the role of MGRS (measured with the MGRSS) and traditional masculinity ideology (measured with the MRNS and the MRNI) in men's aggressive and violent behaviors toward their intimate female partners (measured with the CTS; Straus, 1979). The results indicated that MGRS moderated the relationship between traditional masculinity ideology and aggression against women. Specifically, traditional masculinity ideology only predicted aggression against women among men who also reported high levels of MGRS. This moderation effect of MGRS is similar to the effect of traditional masculinity ideology on the relationship between exposure to violent video games and aggression, discussed earlier in this chapter.

In a related vein, Gallagher and Parrott (2011) examined MGRS as a mediator of the relationship between adherence to specific traditional masculinity norms (measured using the MRNS) and hostility toward women (HTW). Results indicated that MGRS mediated the relation between adherence to the status and antifemininity norms, but not the toughness norm, and HTW. Adherence to the toughness norm maintained a positive direct link with HTW. These findings suggest that men's HTW develops via multiple pathways that are associated with different traditional masculinity norms.

Further, in a study of masculinity and power in men's accounts of domestic violence against their female partners (Anderson & Umberson, 2001), the investigators conducted interviews with 33 domestically violent heterosexual men. They reported that the men used various techniques to present themselves as rational and nonviolent. For example, the men contrasted "effectual male violence with ineffectual female violence," claimed "that female partners were responsible for the violence in their relationships," and viewed "men as victims of a biased criminal justice system" (p. 252). That these domestically violent men would chose to present themselves in this way is not surprising, given Gage and Lease's (2018) findings on IPV myths as previously discussed. To unearth the dynamics, we will have to dig deeper and refer to masculinity's role in establishing a dominance hierarchy of men over women. For example, a recent study found that women earning more than two thirds of the total household income were seven times more likely to experience psychological and physical abuse compared to women who earned less (Knapton, 2014). Could this result from men's sense of masculine dominance being threatened by their women partners' out-earning them? If so, then we are talking about the important role of MGRS in IPV once again; as a reminder, one of the MGRSS subscales is Subordination to Women.

In a related vein, research suggests that men's economic struggles might play a role in their violence toward an intimate female partner. In the previously discussed study by Peralta and Tuttle (2013), it was found that for some men being unemployed or failing to provide for their family can result in anger toward themselves and feeling that they failed in their role as a man. This can cause them to lash out at their wives. They believe that the role that they need to fill was passed down from their father, reflecting the important role that fathers play in the masculine socialization process of their sons. Consider this short excerpt from one of the interviews:

Interviewer: A lot of people say work, employment, is associated with self-esteem. Would it hurt your self-esteem sometimes?
Participant: Yeah, cuz she feels that you ain't the man you should be, but that's how I feel. . . . I'm like my father. My father, he always had work. He was in construction for 44 [years]. He raised all of us. A lot

of times he would do without to make sure we had it. That's the type of person I'm trying to be, even though me and her don't have no kids together. (p. 256)

The pressure to fulfill a role as hard won and easily lost as masculinity can cause great difficulties for men (and those around them). While this in no way excuses IPV, it may help us to understand the processes underlying it, which hopefully can be used to prevent future violence and to help those affected by it.

IPV and Mass Shootings

According to an ABC News report (Keneally, 2019), IPV plays a role in many mass shootings, but receives less attention. A mass shooting is defined by the FBI as an incident where four or more people—not including the suspect—are killed. While there is no publicly accessible federal data base tracking such incidents, various groups keep their own lists, often using different definitions of what qualifies as a mass shooting. Of the 20 mass shootings that ABC News identified in 2018 that fit the FBI's parameters, 10 were instances of either intimate partner or family violence, both of which are forms of domestic violence.

Female-Perpetrated IPV

IPV is typically viewed as male-perpetrated physical violence on female victims in heterosexual and same sex relationships. However, it is generally acknowledged that women also perpetrate physical IPV in heterosexual relationships. There exists controversy in the literature as to whether there is gender symmetry in physical IPV. It is beyond our scope to delve into this controversy, so we simply present both sides here. On the one hand, Dobash and Dobash (2004) concluded:

> The findings suggest that intimate partner violence is primarily an asymmetrical problem of men's violence to women, and women's violence does not equate to men's in terms of frequency, severity, consequences and the victim's sense of safety and well-being. (p. 324)

Whereas Straus (2008) found

> that almost one-third of the female as well as male students physically assaulted a dating partner in the previous 12 months, and that the most frequent pattern was bidirectional, i.e., both were violent,

followed by "female-only" violence. Violence by only the male partner was the least frequent pattern according to both male and female participants. (p. 252)

We will return to the topic of female-perpetrated IPV in Chapter 7 of this volume when we discuss men's trauma.

IPV in Gay Male Relationships

IPV has most often been studied in heterosexual couples, and as a result there has been little research on IPV in gay relationships. Furthermore, few resources exist outside of the LGBT community to help gay men who are victims of IPV. The lack of support from communities outside of the LGBT population can result in survivors feeling ashamed of their experiences, as do some female victims of IPV. Research on prevalence of abuse by sexual orientation suggests that abuse in same-sex couples occurs at the same or even higher frequencies than in heterosexual couples (Balsam, Rothblum, & Beauchaine, 2005; Blosnich & Bossarte, 2009; Finneran & Stephenson, 2013; Messinger, 2011).

There is a similarity between male victims of male-perpetrated violence and those of female-perpetrated violence. Both are dealing with the uncomfortable intersection of being a man and an abuse survivor, which is problematic because masculinity norms require men to be strong and most certainly not a victim. That is, these men may experience discrepancy strain, in which being in an abusive relationship can make the man feel that he does not measure up to the masculine norm of toughness, resulting in a sense of shame. We will return to this topic of IPV in gay male relationships in Chapter 7 of this volume, when we discuss men's trauma.

Hate Crimes

This passage was written the morning after the deadly shooting at the Tree of Life Synagogue in Pittsburgh, by Robert Bowers, an anti-Semitic gunman, which was preceded just days before by the mailing of pipe bombs to political and media figures that President Trump has vilified as his enemies. Also, two Black people were killed in a Kroeger grocery store in Kentucky after the shooter tried and failed to gain entrance into a Black church. Sadly, there have been many such hate crimes, going back to Emmet Till and Mathew Shepard. We will look at the role of masculinity in these horrendous acts.

FBI hate crime statistics for 2017 indicate that most offenders were White (50%) and 18 years of age and older (83 %). Interestingly, they did not post any statistics on the sex of offenders, indicating once again the failure to acknowledge gun violence as perpetrated by boys and men. According to the FBI data, 59% of all hate crimes targeted individuals based on their race/ethnicity/ancestry, 20% were against persons because of their religion, 15% of crimes were a result of bias against an individual's sexual orientation, 1.9% targeted individuals based on their disability, 1.6% were based on bias against gender-identity, and 0.6% were based on gender bias. Of those resulting from race/ethnicity/ancestry bias, the majority of victims were Black/African American individuals. The majority of individuals who experienced hate crimes based on their religion were Jewish (58%), followed by Muslim individuals (18%). According to Weisman (2018), "the FBI reports that hate crimes in the U.S. jumped 17 % in 2017, with a 37 % spike in crimes against Jews and Jewish institutions" (p. 3). Finally, 57% of all antigay hate crimes targeted gay men. This final statistic provides a good transition to begin talking about hate crimes and masculinity.

As the reader may recall, a central masculine norm is to avoid all things feminine. This norm comes into play in heterosexual men's attitudes toward gay men, particularly toward effeminate gay men. In general, men who endorse traditional masculinity norms show higher rates of sexual prejudice against gay men (Barron, Struckman-Johnson, Quevillon, & Banka, 2008), especially men who endorse the avoidance of femininity norm (Parrott, 2009; Parrott, Peterson, & Bakeman, 2011). Animosity toward sexual minorities (which in itself is one of the traditional masculinity norms) is much higher toward gay men than toward lesbian women and is present more in heterosexual men than in heterosexual women (Wellman & McCoy, 2014). So how do we explain this? Perhaps heterosexual men who strongly endorse traditional masculinity ideology might see effeminate gay men as a direct challenge to the masculinity standard that to be a man means to avoid femininity, not embrace it. Alternatively, some heterosexual men might feel a need to secure their own appearance of being masculine by distancing themselves from (and sometimes harming) gay men, hence the previously cited FBI statistics. This leads one to deduce that masculinity norms (primarily antifemininity, but also disdain for sexual minorities[8]) might be a culprit in prejudice against sexual minorities.

Aside from sexual prejudice, hate crimes were highest toward the Black population according to the FBI hate crime statistics. Unfortunately, we could find nothing in the behavioral science literature regarding this matter despite the extremely high rates of prevalence. However, information can be found in online media articles about acts of violence like lynching's and beatings.

---

[8] It should be note that Parrott et al. (2011) measured traditional masculinity ideology using the MRNS, which has an antifemininity subscale but not an antigay subscale. It would be instructive to replicate this study using the MRNI, which has both subscales.

Summary and Conclusions

In this chapter, we have discussed the role of masculinity in gun violence and other major contemporary forms of physical violence. We have seen a clear trend in which the perpetrators are commonly White men and the victims are from a marginalized group such as women, sexual and gender minorities, and people of color. We know that the overwhelming majority of mass shooters are male and that the preponderance of police officers who are involved in shootings of Black men are men. Further, masculinity has been directly linked to negativity toward minority groups and violence toward intimate partners, both women and men. We have also seen that masculinity is linked to aggression and violence in indirect ways. Indirect relationships include traditional masculinity ideology operating as a moderating influence on young men's aggression when exposed to violent video games and MGRS mediating the relationship between adherence to the status and antifemininity masculine norms and hostility toward women. Finally, we also see masculinity's influence in hate crimes, where underneath the violence lays an extreme sensitivity to violations of masculine norms, which results in either creating a distance from gay men or performing hateful acts toward them.

Although we posited in Chapter 2 of this volume that the harmful effects of masculinity are due to the extreme high scores, we are not yet able to answer with any precision the question of why some men commit physical violence and others do not. That is, while we know that traditional masculinity ideology, conformity to masculine norms, and gender role conflict and stress are correlated with various aspects of violence, we do not yet know how these masculinity constructs interact with the personality and individual difference variables and social situations to produce these horrible acts? This is a most urgent task for future research.

We have seen that physical violence is pervasive across situations and people, from teens to adults, and from police to significant others. In our view, violence is a norm in our society, reinforced on a daily basis on the news, in the paper, on our phones, and sometimes physically right in front of us. The idea that a man is violent is not surprising; in fact, we expect it. We normalize it during the early years of a boy's life when we say "Boys will be boys" whenever violent acts occur on the playground, with their friends, or with their siblings. Is it fair of us to say "Boys will be boys" and then shake our heads in disbelief when some of them grow up to commit violent crimes? I (SP) once was involved with a man who behaved in a verbally abusive manner toward me. When I discussed this with one of our mutual friends, he said, "That's just how he is." We make excuses for and pardon the violent behavior in men when we say, "Why didn't she just leave that man if he was abusing her?"; "He wouldn't have been shot if he hadn't dressed in that black hoodie"[9]; and "They were just mentally ill." When victims do come forward to speak out against violence, we might say "Why didn't you say something sooner?"; "Are you sure they would do that?"; and "Quit playing the race card." Our culture excuses violence. Perhaps it is just easier to pretend that there is no problem because the real problem is too complex and daunting to face. One of our goals in writing this book is to raise these uncomfortable questions: What is the problem? Are we doing enough? Are we even doing anything at all? Let us start by recognizing that we have a problem and then let us talk about it.

[9] This is in reference to the case of Trayvon Martin who was fatally shot by a neighborhood watch captain in Miami Gardens, Florida because of his seemingly threatening attire.

‖ 6 ‖

Masculinity's Role in Sexual Violence

In the United States, one in three women and one in six men will be the recipient of some kind of sexual violence in their lifetime (Smith et al., 2017). The Centers for Disease Control and Prevention (CDC, n.d.) define sexual violence as follows: "Sexual violence is defined as a sexual act committed against someone without that person's freely given consent." According to the CDC, sexual violence includes the following acts:

- Penetration of a person, either completed or attempted, and either forced or alcohol or drug-facilitated.
- Acts in which a victim is made to penetrate someone, either completed or attempted, and either forced or alcohol or drug-facilitated.
- Nonphysically forced penetration, which occurs after a person is pressured to consent or submit to being penetrated.
- Unwanted sexual contact (referred to as "sexual harassment" in some contexts, such as a school or workplace).
- Noncontact unwanted sexual experiences in many different settings, such as school, the workplace, in public, or through technology.

Prior Sexual Violence Research

Sexual violence is a very broad topic that is beyond our scope to cover in detail. To give the reader some idea of the extent of the field, Tharp et al. (2013) summarized the results of 191 published studies that investigated the risk and protective factors for sexual violence perpetration, defined very broadly. The review included perpetration by and against adults and adolescents, by female and male perpetrators, and by those who offended against individuals of another or the same sex, but did not include perpetration of child sexual abuse perpetration. In all, 67 risk and protective factors were identified. These encompassed social- and community-level factors, relationship-level factors, and individual-level factors. Of these factors, consistent significant support for their association with sexual violence was found for 35 factors. Of the rest, 22 factors had sample-specific or otherwise limited evidence that they were associated with sexual violence or demonstrated mixed results, and 10 factors had nonsignificant effects. Given the enormous size of this research domain, we focus on the literature that specifically implicates masculinity in men's sexual assault of women.

Hostile Masculinity

Neil Malamuth and colleagues were early leaders in the investigation of men's sexual violence against women (Malamuth, Heavey, & Linz, 1996). They proposed the "confluence model," based on evolutionary and feminist perspectives in psychology, which hypothesized that there are two paths that lead to men's sexual assault perpetration. The first, the hostile masculinity path, is based on the confluence of a number of variables—dominance motives, hostility toward women, sexual arousal in response to aggression, and attitudes facilitating aggression against women—which lead to a controlling and adversarial approach to women. The second path, an impersonal, promiscuous orientation to sexuality, results from delinquent tendencies expressed as sexual acting out, precocious sexual behavior, and reliance on sexual conquest to demonstrate one's masculinity. Of these paths, hostile masculinity has received the most attention. It is measured by combining separate scales that measure negative masculinity, rape myth acceptance, dominance over women, and attitudes supporting aggression or by using selected items from these scales.

Malamuth and colleagues have achieved some important results with this model, including a longitudinal study of men 10 years after first studying them as young adults, in which the model was able to predict which men would be aggressive sexually, nonsexually aggressive, in distressed relationships with women, or a combination of these outcomes (Malamuth, Linz, Heavey, Barnes, & Acker, 1995). The outcomes were assessed by asking the men and some of their female partners about their relationships. Furthermore, Murnen, Wright, and Kaluzny (2002) reported a meta-analysis using 39 studies of male college students' scores on several measures of masculinity; they found several strong effect sizes in relationship to measures of sexual assault perpetration. The largest effects corresponded to Malamuth et al.'s (1991) construct of hostile masculinity and Mosher and Sirkin's (1984) construct of hypermasculinity. More recently, Troche and Herzberg (2017) used the confluence model in their study, which addressed hostile masculinity and impersonal sex as it related to sexual aggression as measured by the Sexual Experience Survey (SES; Krahe, Reimer, Scheinberger-Olwig, & Fritsche, 1999). They reported that these two constructs were indeed linked with sexual aggression; other studies have also found support for this finding (Abbey, Jacques, & LeBreton, 2011; Greene & Davis, 2011; Hines, 2007; Malamuth et al., 1995; Widman, Olson, & Bolen, 2013). Even when impersonal sex was not measured in the study, hostile masculinity continued to predict sexual aggression against women (Anderson & Anderson, 2008; Hall, DeGarmo, Eap, Teten, & Sue, 2006). Finally, Parkhill and Abbey (2008) tested an expanded confluence model, which included alcohol use, hostile masculinity, and impersonal sex attitudes. They found that model fit was significantly improved by including a path between drinking behaviors and hostile masculinity.

Critical Evaluation of Hostile Masculinity Research

It may seem reasonable thus to conclude that constructs included in the rubric of hostile masculinity are positively linked to sexual assault perpetration. However, there are two concerns that weaken that claim. First, apart from Malamuth et al. (1995) and similar to most other research on the impact of masculinities, the hostile masculinity results are primarily from cross-sectional studies, which leaves open the question of whether hostile masculinity is the cause, the result, or a covariate of sexual assault perpetration. Longitudinal studies would address this question.[1] Abbey and McAuslan (2004) found in a longitudinal study that some aspects of hostile masculinity were no longer significant when controlling for past sexual assault. Indeed, as with physical violence, *past sexual assault was the most reliable predictor of future sexual violence perpetration.*

Furthermore, and most important, in a critique of this research literature as it applies to men's sexual assault of college women, McDermott, Kilmartin, McKelvey, and Kridel (2015) astutely pointed out that most studies investigating hostile masculinity simply added up the scores on separate measures of several constructs (which includes various combinations of such variables as hypermasculinity, rape myth acceptance, attitudes toward women, dominance and power over women, and hostility toward women) to create a composite variable that was then called "hostile masculinity." While such a composite measure may appear on first blush to resemble multidimensional masculinity scales (like the Male Role Norms Inventory [MRNI], Conformity to Masculine Norms Inventory [CMNI], and Gender Role Conflict Scale [GRCS], as discussed in

---

[1] We mean true longitudinal studies with repeated measures. Most of the longitudinal work in this area is pseudo-longitudinal and does not use the same measures throughout. Only by controlling for the auto-regressive effects of the same measure's change or stability over time can one really evaluate whether the predicted longitudinal effects between a predictor and criterion are explaining additional variance.

Chapter 2 of this volume), they are not the same by any stretch of the imagination. In fact, it would be necessary to subject the hostile masculinity measure to extensive psychometric analyses to make this claim. These analyses would include both exploratory and confirmatory factor analyses to determine dimensionality and variance composition, multigroup confirmatory factor analyses to assess measurement equivalence, and assessments of reliability and validity. Such studies do not exist. McDermott et al. (2015) found only one study that used confirmatory factor analysis to examine hostile masculinity instruments. They noted that "although the model demonstrated an acceptable fit to their data, only hostility toward women loaded above .50 on their latent hostile masculinity factor. These issues raise serious doubts about the construct validity of hostile masculinity instruments as measures of men's socialized gender roles" (p. 359). These investigators concluded that, while "men's attitudes toward women and violence are strong predictors of sexual assault perpetration . . . research examining men's sexual assault perpetration using constructs central to the psychology of men is generally underdeveloped and underrepresented" (p. 362). Thus, this research program has not provided substantive evidence for the role of masculinity, as it is currently studied in the psychology of men and masculinities, in sexual violence. What it does show is that a combination of variables reflecting hostility toward women are associated with men's sexual violence against women. To move toward the goal of understanding the role of masculinity in sexual violence, we will next put forth a theoretical account of the role that masculinity plays in sexual violence and then evaluate the research from the psychology of men and masculinities. As we will show, there is a good bit of evidence linking masculinity to sexual violence, although aspects of the theory have not yet been put to the test.

Toward a Theory of the Roles That Masculinity Plays in Sexual Violence

There are four aspects of masculinity that we theorize contribute to some men's propensity to engage in sexual violence. The masculinity norm to avoid all things feminine is at the core of men's sexual violence. In addition, the following factors all play a role: privilege, impaired empathy, and the complex pattern largely resulting from traditional fathers' influence on their sons that results in a deep sense of shame and a sense that their attainment of masculinity status is tenuous (e.g., "precarious manhood"). As we have previously stated, precarious manhood can be considered a form of discrepancy strain and is related to masculine gender role stress. We have discussed these aspects of masculinity in Chapter 3 of this volume. Once again, as we stated in regard to gun and other physical violence, *we are not asserting that all men are sexually violent or are proponents of sexual violence nor that masculinity is the sole or even most important cause of sexual violence.* These points are underscored by a nationally representative study that found:

> The frequency with which men reported having perpetrated each form of sexual aggression ranged from 19% of men who indicated that they had obtained sexual contact through the use of coercion to 1% of men who indicated that they had obtained oral or anal penetration through the use of force. (Koss, Gidycz, & Wisniewski, 1987, p. 166)

We are saying, however, that, far and away, most sexual violence is committed by men. Further, we are saying that masculinity does play a role, and this is largely unexamined using the modern toolkit of the psychology of men and masculinities.

Avoid Femininity, Objectification, and Nonrelational Sexuality

As previously stated, a key masculine norm is to avoid all things feminine because masculinity must be clearly demarcated from femininity. By rejecting anything stereotypically feminine, men and boys wind up rejecting, suppressing, and feeling ashamed of essential parts of themselves that are considered feminine— such as empathy, kindness, and compassion. A boy or man displaying these latter traits can invite ridicule or even a beating from other boys or men. Consider that girls who act like boys are often praised; being a tomboy can be a badge of honor for a girl. Consider also that the Boy Scouts have recently opened membership to girls, but can anyone imagine boys seeking membership in the Girl Scouts? We doubt it, because boys who act like girls are called "wuss," "sissy," or worse and made to feel ashamed of themselves. This sweeping rejection of femininity reflects is an underlying misogyny that is built into masculinity.[2] For men who experience poverty in inner city or rural environments or where crime might be rampant, boys and men might be forced to display a tough masculine appearance and avoid femininity in order to protect themselves from being targeted. This would be especially true for adolescent boys who want to fit in with their peers and so would adhere to the status quo of anti-femininity.

---

[2] According to a *New York Times* op-ed, this sweeping rejection of femininity is not just in boys but also in girls: "We have internalized a kind of sexism that values masculinity in both boys and girls, just as it devalues femininity in them" (Selin Davis, 2018).

One consequence of the norm to avoid femininity is that boys lock up the warmer, softer aspects of themselves that are considered feminine. Another is that it promotes the sexual objectification of girls and women. This latter point requires a bit of explanation. The avoid femininity norm is strongly reinforced throughout boys' gender role socialization. Thus, boys tend to play with other boys and avoid contact with girls. Hence, most boys do not have much if any experience interacting with girls as persons. The sociologist Michael Kimmel has advocated cross-sex friendships among children to counter this trend (cf Felmlee, Sweet, & Sinclair, 2012). When puberty arrives, heterosexual boys become interested in girls, but they are largely interested in girls as *sexual objects*, not as persons. As such, they are conforming to an outmoded masculine norm of viewing sex as either recreation or as an award for achieving their masculinity, rather than as the expression of love and intimacy in a close relationship. This orientation to sexuality has been termed "nonrelational" (Levant, 1997b) and is defined as follows:

> Nonrelational sexuality can be defined as the tendency to experience sex as lust without any requirements for relational intimacy, or even for more than a minimal connection with the object of one's desires.... In this mode of sexual experience, objects of sexual desire are often objectified, and at times are in fact objects (as in pornographic books and videos and masturbation toys), which are pursued, in the agentic fashion prescribed by masculinity, to meet a set of needs. These needs include the need to release sexual tension, needs for closeness, connection, and nurturance, and needs for affirming one's sense of adequacy as a man. (p. 10)

Sadly, boys' sex education today comes principally from ubiquitous pornography, most of which, as the Media Education Foundation has demonstrated, is phallocentric and denigrates women (Picker & Sun, 2008). Those boys become men, and some expect their sexual lives to conform to what they have seen in porn, leading to problematic pornography use. A recent study (Borgogna, McDermott, Browning, Beach, & Aita, 2019) examined the links between traditional masculinity ideology (using the MRNI–Short Form) and problematic pornography viewing. Results indicated that men's endorsement of the avoidance of femininity, dominance, restrictive emotionality, and disdain for sexual minorities norms of traditional masculinity ideology predicted men's problematic pornography use.

Some men who view pornography even go as far as to become sexually coercive. Indeed, research has indicated that pornography consumption is a risk factor, among other factors (e.g., substance use, alcohol), for sexual violence perpetration in college men (Carr & VanDeusen, 2004). Baer, Kohut, and Fisher (2015) assessed whether hostile masculinity[3] and sexual promiscuity were associated with pornography use and sexual coercion of women. Sexual promiscuity was assessed by recording the age of first consented intercourse and the number of partners in the previous 5 years. Hostile masculinity was assessed using items that measured attitudes toward violence (e.g., hitting, pushing, abusive language) and attitudes toward women (e.g., "Women mean yes when they say no"; "Women are less intelligent than men"). They found that when men were high in hostile masculinity and sexual promiscuity, pornography use was associated with sexual coercion. Interestingly, pornography use was not found to be associated with sexual coercion in men with low levels of hostile masculinity and sexual promiscuity.

Additionally, endorsing the avoid femininity norm of masculinity may interfere with a person's ability to speak up in a situation where sexual violence may occur. Indeed, research has shown that men who endorse the avoid femininity norm are less likely to intervene in a sexual assault scenario (Leone, Parrott, Swartout, & Tharp, 2016). This suggests that to speak up in a possible sexual assault situation may make the man fear that he would appear less masculine and more feminine, which must be avoided at all costs.

Privilege and Entitlement

As discussed in Chapter 3 of this volume, one major function of the traditional gender roles of masculinity and femininity is to confer a certain degree of privilege on men and reinforce men's dominance over women. This enables some men to think of women as existing for their sexual pleasure and to objectify them. The result for some men is a sense of *entitlement* to women's bodies, ranging from leering (ogling), womanizing, and catcalling to harassment and abuse. A sense of entitlement, by the way, is one of the diagnostic criteria for narcissistic personality disorder.

When I (RL) think of some men's sense of entitlement to women's bodies, a former client comes to mind. I was seeing this middle-aged man and his wife for marital therapy, and the wife complained that he blatantly ogled women in her presence. She described an incident where they were seated at an outdoor table in a restaurant and a buxom young woman was walking along the sidewalk. As the wife described it, her husband locked his eyes on the women's chest like radar, and his head swiveled as in the film *The Exorcist* until the woman was out of sight. The husband's response: "You shouldn't mind where I get my appetite as long as I come home for dinner."

---

[3] Keeping in mind our critique of this construct, these findings must be viewed cautiously.

In a recent study, men's entitlement significantly predicted sexual dominance of women (LeBreton, Baysinger, Abbey, & Jacques-Tiura, 2013). Additionally, men's sense of entitlement affects a man's willingness to obtain consent before initiating sexual activity. Thompson and Cracco (2008) found that in their study of 264 college men, although 64% reported having never asked a woman they didn't know to have sex, half of the men said they hinted at sexual interest by behaving in a sexually aggressive manner such as grabbing a woman's butt or pressing up against her from behind. Furthermore, another study found that 34% of college men reported some proclivity to rape or force sex (Osland, Fitch, & Willis, 1996). Men who reported both proclivities indicated higher rape myth acceptance, offered more justifications for the increasing use of violence against women, were lower in rape empathy, held more gender-stereotyped attitudes toward women, and accepted interpersonal violence more than those who reported no proclivities.

Bushman, Bonacci, van Dijk, and Baumeister (2003) investigated the role that narcissism plays in rape. Over three laboratory analog studies they found (a) narcissism correlated positively with rape-supportive beliefs and negatively with empathy for rape victims; (b) narcissists reported more enjoyment than other men of film depictions that presented consensual, affectionate activity followed by rape (but not in response to either affection or rape alone); and (c), narcissists were more punitive than other men toward a female confederate who refused to read a sexually arousing passage aloud to them.

At the extreme end of the entitlement continuum is the incel phenomenon. Incel is a contraction of the term "involuntarily celibate" and is adopted by a community of predominantly heterosexual men who want sexual or romantic relationships with women but cannot seem to create them. Such men do not accept responsibility for this outcome but rather blame women. They believe they are entitled to sex with women and are bitterly aggrieved that women are not willing to have sex with them. Blume (2018) noted that "they experience 'aggrieved entitlement,' anger and resentment based on a conscious or unconscious sense that they are not getting what they deserve." A central figure in this phenomenon is Jordan Peterson, a psychologist-turned-pop-philosopher whose wide-ranging advice for men includes reasserting their dominance over women and enforced monogamy.

Finally, White male privilege plays a significant role in sexual violence perpetration through racial disparities in sentencing, in which White men (such as Brock Turner and John Enochs) get much lower sentences for their sexual crimes than men of color who have allegedly committed similar crimes (Madkins, 2016). White male privilege as it relates to sexual violence has been examined in fraternities, which house primarily White men. Jozkowski and Wiersma-Mosley (2017) noted that fraternities hold considerable power within the university system, having been recognized institutions in universities for decades. This results in privileging White men in the partying/fraternity culture where sexual violence often occurs by allowing such students convicted of rape to serve very short sentences. For example, a male student who was found guilty of raping a female student was only sentenced for 3 months (Cleary, 2016).

Impaired Empathy

Those men who have difficulty experiencing their own emotions and putting them into words would likely also have difficulty vicariously experiencing another person's emotions. A recent *New York Times* op-ed (Klein, 2018) regarding the #MeToo movement's effect on men reported that some men who are psychotherapy clients are questioning their approach to dating women. These men noted that they have difficulty seeing how their approach affected the women they date—that is, seeing the interaction through the eyes of the woman—in short, being empathic with them. Recall also Aziz Ansari's reaction to learning how "Grace" perceived their sexual encounter, which he thought had been consensual. We have discussed in Chapter 3 of this volume how alexithymic men lack the ability to vicariously experience another person's emotions, which is necessary to be emotionally empathic.

Another example with a different result comes from the *New York Times Sunday Magazine* column, "The Ethicist" (Appiah, 2018). A man wrote about the rupture of a college friendship with a women, following his attempt to kiss her without consent. In trying to understand her reaction, he turned to the #MeToo movement. He wrote:

> When the #MeToo movement was in full swing, I thought about how this friend once told me, tearfully, about being sexually assaulted as a teenager by a guy she knew and trusted. And she now carried that assault with her everywhere she went. I suddenly understood. As much as I know I wasn't—and would never be—that guy, to her I was, or at least I could have been. I broke her trust and our bond by trying to kiss her when she did not want to be kissed.

Fathers, Precarious Manhood, and Womanizing

In regard to womanizing, I (RL) recall a psychotherapy client in his 50s who had married a woman in her 30s and had a family with small children, whom he stated he loved dearly. Yet he had ongoing affairs with multiple women in various cities to which he traveled on business. He also had had a very fraught relationship with his tough and demanding father, a World War II veteran, whom he felt was always down on him and never gave him any credit for anything. Through psychotherapy, he gradually realized that his many infidelities represented an attempt to reassure himself that he was a "real man" despite his father's casting aspersions on his masculinity. This case thus illustrates several concepts: the role of the father in socializing sons to conform to traditional masculinity, precarious manhood, and how some men use sex to demonstrate their masculinity, much as some young men do when they brag about their sexual exploits, real and imagined, to their buddies.[4]

Research Supporting Theory

First, masculinity's general role in sexual violence has been supported using the toolkit of the psychology of men and masculinities.[5] As we have seen in Chapter 4 of this volume, MRNI scores are correlated with attitudes conducive to sexual harassment and sexism. CMNI scores are associated with rape myth acceptance and sexually aggressive behavior. Finally, GRCS scores are correlated with sexually aggressive behaviors and the likelihood of forcing sex, abusive behaviors and coercion, hostile sexism, hostility toward women, rape myth acceptance, and positive attitudes toward and tolerance for sexual harassment. Further GRCS scores significantly predicted general male entitlement, which in turn predicted sexual entitlement, which finally predicted rape-related criterion variables. Finally, studies have shown that high versus low levels of gender role conflict significantly differentiate coercive from noncoercive men, sexually aggressive college men from nonaggressive men, and domestic abusers from nonviolent men. Taken together, the studies indicate that gender role conflict is significantly related to thoughts, attitudes, and behaviors that are abusive and violent toward women. Additional studies, to be discussed next, buttress this support for the general role of masculinity in sexual violence and highlight some aspects of the theory that we put forth regarding specific aspects of masculinity that play a role in sexual violence.

CMNI Studies

A number of studies found links between CMNI scores and aspects of sexual violence. In a study of fraternities, membership in which is associated with

---

[4] Swartout (2013) found that perceiving that peers endorse rape myths is a significant risk factor for college sexual assault.

[5] However, these findings should be viewed as preliminary as they are all from cross-sectional studies. We are not aware of any longitudinal studies on masculinity's general role in sexual violence using the toolkit of the psychology of men and masculinities.

greater perpetration and acceptance of sexual violence, Seabrook, Ward, and Giaccardi (2018) found that conformity to masculine norms, pressure to uphold masculine norms, and acceptance of objectification of women (which, as previously noted is theoretically related to the avoid femininity norm) mediated (transmitted) the relationship between fraternity membership and acceptance of sexual violence.

Locke and Mahalik (2005) found that college men who use alcohol problematically and conform to certain masculine norms using the CMNI (power over women, playboy, dominance, violence, risk-taking, disdain for gay men) tended to accept rape myths and engage in sexual aggression as measured by the Illinois Rape Myth Scale and the Sexual Experiences Survey, respectively.

Mikorski and Szymanski (2017) found that the CMNI playboy and violence subscales and higher levels of pornography use uniquely predicted more body evaluation (i.e., objectification) of women among college men. Pornography use and the individual interactions of the playboy, power over women, and violence subscales with a scale measuring a man's association with abusive male peers were all unique predictors of making unwanted sexual advances. Conformity to the playboy, power over women, and violence masculine norms each predicted making unwanted sexual advances toward women for men with high levels of association with abusive male peers but not for those with moderate or low levels of association with abusive male peers.

Hermann, Liang, and DeSipio (2018) investigated the relationship between college men's conformity to three masculine norms (playboy, power over women, and violence) using the CMNI and their intentions to engage in consensual sexual behaviors. A path analysis revealed that men who conformed to these norms reported a greater lack of control over asking for consent, more negative attitudes toward consent, and more indirect consent behaviors (e.g., "Typically I communicate sexual consent to my partner using nonverbal signals and body language"; p. 494).

Discrepancy Stress, Masculine Gender Role Stress, and Precarious Manhood

In a study of middle and high school boys, Reidy, Smith-Darden, Cortina, Kernsmith, and Kernsmith (2015), found that boys who experience masculine gender role discrepancy stress about being perceived as "submasculine" were more likely to engage in acts of sexual violence but not necessarily physical violence. The researchers speculated that such boys may be more likely to engage in sexual violence as a means of demonstrating their masculinity to self and/or others. As we have noted before, experiencing discrepancy strain results in a sense of shame that some men dispel by forcefully demonstrating their masculinity. In this context, sexual violence can be seen as a resource for doing masculinity.

Smith, Parrott, Swartout, and Tharp (2015) found that adherence to the avoid femininity norm on the MRNI and the tendency to experience masculine gender role stress when in subordinate positions to women on the Masculine Gender Role Stress Scale (MGRSS) were indirectly related to sexual aggression perpetration through their adherence to sexual dominance (using the Sexual Dominance Scale). Thus, the men who adhere to the avoid femininity norm and endorse sexual dominance may feel compelled to be sexually aggressive and/or coercive toward an intimate partner when experiencing masculine gender role stress (i.e., discrepancy strain) to demonstrate their masculinity.

Munsch and Willer (2012) conducted an experiment that investigated the effects of gender threat (masculinity and femininity) on men's and women's perceptions of date rape and sexual coercion. They found that masculinity-threatened men blamed the victim and exonerated the perpetrator, whereas femininity-threatened women blamed male perpetrators and placed less blame on female victims. Men's response to threats was more pronounced than women's, illustrating how much more powerful masculinity threat is to men as compared to femininity threat to women.

Masculine Honor Beliefs

Masculine honor beliefs are beliefs that compel men to defend their reputations against threats and insults. Masculine honor beliefs is one of the theories of aggression that I (RL) cover in my social psychology class. Honor cultures are social institutions exemplifying patriarchy and entitlement. In the United States, southern states are honor states, but honor cultures are not limited to U.S. southerners. Examples outside the U.S. include Italian and Arabic cultures.

Brown, Baughman, and Carvallo (2018) tested (using census data) the hypothesis that masculine honor beliefs would be associated with an increased likelihood of men engaging in violent and sexually coercive behaviors toward women. Comparisons between honor states (southern states per the U.S. Census Bureau) and nonhonor states in the United States show that rape by White male perpetrators and experiences of rape anonymously reported by White female teenagers were higher in honor states, controlling for a variety of potential confounds. These results extend prior laboratory research on honor-based beliefs into the realm of real-world behavior.

Do masculine honor beliefs play a role in men responding aggressively (e.g., name calling, physical aggression) to women who reject their romantic advances? Stratmoen, Greer, Martens, and Saucier (2018) hypothesized that masculine honor beliefs would be positively associated with perceptions that men's aggressive responses to rejection are appropriate. As participants' level of adherence to masculine honor beliefs increased, so did their perceptions that the man responding aggressively to a woman for rejecting his attempt to initiate a relationship with her was appropriate. Interestingly, higher levels of masculine honor beliefs were not associated with the perception that the man's aggressive responses were more appropriate when the rejection, and his consequent response, were more public. This research suggests these antisocial responses may be rooted in the defense and maintenance of their perceived social (i.e., honor) reputations. Once again, this seems to be another form of discrepancy strain, where the rejection induces in the man a feeling that in being rejected, he has not lived up to his internalized masculinity ideals.

Summary of Research Supportive of Theory

First, there appear to be links between sexual violence and men's endorsement of and conformity to traditional masculinity norms and their gender role conflict. Furthermore, there is evidence supporting some of our theorized components of masculinity's role in sexual violence—specifically avoiding femininity, privilege, and discrepancy strain/masculine gender role stress/precarious manhood. Future research might further investigate these variables and the role of impaired empathy in sexual violence.

Summary and Conclusions

We have discussed several directions that researchers have taken in trying to understand masculinity's role in sexual violence. We discussed and critiqued the construct of hostile masculinity in the sexual violence literature, which was an early forerunner in the field. We dug a little deeper into the literature on the psychology of men and masculinities and explored the possible ways that masculinity might relate to sexual violence. Several factors were theorized, including avoidance of femininity, objectification, privilege, impaired empathy, and precarious manhood/discrepancy strain. We then reviewed research on the roles that conformity to masculine norms, masculine gender role stress, and honor beliefs play in sexual violence, finding some support for the theorized masculinity components that we posited.

The research that was reviewed and analyzed in this chapter approach the relationship between masculinity and sexual violence in different ways. However, they all lead to the same conclusion—namely, that masculinity plays a role in sexual violence. Having sex is a rite of passage and even a way to prove one's masculinity for many young men. Men who have not had sex are not able to show their prowess to their peers, which they find very distressing. Like Elliott Rodger, the Isla Vista shooter, who killed several people over his anguish about being rejected sexually by women, some men who feel rejected by women grow to hate them for spurning their advances. In less extreme cases, some men might feel like lesser men for being a virgin or not having as much sex as others seem to. While only a minority of men will be sexually violent, the norms of masculinity (e.g., avoid femininity, restrictive emotionality, self-reliance, toughness, dominance, disdain for sexual minority men, and placing a great deal of importance on sex) continue to be a negative influence on developing boys as they reach puberty and go on to college, as well as on older men as they go through life. Although we have found links between masculinity and sexual violence using the modern toolkit of the psychology of men and masculinities and although we posited in Chapter 2 of this volume that the harmful effects of masculinity are due to the extreme high scores, we are not yet able to answer with any precision the question of why some men commit acts of sexual violence and others do not. Echoing our statement at the end of Chapter 5 of this volume, we ask how traditional masculinity ideology, conformity to masculine norms, and gender role conflict and stress interact with the personality and individual difference variables and social situations that are necessary to lead men to do these horrible things. This is a most urgent task for future research.

Before we end this chapter, I (SP) wanted to say that I have spent a lot of time working with the topic of sexual violence, and as a survivor myself, I want to end with a small but important idea that I learned from my time serving in Defined Lines.[6] When people think of sexual violence, it is not uncommon to think of some scary man jumping out of the bushes and sexually attacking someone, but that is rarely the case. In many cases, the perpetrator and victim know each other. Sometimes, sexual violence can come from being sexually coercive on a date or manipulatively buying drinks for someone with whom you hope to have sex. Perpetrators might not be completely aware that the woman does not want to have sex. Sexual violence is complicated, and the hard truth is that we all can be capable of it to some degree. It is important to note the helpful and unhelpful things in our sexual lives. Based on the research that we have discussed, masculinity is associated with unhealthy and unsafe sex.

---

[6] Defined Lines is a student organization at the University of Akron in Ohio that works to eliminate rape culture on college campuses.

Coda: Masculinity's Roles in Gun and
Sexual Violence

As a coda to this and the prior chapter, we compare the pathways for gun and sexual violence and reflect on these topics. We have shown that outmoded masculinity norms influence gun and sexual violence, albeit in seemingly different ways. While we know something about this topic, there is still much more to learn. Masculinity's role in gun and other physical violence stems in theory from normative male alexithymia and the resultant inability to resolve personal problems and address hurt feelings through having an emotionally honest conversation and the tendency of some men to transform vulnerable feelings into anger and rage, and the tendency of depressed men to externalize their distress as aggression and violence. For example, consider the school shooters that we profiled in Chapter 5 of this volume. Feelings of sadness felt by these shooters who experienced rejection, bullying, and loneliness and depression were transformed into anger and aggression, including violence. On the other hand, masculinity's role in sexual violence is theorized to be due most centrally to the masculine norm of avoiding femininity, as well as privilege, impaired empathy, and the fathers' role in masculine socialization, shame, and precarious manhood. However, sometimes the pathways merge, as seen in those deceased shooters who left behind manifestos in which they complained of not living up to society's expectation of being a man and rejections from women. Some of these are part of the incel phenomenon, endorsed by Alek Minassian, the man accused of plowing into pedestrians with a rented van in Toronto, killing 10 and injuring 13, mostly women.

And so half a century after women's roles began to change, the country is experiencing a new iteration of the masculinity crisis, now due to sexual and gun violence. In this light, it is noteworthy that two articles appeared several days apart in the *New York Times* on the current iteration of the masculinity crisis, each one focusing on one of these major problems (Black, 2018; Velasquez-Manoff, 2018). A recent survey (Koeze & Barry-Jester, 2018) asked 1,615 men whether #MeToo changed their thinking on masculinity, finding that 60% of the men agreed that society pressures men in unhealthy ways. The younger the man, the more likely he was to agree with this. But the men disagreed on the type of pressure, some noting pressure to conform to traditional masculine norms and others mentioning pressure to develop new norms.

Finally, the current ethos is causing a re-examination of bits and pieces of our culture that had been taken for granted. We refer here to the controversy surrounding the 1940s duet "Baby, It's Cold Outside," a holiday classic. Listening with the "wokeness" of the #MeToo era, the lyrics are unnerving and creepy.

They may have been creepy in the 1940s, but back then people may have lacked the vocabulary to address it. The women repeatedly says "No" to the man's advances, and the man keeps pushing. At one point she asks what is in this drink, raising the question of a date rape drug. Several radio stations have pulled the song from the air during the holidays in 2018. Arguments have erupted on social media, and commentators from across the political spectrum, from Fox News to CNN, have amplified the debate (Fortin, 2018). The cultural re-evaluation of this song is similar to the recent cultural process of recognizing that memorial statuary throughout the South honored slave-holding confederate leaders or that current political leaders in southern states like Virginia have pictures of themselves in Blackface in their college and medical school yearbooks.

7

Men's Health and Experiences
of Trauma

We have devoted the greater part of this book to discussing the role of masculinity in boys and men harming other people through various forms of violence. We did not spend much time on how masculinity can harm the boys and
men themselves—that is, the violence that masculinity does to the self. In this
chapter, we look at masculinity's links with boys' and men's physical and mental
health problems. We also discuss men's experiences as victims of interpersonal
trauma, including both sexual trauma and intimate partner violence (IPV), and
how they are impacted by masculinity, which are relatively unexplored topics.

Masculinity and Men's Physical Health

The role of gender in men's health received little research attention until the
1990s. According to Gough and Robertson (2017), "historically, men have
been central to health-related research (e.g., new drugs tested on men but not
women), but have not been understood as gendered beings" (p. 198). The central questions now are, Why do men have higher mortality rates than women,
and how has research indicated that masculinity is linked with men's health risk
behaviors (Gough, 2013; Gough & Robertson, 2017)?

The Role of Masculinity

From a theoretical perspective, the norms of masculinity include proscriptions
and prescriptions such as restrictive emotionality, toughness, risk-taking, avoidance of femininity, self-reliance, and being a playboy, all of which have a clear conceptual linkage to taking health risks or avoiding health promotion behaviors. In

regard to wellness in general, some men might not take the needed steps to stay healthy such as attending regular medical check-ups and eating healthy diets because these things may appear more feminine or unmanly. Continuing with the norm to avoid femininity, men who endorse this norm may be likely to visit a doctor or nurse only when their condition has become severe and they can no longer avoid it, and even then, some may resist. In addition, men who conform to the self-reliant norm may be reluctant to ask for help about a medical condition because it could cause them to feel weak and unmanly. After all, talking about one's health concerns is a private and vulnerable experience, which is something that some men try to avoid. Readers, can you think of a man in your life who waited until the last minute to seek medical attention? If you are a man, have you ever waited until last minute? If so, why do you think you did that?

Men's Morbidity Rates

National health statistics indicate that under the age of 65 men are at a higher risk for heart disease and certain cancers than women (Centers for Disease Control [CDC], 2015). Heart disease (24%) and cancer (22%) remain the top causes of death for males of all ages and races/ethnicities (CDC, 2015). Prostate cancer is the most frequent cancer for men, followed by lung and bronchus cancer, and then cancer of the rectum and colon (American Cancer Society, 2015). For all male deaths, 6.8% are from unintentional injuries (i.e., accidents). However, of male deaths between the ages 20 and 24, 42.3% are from these unintentional injuries (CDC, 2015), and this remains the number one cause of death in men until age 45. Of course this reflects the fact that most causes of mortality (heart disease, cancer, and other chronic life-threatening illnesses) are unexpected among the young. In addition, men have higher rates of infectious disease (mostly due to HIV/AIDS), suicide (as will be discussed), and liver disease (due to alcohol abuse; Creighton & Oliffe, 2010).

Longevity Disparity and Health Behaviors

As we mentioned previously, in the United States, men do not live as long as women. Although men have certain social and economic advantages by virtue of being male, they also have higher mortality rates than women for 14 of the top 15 leading causes of death (Brayboy Jackson & Williams, 2006). A National Center for Health Statistics data brief on mortality reports that, on average, women who live to the age of 65 have a life expectancy of 85.6 years while men who do so live to 83.1 years (Murphy, Xu, Kochanek, & Arias, 2017). The age gap was twice as large 50 years ago, indicating that it has improved over this time span, but it seems to be getting worse very recently: In 2016, the difference in overall[1] life expectancy between females and males increased 0.2 year from 2015 to 5.0 years (Kochanek et al., 2017). Some might assume that this longevity disparity is due to some sex-linked biological anomaly related to hormones or the XY chromosome pattern. Although there is some evidence of boys' and men's greater biological fragility (Kraemer, 2000), McGinnis, Williams-Russo, and Knickman (2002) found that behaviors that constitute a risk to health account for around 40% of mortality rates irrespective of sex. In other words, regardless of your biological sex or gender identity, if you do things that can negatively impact your health, such as smoking tobacco, that behavior can lead to a higher mortality rate through an elevated risk for a life-threatening physical illness such as lung and bronchus cancer.

According to Griffith and Thorpe (2016), "health behaviors often are associated with femininity, and health-harming behaviors are linked with masculinity" (p. 709). Furthermore Courtenay (2000a, 2000b) observed that American men tend to engage in more than 30 controllable behaviors that increase their risk for disease, injury, and death. Men spend less time with their physicians, engage in fewer preventive health behaviors; consume more alcohol; use more tobacco products; take more risks; have poorer diets, sleep hygiene, and weight management; and lower physical activity than women (Galuska, Serdula, Pamuk, Siegal, & Byers, 1996; Garfield, Isacco, & Rogers, 2008).

Masculinity and Men's Health Behaviors: What Does the Research Show?

Over 40 years ago, Harrison (1978) warned, "The male sex role may be dangerous to your health" (p. 65). However, since then, the picture has become much more complicated. Early studies focused on masculinity's relationship to alcohol use. McCreary, Newcombe, and Sadava (1999) found a direct relationship for men between alcohol consumption and the endorsement of the status, toughness, and antifemininity norms using the Male Role Norms Scale (MRNS). They also found that higher scores on the Masculine Gender Role Stress Scale were related to problematic alcohol use for men. More recent studies have examined a wider range of health behaviors in relation to diverse groups of men, including American and Kenyan men (Mahalik, Lagan, & Morrison, 2006), Australian men (Mahalik, Levi-Minzi, & Walker, 2007), African American men (Wade, 2009), older men (Tannenbaum & Frank, 2011), alcohol dependent men (Uy et al., 2013), and gay men (Hamilton & Mahalik, 2009). Of particular note,

---

[1] That is, not limited to those who are 65 or older.

Mahalik, Burns, and Syzdek (2007) found that men who perceive healthy behaviors as normative for men (i.e., if they notice other men taking care of their health) are more likely to adopt healthier practices.

With regard to specific health behaviors, several studies have investigated masculinity and diet. Mahalik, Levi-Minzi et al. (2007) found that the Conformity to Masculine Norms Inventory (CMNI) scores of Australian men were inversely related to consuming fiber and fruit, and Rothgerber (2013) reported that endorsing traditional masculinity ideology using the MRNS was related to men's increased meat consumption. Another study with a U.K. sample (Sloan, Conner, & Gough, 2015) found that endorsing the toughness norm of the MRNS was predictive of high saturated fat consumption and low fruit intake for men.

Then there are studies that found that masculinity may be a two-edged sword, associated with both health risk and health promotion behaviors. A review of 12 studies by Levant, Wimer, Williams, Smalley, and Noronha (2009) reported that gender role conflict (using the Gender Role Conflict Scale [GRCS]) was directly associated with men's risky health behaviors, but traditional masculinity ideology (using the Male Role Norms Inventory [MRNI]) was, unexpectedly, negatively associated with risky health behaviors, which meant that higher scores on the MRNI was associated with health promotion behaviors. Iwamoto, Corbin, Lejuez, and MacPherson (2013) found that conforming to the playboy and risk-taking norms on the CMNI were predictive of increased alcohol use, while endorsing the emotional control and heterosexual self-presentation norms were related to less alcohol use.

Levant, Wimer, and Williams (2011) found a host of relationships between specific masculinity factors and specific health risk behaviors. They found that some masculinity factors were associated with health risks: (a) the CMNI dominance and self-reliance scales were negatively associated with avoidance of anger and stress; (b) the CMNI dominance and playboy scales and the GRCS restrictive emotionality scale were positively associated with substance use; (c) the CMNI risk-taking, playboy, and GRCS restrictive emotionality were negatively associated with appropriate use of health-care resources; and (d) the CMNI pursuit of status scale was negatively associated with preventive self-care. But they also found that some masculinity factors were linked to health-promoting behaviors. The CMNI dominance and primacy of work scales were linked with preventative self-care, while the CMNI winning scale was associated with avoidance of substance use, and the CMNI emotional control and primacy of work scales were positively associated with avoiding anger and stress. Levant et al. (2011) concluded: "The relationship between health behavior and masculinity depends on which dimension of health behavior one is interested in predicting, and which facets of masculinity one is using as predictors" (p. 38). To complicate matters further, some masculinity factors were associated with both risky and health-promoting behaviors; as previously noted, higher scores on the CMNI dominance scale was related to less avoidance of anger and stress and more substance use—but also to greater preventative health care. The links between masculinity norms and health behavior and outcomes have been at least partly replicated with a larger, more diverse sample (Levant & Wimer, 2014). Levant and Wimer (2014) noted: "The vast majority of the findings that were replicated were risk factors, suggesting that traditional masculinity is more of risk than a buffer, and occurred in the analyses involving avoiding anger and stress and avoiding substance use subscales, suggesting that these health behaviors are most closely associated with masculinity" (p. 110). Clearly, there is more work to be done with both larger and more diverse samples of men, employing specific measures of masculinity and specific indicators of health behaviors.

Masculinity and Men's Current Health Status

We could not find many studies linking masculinity to men's current health status. Burns and Mahalik (2008) found that conforming to the norm of emotional control was associated with poorer physical well-being in men treated for prostate cancer. Then there is the study focusing on energy drinks that was mentioned in an earlier chapter that linked the endorsement of traditional masculinity ideology to health behaviors (energy drink consumption) and then to health consequences (e.g., sleep disturbance; Levant et al., 2015). Finally, in another study mentioned in an earlier chapter, Levant et al. (2018) found that the MRNI was associated with positive general health status for self-identified men, regardless of their sex assigned at birth (and thus included transgender men).

Masculinity, Stress, and Coping

Stress has a monumental influence on health; in fact, it has been found to greatly contribute to men's higher mortality rates (Williams, 2003). Masculinity norms create a lot of stress for men. These norms encourage men to be breadwinners and initiators, always ready for sex, and tough protectors, while being pressured to not show their emotions or vulnerabilities and not being allowed to receive emotional support. It can take a lot of emotional energy to act manly, especially when you might not feel like the toughest or most confident person that day. When life gets difficult, men influenced by masculinity norms are also limited in coping strategies. Coping mechanisms that are beneficial to health such as meditation, yoga, crying, and asking for help are often off limits to men because they appear feminine. Furthermore (as discussed in Chapter 3 of this volume), some men may be alexithymic and therefore unable to put their inner experiences into words. Instead, such men might be more likely to use substances, eat unhealthily, smoke, and engage in risky behaviors like having unprotected sex. We would ask our men readers: How do you cope when things get very hard?

Racial/Ethnic Variations

There are also differences between men of different races and ethnicities in physical health. For example, Black American men have been shown to have a higher risk for certain physical illnesses (such as hypertension and sickle cell disease) than White American men (Jackson, Knight, & Rafferty, 2010). There is probably an environmental component to this where if one does not live near resources like gyms or stores that sell healthy food (i.e., in a food desert, as many inner city Black neighborhoods are), one may be more likely to use negative coping mechanisms like substance use or eating foods high in fat and sodium, which can contribute to greater physical health concerns (Jackson & Knight, 2006). Additionally, experiencing racism is very stressful and, as previously noted, stress creates physical health concerns.

Furthermore, Latino men have higher rates of physical illness like diabetes and cancer than do White men (Vega, Rodriguez, & Gruskin, 2009). This is truer for Latino men born in the United States than it is for foreign-born Latinos. Lack of knowledge of cancer screenings, poverty, and limited access to health care are contributing factors to this disparity. Even so, Latino men who have immigrated to the United States from Mexico experience many stressors. These include the stress of being separated from family members and others who provide social support who might not be residing in the United States and providing financial support for these family members who live abroad, language learning, acculturation, working several jobs to make a living, harassment, lack of insurance, and dealing with their immigration status, all of which impact their health status (Daniel-Ulloa, Sun, & Rhodes, 2017).

Finally, there are health disparities that put men of color at greater health risk than White men. According to the Kaiser Family Foundation (Orgera & Artiga, 2019),

> many groups are at disproportionate risk of being uninsured, lacking access to care, and experiencing worse health outcomes. For example, people of color and low-income individuals are more likely to be uninsured, face barriers to accessing care, and have higher rates of certain conditions compared to Whites and those at higher incomes.

In summary, then, men have greater mortality and have poorer health behaviors than women. While masculinity is linked with many poor health behaviors, it is also linked with a smaller number of health promotion behaviors. There are only a few studies on masculinity and current health status, and those that exist have found opposite results. There are also racial and ethnic differences in health status and disparities in access to health care resources. Clearly, more research is needed to understand why some facets of masculinity are linked with health risk behaviors and statuses and others are linked with positive health behaviors and statuses.

Masculinity and Boys' and Men's Mental Health

Mental health is a topic that has been gaining momentum over the past decade. Unlike physical health, mental health has long been stigmatized, and as result the idea of supporting one's personal mental health is not often discussed or encouraged for men. In fact, many of the activities done to foster mental health fly in the face of masculinity (e.g., showing vulnerability, talking about one's feelings, crying, seeking help from another) and are strictly discouraged in boys and men. In this section, we will discuss the role that masculinity plays in mental health. We will first review the sex differences in diagnoses of mental illnesses, discuss externalizing versus internalizing symptoms and several theoretical frameworks for understanding men's depression, take a closer look at how masculinity influences how men cope with depression, and, finally, as a coda to this section, discuss how patriarchal social norms negatively influence men's depression.

Sex-Based Diagnostic Differences

Boys and men experience mental health problems as do girls, women, and nonbinary persons, but the types of problems can differ by gender. The fifth edition of the *Diagnostic and Statistical Manual of Mental Disorders* (DSM-5; American Psychiatric Association, 2013) covers a variety of disorders that are more common in boys than girls. According to the DSM-5, boys experience a disproportionate number of childhood disorders, including attention-deficit/hyperactivity disorder (ADHD), learning disabilities, conduct disorder, and autistic spectrum disorder. The DSM-5 also highlights several adult disorders that are diagnosed much more frequently in men than women. These are the so-called acting out or externalizing disorders, such as substance abuse. For alcohol use disorder, men are diagnosed twice as often as women (National Institute on Alcohol Abuse and Alcoholism, 2019). For other drug abuse disorders, men are diagnosed two to three times as often as women (Becker & Hu, 2007). Men are also diagnosed more frequently with disorders of sexual excess (e.g., sex addiction), paraphilias (e.g., foot fetishism), and conduct problems like pyromania (fire-setting), compulsive gambling, and intermittent explosive disorder (also known colloquially as "rage-aholism").

Girls and women are more likely to be diagnosed with internalizing disorders like depression (about twice as often as men), anxiety, and eating disorders (World Health Organization, 2002). However, there is a growing problem of body dysmorphic disorders among men, related to a "drive for musculature," called colloquially "bigorexia" (Griffiths, Mond, Murray, & Touyz, 2015), which is too often linked with steroid use.

There are sex differences in the diagnosis of different types of personality disorders as defined in the DSM-5. Six personality disorders affect men more often than women: paranoid (overly suspicious, guarded, fear losing autonomy), schizoid (severely withdrawn), schizotypal (odd thinking, poor relationships), narcissistic (grandiose, self-absorbed, fragile self-esteem), antisocial (violate others' rights, little remorse, criminals), and obsessive-compulsive (perfectionists, push people away with their unreasonable expectations; APA, 2013). However more women than men are diagnosed with borderline personality disorder (unstable personality, inability to tolerate separation, abrupt change in feelings toward another, self–harm; APA, 2013). The big differences are seen in depression and suicide, which we take up next.

As previously noted, women are diagnosed with major depressive disorder (MDD) approximately twice as often as men. The National Comorbidity Survey–Replication (NCS-R; Kessler et al., 2003) is one of the most frequently cited reports of sex differences in MDD. It assessed the prevalence of MDD in a sample of over 9,000 Americans selected using a stratified sample who were reached by cold-calling. They found that women have a lifetime prevalence rate for depression that is about 1.7 times as high as that of men. Studies like the NCS-R present significant advantages over epidemiological research based on clinical data. As we discuss later, men tend to be reluctant to seek professional help for depression; as a result, clinical data are likely to underestimate the prevalence of depression in men relative to women.

However, men complete 7 of 10 of all suicide attempts (CDC, 2016). Readers might be surprised to learn this statistic because of women's more frequent diagnosis with depression and the link between depression and suicide. According to the CDC (2016), men are 5.5 times more likely to complete suicide than women. This further suggests that estimates of depression in men may undercount its prevalence. The reason that men complete suicide more often is they tend to choose more lethal methods, such as firearms, hanging, and asphyxiation, whereas women are more likely to overdose on medications, drugs, or alcohol or cut their wrists.

Another factor to consider is that some depressed men do not display the prototypic symptoms of depression such as sadness, depressed mood, feelings of worthlessness and guilt, loss of energy, and recurrent thoughts of death. This might be explained by the fact that the prototypical symptoms of depression are more congruent with women's gender norms than with men's. In the next section, we will discuss two different ways that symptoms of depression can be expressed.

Externalizing Versus Internalizing Symptoms

Mental health problems can be mapped through either externalizing or internalizing symptoms. The DSM-5, which is used by psychologists and other mental health practitioners, uses this framework. Externalizing symptoms are behavioral and tend to be maladaptive in nature (e.g., drinking or drug use, risk-taking, violence, sexual promiscuity). These type of symptoms are thought to "act out" the internal conflicts or problems. Internalizing symptoms on the other hand are painfully experienced within the mind and body as negative emotions like grief, despair, hopelessness, guilt, fear, anxiety and panic and contribute to such problems as social isolation, emotional distress, and somatic complaints like pain or fatigue. Traditional masculinity norms can influence how men experience serious psychopathology like depression by encouraging them to suppress what they feel within themselves (i.e., the internalizing symptoms) and to discharge these unpleasant feelings through action (i.e., externalizing symptoms). That is, depressed men might recognize that they feel bad but externalize it with irritation/anger/aggression/violence, drinking, drug use, dangerous driving, sexual promiscuity and other unhealthy behaviors, up to and including suicide. Externalizing symptoms have been found to be associated with suicide (Verona, Sachs-Ericsson, & Joiner, 2004), which provides some insight into the disparity in suicide completion mentioned earlier. In the next section, we will discuss four theoretical frameworks on depression in men.

Theoretical Frameworks on Depression in Men

In 2008, Michael Addis published an article outlining four theoretical frameworks on depression in men based on the clinical and research literature: (a) sex differences, (b) masked depression, (c) masculine depression, and (d) gendered responding. The idea that there are certain differences in the presentation of depression in men and women comes from the sex differences framework, which states that depression for men and women are really the same phenomenon, but there are phenotypic differences in presentation. For example, clinicians have observed that their men clients are more likely to experience anger than sadness. The problem with this perspective is that psychological research has found that men and women are much more alike than different. Hyde (2005) found that 78% of the psychological sex differences reported in the research literature are either small or trivial. Such research tends to make one skeptical of sex differences as profound as the 2:1 ratio.

The masked depression framework suggests that there is some concealed depression that is hidden behind a masculine front (i.e., the mask). Proponents of this view point to men's higher rates of substance use disorders as evidence of an underlying but hidden depression. However, there is no direct evidence to support this view.

The masculine depression framework has the most evidence to support it, and it states that men will express depression symptoms based on masculinity norms. That is, masculinity norms influence how men recognize and cope with depression. Men who as boys learned to transform their vulnerable emotions into aggression will likely express depression with externalizing symptoms such as anger and aggression, as we have seen with some of the school shooters. This framework is supported by research linking gender role conflict and conformity to masculine norms with depression. Gender role conflict is defined as distress caused by adherence to traditional masculine norms. In effect, these findings suggest that masculine norms can cause so much strain from their unattainable nature as to cause depression in some men.

Finally, the gendered responding framework states that men and women will respond to depression (and negative emotions in general) differently. For example, women may focus on their internal feelings to a fault, even going so far as to ruminate on them, which in and of itself is associated with greater likelihood of a diagnosis of depression, whereas men may avoid, distract, or numb themselves from their feelings, never really focusing on them. This framework would say that men's tendency to restrict emotionality and avoid feelings of vulnerability (as required by masculine norms) will influence how men respond and cope with depression.

Not included in these theoretical frameworks is the impact that discrimination and oppression have on men of color and sexual and gender minority men. These men might experience depression due to the additive effect that being a man and also having a minority status. This should be integrated into current frameworks on masculinity and depression.

Traditional Masculinity, Help-Seeking, and Depression

The *Journal of the American Medical Association* (JAMA) published an interesting study in 2013 which reanalyzed the NCS-R and found similar rates for men and women when they considered the different ways symptoms might be expressed (externalized vs. internalized, as we discussed earlier). For example, this study found that men tend to endorse higher risk-taking behavior, aggression, and substance use as symptoms of depression whereas women endorsed sleep problems, stress, and loss of interest in activities (Martin, Neighbors, & Griffith, 2013). This is echoed on online websites like WebMD (2018), which report that men tend to become more irritable, aggressive, and/or hostile when experiencing depression. It is also possible that women are more likely than men to report symptoms (hence, their higher rates) and to seek help for it (which we know to be a fact) and, further, that the standard diagnostic criteria may be biased toward symptoms more common in women.

Masculinity also impacts men's depression through its effects on men not seeking psychological help as often as do women. Many masculinity norms (e.g., self-reliance, emotional control, toughness, avoidance of femininity) carry the implication that to seek help (i.e., therapy, seeing a doctor) is "unmanly." Research has indicated that conformity to and endorsement of traditional masculinity norms predicted negative attitudes about psychological help-seeking (Levant, Wimer & Williams, 2011; Parnell & Hammer, 2018; Ramaeker & Petrie, 2019). For men experiencing suicidal thoughts, conforming to norms of self-reliance and emotional control predicted negative attitudes toward psychological help-seeking, such as seeing a psychotherapist (McDermott, Smith, Borgogna, Booth, Granato, & Servig, 2018). These attitudes about seeking help not only affect men and their mental health but also the health of their relationships. Specifically, men who scored high in conformity to these same two norms, self-reliance and emotional control, held negative views about seeking couples counseling (Parnell & Hammer, 2018). Some men of color or sexual/ gender minority men might have a mistrust of mental health professionals. They also may not have access to mental health counseling because they live in a community that does not have any of those options available or because they lack transportation, money, or health insurance.

It is easier to understand how masculinity might negatively affect men's depression and mental health if we examine the specific norms that research indicates are problematic. In the CMNI meta-analysis of mental health correlates (discussed in Chapter 4 of this volume), the investigators found that conforming to the emotional control norm was associated with negative mental health (Wong et al., 2017). Further, these investigators found that conforming to the power over women, self-reliance, and playboy norms were also related to negative mental health. Out of all of the masculinity constructs, the gender role conflict pattern of restrictive emotionality has been shown to be the strongest predictor of men's depression (O'Neil, 2008). This is understandable because restrictive emotionality is linked with alexithymia. Thus, if men are depressed but do not have the ability due to alexithymia to express those vulnerable feelings or, if they do, do not have a safe and secure outlet due to their reluctance to show vulnerability, then depression may go unchecked and unmanaged until it gets quite severe. Another masculine norm associated with negative mental health is self-reliance; stereotypically, men are known to rarely stop to ask for directions and to have a hard time asking for help. The same applies for mental health where men who conform to the masculine norm of self-reliance tend to avoid seeking psychological treatment (Berger, Addis, Green, Mackowiak, & Goldberg, 2013). Thus, the combined effects of not being able to express their innermost vulnerable feelings of depression and not being able to ask for help creates a double jeopardy for such men. There is nowhere for the depression to go except through externalizing behaviors like drinking, substance use, violence, and possibly suicide.

Interestingly, as previously noted in regard to physical health, research has also indicated that some norms of masculinity can be of positive benefit to men's mental health. For example, using the CMNI, Mahalik and Rochlen (2006) found that men who conformed to the winning norm chose to exercise more when feeling depressed, which is helpful because exercise has been known to decrease anxiety and depression. However, men who conformed to the norms of violence, power over women, playboy, disdain for sexual minorities, and pursuit of status were likely to drink alcohol when feeling depressed, which can exacerbate anxiety and depression. As mentioned earlier in Chapter 4 of this volume, some norms of masculinity may be more harmful than others. This demonstrates the complicated relationship that masculinity has with men's mental health. While we have demonstrated that masculinity creates a host of problems for men, there are some aspects of it that help men in certain situations, and we need more research to better understand the conditions under which that occurs.

Patriarchal Social Norms and Men's Depression

Not only do masculine norms play a role in men's mental and physical health, the larger societal expectations that they uphold (i.e., patriarchy) can also impact men. When we hear about patriarchy, or a male-dominated society, we assume that the conversation is going to talk about the negative effects that it has on women and minorities. Although a patriarchal society is indeed negative for women and minorities, it is also negative for the men themselves. An article by Kavanagh and Graham (2019) reviewed research showing that gender inequality can worsen men's physical and mental health. They found that men exhibit a range of unhealthy behaviors that allow them to appear masculine to meet social expectations but doing so undermines their physical and mental health. These social expectations are largely unattainable (e.g., toughness, emotional restrictiveness, self-reliance, dominance); hence, gender inequality effectively restricts men from behaviors that would improve their own physical and mental needs. If men cannot meet their own needs, then they will not be able to meet the needs of others around them, causing their loved one's undue strain. Kavanagh and Graham argue that gender equality will allow men to live by more realistic norms that can allow them to take care of themselves as well as others, in addition to improving the general welfare of society.

Patriarchy assigns men to a gender role that operates in a very narrow framework and comes with a lot of pressure to conform to that role. Many men strive to be breadwinners, bringing home the majority of the family income, and to be strong, physically and emotionally. This role gives them power and privilege as discussed in Chapter 3 of this volume, from which they gain benefits. As we have seen in Chapter 3 of this volume, the benefits that men receive also come with some serious limitations. On the other hand, research has indicated that equally sharing roles with a partner is beneficial to men's physical and mental health (Barnett, 2008), suggesting that gender inequality is not only ineffective but also harmful to men themselves.

Consider these contrasting scenarios. At work, you are tasked with ensuring that everything gets completed and everyone is cared for at all times. Your job is stressful, and you work double the normal hours trying to make it all work out. As a result you are tired, achy, irritable, and just plain unhappy. Then you get another person to share those tasks, and now the pressure you had to make it all work out is reduced, allowing for less hours at work and more energy to do other things that you could not do before. On top of that, this person is in a similar boat so you can confide in this person when you feel pressure and stress from work.

The contrasting scenarios represent going it alone versus sharing responsibilities and stressors with your partner, friend, or family member. It is a simple case of "Two is better than one," but it is easier said than done. In many respects, men often strive to be superheroes but don't realize that being a man also means being human and with that comes limitations.

Men's Interpersonal Trauma and Masculinity

In Chapters 5 and 6 of this volume, we discussed how masculinity is implicated in men becoming perpetrators of gun/physical and sexual violence. This section of the present chapter will discuss men as trauma victims/survivors of interpersonal trauma, which includes sexual and IPV. The terms "survivor" and "victim" will be used interchangeably in this section, as not all readers who have experienced trauma feel like survivors. Here, we consider how masculinity affects men trying to cope or heal from trauma. We will see that masculinity is associated with some serious deleterious effects on the well-being, healing, and growth of trauma survivors. We cover men's sexual trauma resulting from both female and male perpetrators, looking at sexual violence among gay men for the latter. We finish the section with a discussion of IPV in gay male relationships and in heterosexual relationships with women as the perpetrators. This section will also not only cover cisgender men but also transgender people as well.

The idea that men can experience sexual violence and IPV is surprising to many people. Stereotypically, men have been viewed as heroes and women as damsels-in-distress, which created a narrative in which we expect women to experience trauma; at the very least, we are less likely to be surprised by its occurrence. For men, however, the idea of male victims of trauma just does not fit with the narrative, so much so that men might not even consider such an idea. Many men might go through their whole lives never identifying as having experienced abuse or coercion.

When I (SP) first began my journey as a fledgling psychologist, I volunteered for a rape crisis hotline. Back then, I was convinced that I was going to work with women and trauma; however, several men callers changed my mind. I got phone calls from men who experienced sexual abuse or assault; at the end of the conversation many would say, "Thanks for not judging me." I must admit that, before those experiences, I had never considered the idea that men could be victims of interpersonal trauma; after all, I had never really encountered it before. I began to wonder how many other men might be going through trauma and that sparked a series of actions that lead me to where I am today, writing about men's experiences of interpersonal trauma in this book.

Men's Sexual Trauma and Masculinity

Many people are familiar with the statistic of one in four, which is the number of women who will experience sexual violence in their lifetime. Very few know that one in six men will also experience sexual violence (Smith et al., 2017). When thinking about men's sexual trauma, it is important to understand that these rates represent the lifetime incidence, with many traumatic experiences coming from childhood. It is also likely an undercount, as many sexual assaults are never reported. Men who have experienced sexual trauma have been reported to experience depressive symptoms, alcohol abuse, risk-taking, and sexual dysfunction (Turchik, 2012), as well as hostility, general distress, and posttraumatic stress (Aosved, Long, & Voller, 2011).

Male survivors of sexual trauma face a unique challenge in that they are both victims and men influenced by traditional masculinity ideology. We know that traditional masculinity ideology does not allow for a victimization status for men, especially for men who have experienced interpersonal trauma. Even men who experience combat trauma, a more gender-congruent and expected trauma for men, can be seen as weak. For example, then-presidential candidate Donald Trump remarked that the late Senator John McCain was not a war hero because he was captured, insinuating that John McCain did not deserve the status of hero (Sonmez, 2018). Indeed, failing to fight off a foe and come out on top can be seen as a failure for a man. This is certainly the case for many male trauma survivors, who are sometimes questioned why they did not just fight their assailant off. Some victims can even feel responsible for their trauma, because they expected themselves to prevent it. Men who have experienced interpersonal trauma might feel a need to cover up what happened by displaying traditional masculinity characteristics. To some victims, this may feel like they are attempting to blend in and feel like they are "one of the guys" when they may secretly feel like an outcast. A study by Kia-Keating, Grossman, Sorsoli, and Epstein (2005) found that male survivors struggle with masculine expectations such as toughness, stoicism, and sexual readiness. The study highlighted the struggle that these men endured when living the secret life of a sexual abuse survivor while also grappling with masculinity expectations. Consider the experience of this participant: "We [men] have an extra layer of shame and everything else because after all, we're supposed to enjoy [sexual intimacy] . . . and we're supposed to be strong enough to be able to just like fight it off or something" (Kia-Keating et al., 2005, p. 179).

Unfortunately, the pressure to be masculine while also carrying the burden of having experienced sexual trauma does not end there. Masculinity may potentiate long-term negative effects in these men. Research indicates that conforming to masculine norms, as measured by the CMNI, has a negative relationship with posttraumatic growth (Easton, Coohey, Rhodes, & Moorthy, 2013). That is, it seems to interfere with the survivor's ability to process the trauma and heal and grow in a positive way, which is a critical part of the treatment of trauma. Tools that can be helpful for healing after trauma such as emotional expression and processing the abuse are often not an option for many male survivors. As mentioned in the section on mental health when discussing men's depression, the effects of trauma can also go unchecked and cause potentially harmful results. A shocking finding came from a study that discovered that men who conformed strongly to masculine norms (as measured by the CMNI) had a 230% greater chance of having attempted suicide within that year than men who conformed less to masculine norms (Easton, Renner, & O'Leary, 2013). We previously mentioned in the mental health section that men's rates of completed suicide was much higher than that of women. It is possible that trauma plays a role in these higher suicide rates. Men who experience sexual trauma (and interpersonal trauma in general) have fewer resources, less support, more stigma, and typically a massive amount of shame; therefore, it is possible that such men will suffer the more severe outcomes up to and including suicide.

Gender of the Perpetrator

The gender of the perpetrator is also an important factor for many men. If the perpetrator was a woman they may be less likely to see it as abuse. I (RL) had a client who had been raped by an adult woman when he was a teen, but he did not consider it rape; rather, he considered himself "lucky." As previously noted, men are expected to enjoy sexual advances from women, and it is considered "manly" to always be ready to have sex. To reprise, many men are not aware that they can be sexually assaulted, and they see women as victims and not perpetrators, which together may cause many male survivors to question whether what happened to them was truly sexual assault.

On the other hand, if the perpetrator was the same sex as the victim, and the victim identifies as heterosexual, the survivor may struggle with confusion about their sexual orientation. Furthermore, it is common for men to obtain an erection during the abuse, which is a nonconscious bodily reaction to the experience, but that might bring confusion as to whether it was actually abuse or that they enjoyed it. There is not enough public discourse about male survivors of sexual trauma to assure these men that having an erection during a sexual assault does not indicate enjoyment. A common myth is that male rape and abuse happens only in prisons, and while sexual assault certainly occurs in the detention system, rape and abuse also occurs with friends, family members, or significant others. It also happens among same-sex couples, which is often ignored when discussing interpersonal trauma. This will be discussed more fully later in this section.

Disclosure

Masculinity not only negatively influences how sexual trauma affects men, it also has an impact on disclosure. Easton, Saltzman, and Willis (2014) interviewed male survivors on barriers to disclosing their traumatic experience and found that one of the most common barriers to disclosure was fear of being stigmatized. Masculinity ideals include self-reliance, toughness, and stoicism. As a result, male survivors might experience shame from being questioned on why they didn't fight back or somehow stop the abuse from happening. When the perpetrator is a woman, this is even more the case. Additionally, men are taught to consider sexual attention from women as a win, since men should always be ready to have sex, they could assume that they should have enjoyed it if the perpetrator was a female. These messages can be damaging for the individual and likely offer an explanation for why men are often found to have lower disclosure rates than women (Boudewyn & Liem, 1995; O'Leary & Barber, 2008; Ullman & Filipas, 2005). On the lower disclosure rates, we want to note that although many studies have found this to be the case, it is not a consistent finding across studies. Furthermore, because of low rates of reporting, we might never know the actual rates of disclosure. Men also reported fearing the strong vulnerable emotions (e.g., shame, sadness, guilt, fear) that likely come with disclosure (Easton, Saltzman, & Willis, 2014). We know that men are expected to avoid displaying vulnerable emotions even if there had been no abuse due to the masculine norm of restrictive emotionality. To avoid these emotions, many abused men do not disclose at all or may take a very long time to do so. For many men, disclosing an experience of abuse is akin to being weak and less of a man, both in his eyes and that of others, which serves as yet another barrier that abused men may face.

Transgender Survivors

Very little is known about trauma among transgender people as there is scant research. In this section, to respect gender fluidity, we have included transgender men, transgender women, and nonbinary people. Recently, the transgender population has been regarded negatively by society, ranging from fears that transgender people will assault others in bathrooms to actions barring them from the military. Just recently, a transgender woman was sexually assaulted in a bar by two other women in North Carolina (Caron, 2019), and President Trump released a policy banning any transgender person from serving in the military (Liptake, 2019).

In regard to the military, research is beginning to emerge regarding military sexual trauma (MST) of transgender people. Reports indicate that 19% of transgender men and 13% of transgender women experience MST (Lindsay et al., 2016). It was found that following trauma, transgender men were at an increased risk for posttraumatic stress disorder (PTSD) and personality disorders. Transgender women who experienced MST were likely to be diagnosed with depression, bipolar disorder, personality disorders, and PTSD. A study supported by the National Institute of Health found that a massive 84% of their sample of transgender women experienced physical or sexual abuse at some point in their lifetime (Kussin-Shoptaw, Fletcher, & Reback, 2017). The effects of masculinity may be different for transgender men as compared to cisgender men, since they transitioned from female to male, were socialized as girls, and experienced both gender identities. Research with the transgender population is limited and more needs to be done to understand the lives and struggles of these individuals.

Resources for Male Survivors

While research and resources for male survivors of sexual trauma are limited, they are growing as more people see that men can and do experience sexual trauma. One of the most accessible and anonymous options are hotlines, which offer their service 24/7. Websites dedicated to sexual trauma are also an option; there are some sites dedicated to male survivors if that is desired. The nice thing about these websites is that they can offer a sense of community as these sites have forums for online anonymous chat, and some have support groups as well as other resources that might be specific to a geographical location. Other options include individual or group therapy where survivors can talk about their experiences and get on a course of treatment if necessary.

Sexual trauma creates numerous hardships for men. There is still much to learn to aid them in their recovery, and the needs of transgender survivors of sexual trauma need to be addressed more in the community and in the scientific literature. Support for male survivors of sexual trauma is growing in the behavioral sciences, but more needs to be done to get information found in the research labs out into the community and to mental health professionals who may encounter men who have experienced sexual abuse.

Female-Perpetrated IPV and Masculinity

We left off with female-perpetrated IPV in Chapter 5 of this volume; we thought it was most appropriate to talk about how IPV effects men in this chapter. As we stated there, one in nine men will experience some form of IPV/domestic violence (Smith et al., 2017). Men as victims of IPV are generally overlooked as seen in a study by Bates, Kaye, Pennington, and Hamlin (2019), who found that when participants were given a hypothetical scenario they were less likely to identify a situation as IPV and reported being less likely to intervene or report an instance of IPV if the victim was a male. As we have noted, thinking about women as perpetrators of IPV may seem odd since it is more common to view men as the perpetrators. However, it is important to cover this topic especially because it is infrequently discussed. Before we get into the gendered parts of this section, let us dive a little more deeply into what IPV is. There are two types of IPV according to Johnson (1995). One is situational and escalates between the couple; the second is intimate terrorism, which is the extreme and severe violence with which we might be more familiar. In situational violence, the perpetrator can be either partner or even both partners in a repetitive negative cycle. With intimate terrorism, the perpetrator (most commonly a man) targets and aims to harass and harm the victim (generally a woman), but we will see that this can also occur with men as the victim and women as the perpetrators. We likely see survivors of intimate terrorism at battered women's shelters, and we are most exposed to this form of violence in the media.

Men who survive intimate terrorism are studied infrequently largely because gaining access to that population is very difficult. That changed in 2000 when the first Domestic Abuse Helpline for Men appeared. Since its creation, calls have steadily increased as more and more men call the line for support, resources, or legal assistance. Hines, Brown, and Dunning (2007) conducted a study using the callers of this hotline to map characteristics of abuse, which was rarely studied before this time. They found that 54% of men reported being involved in an abusive relationship where a serious injury could result if the other partner found out that they were calling a hotline. The most frequent physically abusive behavior reported was slapping or hitting, which occurred in 43% of participants followed by pushing (41%), kicking (39%), grabbing (31%), and punching (24%). Many participants reported that the aggression focused on their groin area or threatened to seriously harm them by cutting off their genitals or kicking them repeatedly in the groin. Ninety-five percent of participants reported controlling behavior (i.e., threats and coercion, not allowing access to checkbook).

Psychological Aggression

Psychological aggression includes what was defined by the CDC (2018) as "expressive aggression" (such as name calling, insulting or humiliating an intimate partner) and "coercive control," which includes behaviors that are intended to monitor and control or threaten an intimate partner." Hines et al. (2007) reported that 77% of their participants recalled an incident where their partner threatened to have them falsely arrested, or to kill themselves, or to leave them. In addition, 74% of their participants reported experiencing emotional abuse, where they were called names, put down, made to feel crazy or guilty, and were subjected to mind games. Sixty-five percent of participants experienced intimidation through the smashing of objects, abusing pets, using weapons, or damaging/destroying their personal property. As we have seen, many men are reluctant to seek help for physical and mental health. So too, men who are experiencing psychological aggression from their partner may have difficulty reaching out to others about their experience. Additionally, with limited resources for men experiencing IPV perpetrated by a woman, many may not know where to go for help if they are interested.

Legal and Administrative Aggression

A topic that has emerged in the last decade is women's use of legal and administrative (LA) aggression (Tilbrook, Allan, & Dear, 2010). LA aggression is an attempt or threat to utilize legal systems and related resources as a way to exert control over a partner or to harm them. Examples include a woman making threats or taking steps to prevent her partner from seeing their children or falsely accusing the victim of abuse or of some other crime. Hines et al. (2007) found that 49% of survivors in their study experienced threats by their partner to take sole custody of children or otherwise keep their children away from them. Berger, Douglas, and Hines (2016) examined the effects of LA aggression on male victims of physical IPV, focusing on negative mental health consequences such as PTSD and depression. Berger et al. (2016) measured LA aggression using the LA Aggression Scale, which Hines, Douglas, and Berger (2014) found to be reliable and valid for measuring both threatened and actual LA aggression in their sample of men with histories of physical IPV victimization. Berger et al. (2016) found that LA aggression was associated with PTSD as well as depression in male victims of IPV, indicating that this kind of aggression has serious consequences.

Gay Male IPV and Masculinity

As with female-perpetrated IPV, we left off talking about this in Chapter 5 of this volume, as the traumatic effects on men are best discussed here. As previously noted, IPV is generally viewed as women being the victims and men being the perpetrators. Research and support resources are generally allocated toward that configuration. As a result, IPV in gay male couples is less apparent, even though same-sex IPV has been reported to have rates similar to that in heterosexual couples (Blosnich & Bossarte, 2009) and sometimes even higher rates (Greenwood et al., 2002; Jolly, 2014; Tjaden, Thoennes, & Allison, 1999). Gay men have been found to have significantly higher rates of IPV than heterosexual and bisexual men (Goldberg & Meyer, 2013). Additionally, a study by Miller and Irvin (2017) found that victims in same-sex couple IPV are 70% more likely to be diagnosed with depression and 60% more likely to have anxiety than their heterosexual counterparts. Since many IPV programs and resources have focused on women, some gay men report that organizations and people in the community have not taken their situations adequately into account (Freeland, Goldenberg, & Stephenson, 2018). In regard to community resources, many men may not even know that those resources exist, or the resources in their area do not have enough knowledge or experience in working with gay men going through partner abuse to be of help.

Homophobia

Gay men who are survivors of IPV not only have to deal with the struggles that come with being a man and experiencing interpersonal violence, but they also have to deal with homophobia and the way that they might be treated by law enforcement or the court system because of their sexual orientation. They are often victims of dual stigmatization. This can cause them to keep their abuse secret because reporting it could "out" them, which would create additional stress if they are not open to sharing their sexual orientation. The treatment that these men receive by police when reporting a situation of abuse can range from the police not knowing how to handle the situation to hostility due to homophobia. Experiences in the court system also reflect this lack of acceptance and understanding of same-sex IPV. Here is a short passage regarding one man's experience with the court:

> We had to go to court on the issue where you could actually look at me and tell something had gone on. I had pictures to prove it, I had tons of stories to tell. And because I get in front of the judge, and the judge kind of like dismisses it.... But I felt slighted because I felt like I wasn't taken seriously. (Freeland, Goldenberg, & Stephenson, 2018, p. 307)

A Brief Comment on Intersectionality

Gay men who are experiencing abuse from a male partner thus have these added struggles. The same can be said for many people as identities like race, ethnicity, sexual orientation, and gender intersect (more on this in the next chapter). For example, men of color who are gay and also experiencing IPV from a same sex partner have even more difficulties as they struggle with being gay in a straight society, being an abuse survivor while also being a man, and also being a man of color in a predominately White society. In fact, research has indicated that people of color (i.e., Black, Latinx, Native American) have higher rates of IPV than White people for both men and women (Rennison & Welchans, 2000; Tjaden & Tjoennes, 2000). These statistics suggests that trauma and the effects of trauma could differ depending on the identities of the individual. More attention needs to be given to this as understanding the way identities intersect can greatly affect treatment in a mental health setting.

Unique Aspects of Same-Sex IPV

There are several aspects of IPV that are unique to same-sex relationships. One concerns differences in being out as gay (Carvalho, Lewis, Derlega, Winsted, & Viggiano, 2011). One partner might threaten to out the other partner as a form of control and a way of keeping power over the other partner. This can result in the outed person losing their job, losing other relationships, experiencing additional homophobia, and generally leaving them with a sense of feeling violated and vulnerable. In this scenario, threatening to out the partner is a way to exhibit control while also instilling terror. Perpetrator/victim roles in same-sex relationships also tend to be interchangeable, with both partners each giving and receiving violence throughout the relationship. Indeed, a study on the topic indicated that up to 42% of the sample of gay men reported that both partners experienced physical and sexual abuse in their relationship and also perpetrated physical and sexual abuse themselves (Oringher & Samuelson, 2011). Finally, social support may be lacking in the lives of gay men as the stigma for being gay is high, resulting in some families and loved ones withholding support that is vital to the well-being of someone experiencing trauma.

IPV Triggers

An important study by Finneran and Stephenson (2013) that used a sample of gay and bisexual men found several phenomena that they viewed as triggers that might cause IPV to erupt in relationships. Some triggers were educational differences in which one partner is more educated than the other, disagreements about sex, lack of trust, religious differences, acting disrespectful toward one partner, both men being "alpha males," jealousy, finances, drug use, age differences, disagreements about relationship dynamics (e.g., time spent together, intimacy), and alcohol. These triggers by themselves are not enough to result in violence. This study found that triggers were more likely to escalate into violence in men who experienced IPV in the past as compared to men who have not experienced IPV before. Non-White men and men who were HIV-positive were also more likely to escalate to violence following triggers. This study demonstrated that IPV is a complex problem with diverse causes that can vary across couples. More research and attention need to be given to the idea of triggers and interpersonal violence in same-sex relationships.

Resources for Male Survivors of IPV

The resources for male survivors of IPV are very similar to those for sexual assault. There are hotlines in place to take anonymous calls 24/7 as well as provide an option for individual and group therapy. The National Coalition Against Domestic Violence and the National Domestic Violence Hotline websites provide many resources for support and information for both men and women. These organizations also have sites that allows for a quick exit out of the webpage if necessary, which adds some security for viewers who might fear getting caught by their abuser.

Summary and Conclusions

This chapter has examined how masculinity is not only linked with violence against those close to boys and men as well as society at large but is also linked to violence against the self for boys and men, in terms of its effects on health, mental health, and trauma. Masculinity has been found to be linked to a host of physical and mental health problems as well as issues in help-seeking and coping. Men are not often seen as victims by society, and this can make men who have been victimized feel alone in their struggle, never going to seek help and living with their experiences as heavy burdens that they must carry alone. In male survivors of interpersonal trauma, masculinity can cause shame, guilt, and isolation with many men either not knowing that they are actually experiencing interpersonal violence or feeling silenced by messages from society. Fortunately, some areas of masculinity have been shown to be helpful factors in regard to physical and mental health, and when men do get together to talk about their hardships amazing things can happen. More needs to be done to understand and harness what can be helpful in masculinity and change what is unhelpful. Unfortunately, it can be hard to get men to discuss these issues as it goes against the norms that men are supposed to be tough and self-reliant, the heroes. In actual fact, there is nothing feminine about trauma or abuse, and there is nothing feminine about being a victim. The fact that we can sometimes believe that abuse is a woman's issue is insulting to both men and women.

8

Many Masculinities

As we have stated before, masculinity is a cultural construction, and there are many cultures in the United States; therefore, there are multiple masculinities. This phenomenon has been conceptualized in the psychology of men and masculinities by borrowing the theory of intersectionality. The intersectional perspective underscores the mutually constitutive relationships among different social identities such as race, ethnicity, gender, sexual orientation, social class, ability status, and age. In particular, this framework focusses on the manner in which multiple social identities are dependent on each other for meaning (Cole, 2009). It further addresses how multiple interlocking social identities reflect diverse systems of privilege, power, and oppression (Bowleg, 2012; Shields, 2008). The concept of intersectionality was first introduced by critical race theorist and legal scholar Kimberlé Crenshaw (1991) to describe the marginalization of Black women in such locations as feminist theory (which equated women with White women) and antidiscrimination law (which equated Black people with Black men).

Although the theory of intersectionality was developed based on the experiences of Black women, it has proven useful in the study of masculinities. For example, an intersectional approach illuminates the ways that groups of men, particularly men of color, will construct distinctive masculinities because of their relationship to more than one social group. The positions men occupy within other power structures can exacerbate or mitigate gender role strain. The gender structure is largely hierarchical but intersects with other axes of social stratification (e.g., race, social class, age, and sexual orientation). Intersectionality theory is a useful framework to consider how the inequitable distribution of male privilege and power determines how relatively marginalized or subordinated men experience gender role strain. We had earlier given the example of African American men, who, due to racism and gender role strain, not only constructed a culturally unique version of masculinity in which they viewed their masculinity in a broader frame than traditional masculine norms to also include family, community, and spiritual emphases. (Rogers et al., 2015) but also experienced impediments to meeting the requirement of manhood, which is termed "racist gender role strain."

Wong, Liu, and Klann (2017) acknowledged the challenges in applying the intersectional perspective to empirical research. In particular, they highlighted the flaws with what they termed the "additive approach" (p. 262), in which investigators sum the independent effects of multiple identities, such as race and gender. This is a flaw because there is something more about, say, being a Black women, than being Black and being a women. This flaw is hard to avoid in quantitative research. Another flaw is that cultural categories such as race and gender are sometimes used as proxies for underlying constructs (e.g., minority stress, gender role strain), yet these constructs are not explicitly examined (Cole, 2009). Simply showing that Black and White men differ on several variables does not enlighten us as to why these differences exist. Furthermore, the unintended effect of stereotyping minority groups might result from focusing on differences across social categories, rather than on the underlying constructs associated with these social categories. Wong et al. (2017) also observed that there are multiple approaches to studying intersectionality and categorized them into three research paradigms: The intergroup paradigm, the interconstruct paradigm, and the intersectional uniqueness paradigm. We will borrow their classification for this chapter and discuss a number of different approaches to studying multiple masculinities. We will say at the outset that this is a vast research domain. For illustration, the *APA Handbook of Men and Masculinities* (Wong & Wester, 2016) has eight chapters on diverse masculinities, covering race and ethnicity, social class, sexual orientation, and age. And even with that amount of information, investigators have barely scratched the surface of this topic; there is so much more to be learned. Hence, the aim of our presentation here will be to illuminate certain aspects of diverse masculinities, but presenting all that is known is well beyond our scope, which we think is justified because we are nowhere near being able to fully describe the masculinities of the major cultural groups in our society.

The Intergroup Paradigm

My (RL) research in the late 1990s and early 2000s focused on the comparison of different groups on the endorsement of traditional masculinity ideology (TMI) using the Male Role Norms Inventory (MRNI). The goal was to discover evidence that would either support or refute the central point by which the gender role strain paradigm departed from the older gender role identity paradigm— namely, that gender was socially constructed rather than biologically determined.

To do this, we had to determine whether there were differences in TMI based on cultural dimensions of identity. Differences in the overall endorsement and in the weighting of subscales of measures of TMI (such as the MRNI) were indeed found, corresponding to differences in sex, sexual orientation, race/ethnicity, nationality, social class, age, geographic region of residence, generation within a family, and disability status (see Levant & Richmond, 2016, for a summary). Some of these results are displayed in Figure 8.1 in the Appendix, and these will be more fully described below.

U.S. Studies of Cultural Variations in Masculinity Endorsement

Levant and Majors (1997) compared European American and African American college students, men and women, and found, first, that women tended to score lower than men in endorsing TMI in both racial groups, a finding which was replicated in all studies using U.S. data. This means that women tended to reject more strongly than men[1] the belief that men should conform to TMI, which makes sense because these norms are at their core misogynistic. Second, African American men and women tended to endorse these norms more strongly than their European American counterparts, which may reflect African American's stronger commitment to traditional values, as observed by other investigators (e.g., Hunter & Davis, 1992, 1994).

To further examine the role of culture in masculinity ideology endorsement, Levant, Majors, and Kelly (1998) compared African American college men and women from the rural southern United States with those in the metropolitan mid-Atlantic and northeastern United States. They expected those from the rural southern states to more strongly endorse TMI, because African American people from that region are more traditional in gender roles than those from the metropolitan areas in the mid-Atlantic and northeast. Furthermore, it could be argued that African American people from the mid-Atlantic and northeast adhere less strongly to these norms as a result of their acculturation in a metropolitan environment, one that is more influenced by modern conceptions of gender and less tied to traditional values. Once again, women tended to score lower than men in endorsing traditional masculinity norms in both geographic groups. Further, men and women from the South tended to endorse these norms more strongly than their mid-Atlantic/northeastern counterparts, as predicted, further supporting the cultural nature of masculinity ideology.

---

[1] As we discussed in Chapter 2 of this volume, most men do not endorse most traditional masculine norms.

Finally, Levant et al. (2003) compared White, Latin*x*, and Black men and women, finding that men endorsed TMI more strongly that women in all three race/ethnicity groups, replicating and extending prior research on gender differences in MRNI endorsement in the United States. Black men and women showed the strongest endorsement of TMI, while White men and women showed the weakest endorsement, and Latin*x* men and women fell in between. The cultural differences in masculinity endorsement in this study as well as those in Levant and Majors (1997) and Levant et al. (1998) reflect differences in beliefs about *gender equality* in different cultural groups in the United States.[2] This research does not tell us why these differences exist. These variations might be explained by a number of factors, including the interplay of TMI and privilege. Teasing this out is an important task for future research.

Cross National Studies of Variations in Masculinity Endorsement

We next went overseas to conduct cross-national studies of variations in masculinity endorsement. This required using the systematic method of back translation as developed by Brislin (1970), through which the MRNI and any other instruments in the study were adapted into another language (e.g., Chinese, Russian) through a series of steps to ensure equivalency of meaning and absence of cultural bias. These steps are (a) an original translation from English to the other language; (b) blind back-translation (translation from the other language to English without knowledge of the original English version); and (c) comparison of the back-translated English version with the original English and resolution of any differences in wording. The translations were then compared and corrected for discrepancies in vocabulary, phrasing, and syntax and cast into a single, modified version.

Levant, Wu, and Fischer (1996) compared male and female university undergraduates in the United States and China, drawing samples in 1994. The U.S. women rejected TMI more strongly than did the U.S. men, replicating prior results, and the Chinese men and women scored significantly higher than their U.S. counterparts. However, the scores of Chinese men and women were not significantly different, with both Chinese gender groups endorsing TMI. We interpreted this finding in light of the fact that China has long been a society low in gender equality, in which women may feel that they have little choice but to

---

[2] It should be noted that none of the groups strongly endorsed TMI, corresponding to our discussion in Chapter 2 of this volume regarding the findings that most people do not strongly endorse masculine norms.

accept patriarchal norms. For illustration, female infanticide reached epidemic proportions under China's one-child policy, illustrating the bias against females. According to United Nations data,[3] China's gender equality index ranged from 0.50 to 0.75 over the period from 1990 to 2017, compared to nations which rank high in gender equality, such as Norway, which ranged from 0.85 to 0.95 or the United States, which ranged from 0.86 to 0.92, over the same period.

The Chinese MRNI study was repeated after the Fourth World Conference on Women: Action for Equality, Development and Peace, convened by the United Nations from September 1995 in Beijing, China, drawing samples in 1998. It was a measure of my (RL) naïve idealism at the time that I thought that we might find greater gender differences on the MRNI among Chinese students as a result of the conference. We did not (Wu, Levant, & Sellers, 2001).

Levant et al. (2003) compared United States and Russian men and women on the MRNI. Once again, the U.S. women rejected TMI (as reflected in the MRNI total traditional score) more strongly than did the U.S. men, replicating prior results. The Russian men and women scored significantly higher than their U.S. counterparts. However, unlike the Chinese studies, the scores of Russian men and women were significantly different, but both Russian gender groups endorsed TMI (i.e., with mean scores above the neutral point of 4). This makes sense given that the Russian gender equality index ranged from 0.73 to 0.82 over the period from 1990 to 2017. However, the order of magnitude (the effect size[4]) of the gender differences in the scores between the two countries was different. Russia's was medium (0.79), whereas the United States' was large (1.06).

In sum, what we have learned from the intergroup paradigm research discussed here is that TMI endorsement does indeed vary by culture and thus cannot be based in biology and further that these variations reflect differences between cultural groups on their beliefs in gender equality. The studies in the next paradigm will take us a little further by showing how specific norms may complement or conflict with ethnic and racial group cultural norms.

The Interconstruct Paradigm

Although realization of the full advantages of the intersectional perspective for the psychology of men and masculinities may require qualitative research, some information can be obtained by examining of the role of social identities such as culture (race and ethnicity) and gender as moderators of the relationship

---

[3] http://hdr.undp.org/en/data

[4] Effect sizes were measured here by the differences in the mean scores of the two groups, and were classified as small ≤0.2, medium ≤0.5 and large ≥08.

between other variables. As we have discussed previously, moderation occurs when a third variable changes the strength and/or direction of the relationship between two other variables, typically a predictor and an outcome. Using an intersectional approach, Levant and Wong (2013) examined the role of gender and race as moderators of the positive linear relationship between alexithymia and the endorsement of TMI found by Levant et al. (2003). Race was shown to moderate the relationship between alexithymia and the endorsement of TMI, and this in turn was strongly affected by gender, which had a second-order moderation effect.[5] Specifically, this study found that the endorsement of TMI was more strongly related to alexithymia for White men than it was for racial minority men. On the other hand, the endorsement of TMI was more strongly related to alexithymia for racial minority women than for White women.

Levant, Wong, Karakis, and Welsh (2015) found that men's conformity to the masculine norm of emotional control mediated (transmitted) the positive relationship between beliefs in the restrictive emotionality norm and the personal experience of alexithymia. That is, the personal performance of the norm by conforming to it transmits the effect of believing in the norm on a measurable deficit in emotional functioning. Additionally, the relationship between restrictive emotionality and alexithymia was moderated by culture. It was stronger for Latino men versus men from other racial groups, but weaker for Asian American men versus men from other racial groups. That is, Latino men had greater alexithymia for a given level of belief in the norm as compared to other men, whereas Asian American men had less alexithymia for a given level of belief in the norm as compared to other men. These results highlight how useful it can be to investigate hypothesized mediation and moderation of established relationships between variables to further knowledge of cultural variations and social identity differences in the endorsement of TMI and its consequences, as we shall see.

As we previously stated, intersectionality theory suggests that cultural norms based on race and gender interact so that each contributes to a person's social identity. Levant et al. (2015) proposed the "masculinity cultural incongruence hypothesis" to explain potential cultural differences in the association between the endorsement of TMI and well-being (p. 460). Specifically, they theorized that men's endorsement of the restrictive emotionality masculinity norm is likely to lead to greater psychosocial stress when this endorsement conflicts with norms of the men's cultural group. Latino cultures have as a central value familism (Kuhlberg, Peña, & Zayas, 2010), which is part of the Latino masculinity ideology of *caballerismo* (Ojeda & Piña, 2014). *Caballerismo* allows Latino

[5] For readers who are more knowledgeable about statistics, moderation is an interaction, and second-order moderation is a three-way interaction.

men to have greater emotional expressivity (De La Mora, 2006). Latino cultural norms therefore conflict with the White masculinity norm of restrictive emotionality. This creates a situation in which some Latino men may be caught in masculinity cultural incongruence in which conforming to the White masculine norm of restrictive emotionality renders them in conflict with the Latino masculinity ideology of *caballerismo*. This in turn creates acculturative stress arising from having to negotiate two competing masculinity norms, which contributes to a greater emotional deficit.

On the other hand, Asian cultural norms require emotional restraint (Kim, Atkinson, & Umemoto, 2001; Wong et al., 2012). From an Asian cultural perspective, the expression of strong emotions is discouraged because that would potentially disrupt interpersonal harmony, and emotional restraint is viewed as a sign of strength (Kim, Atkinson, & Umemoto, 2001). Further, emotional toughness is one of the most central masculinity norms in some Asian societies (Wong, Ho, Wang, & Fisher, 2016). Of course, the cultural norm of emotional toughness complements the White Western masculinity norm of restrictive emotionality. Given the compatibility between these two norms, Asian American men may experience less masculinity cultural incongruence, less acculturative stress, and less emotional deficit arising from having to negotiate two sets of competing masculine norms on emotionality.

In sum, we have learned from studies in the interconstruct paradigm how specific masculinity norms may complement or conflict with ethnic and racial group norms, creating acculturative stress and greater effects when they do conflict.

Intersectional Uniqueness Paradigm

The intersectional uniqueness paradigm focuses on how the intersection of cultural identities creates unique, nonadditive experiences. This focus on unique experiences is based on the idea that cultural identities are intertwined. That is, experiences associated with multiple identities cannot be separated, just as they cannot be simply added together to account for individuals' overall experiences. There are several areas of intersectional uniqueness research. One area is how men of color conceptualize their own identities based on the intersection of race, ethnicity, and gender. Researchers who are interested in this topic might address the question, "What does it mean to be an African American man?" using qualitative methods. We will provide an example of that from work in our lab (Rogers, Sperry, & Levant, 2015). A second area is the investigation of masculinity norms in specific cultural groups, based on social identity variables. We will present two examples of this from work in our lab with respect to age, specifically adolescence and aging men.

African American Masculinity Ideologies

African American men construe masculinity with a stronger family- and community-oriented perspective than do White men. Hunter and Davis (1992, 1994) asked their participants, "What do you think it means to be a man?" and found that African American men defined manhood in terms of four major domains with 15 separate concepts. At the center of the map was self-definition and accountability with other themes such as family, pride, and spirituality prominent. Notably, the participants identified themes salient to the African American community, and none of the 15 clusters of ideas overlapped with White masculinity norms.

Hammond and Mattis (2005) found 15 categories relating to African American men's conceptualization of masculinity. They used open-ended survey questions and content analysis to discover and rank order themes. Similar to Hunter and Davis (1992), they found that responsibility and accountability were viewed as the most salient features of manhood, endorsed by almost half of the participants, with autonomy next most frequent. Other frequently endorsed themes were spirituality/religiosity, moral rectitude/virtues, family centeredness, and being emotionally connected.

Although Hammond and Mattis (2005) and Hunter and Davis (1992, 1994) made major contributions to our understanding of Black men, they did so with respect to how Black men conceptualized masculinity as unrelated to their race by asking questions like "What does manhood mean to you?"

One of my (RL) students did his senior (undergraduate) honors thesis on African American men's concepts of masculinity, using an intersectional perspective, which was subsequently published (Rogers et al., 2015). This was a qualitative study in which participants recruited from a Midwestern public research university and a nearby barbershop were interviewed. Rogers developed a clever strategy to get at the intersection of gender and race. The participants were first asked a set of 10 questions concerning masculinity-in-general (e.g., What does it mean to be a man?). Race was then brought into the picture in the second set of seven questions, which inquired about the intersection of masculinity with race (e.g., What does it mean to be an African American man?). Results indicated, first, that the African American participants' views of masculinity consisted of six themes, each of which had a number of subthemes: African American values, familial relationships, self-definition, leadership, structural oppression, and traditional masculinity. Second, African American men viewed their masculinity as a reflection of traditional masculine norms hindered by the systemic barriers resulting from racism, which was termed "racist gender role strain." As a result, they adopted specific strategies and techniques to deal with the obstacles, in the course of which they constructed a culturally unique version of masculinity.

Rogers then used these results to construct a scale for his master's degree thesis, which has been submitted for publication (Rogers & Levant, 2018). The scale is the Racist Gender Role Strain Scale (RGRSS). A set of items was written using actual statements made by the participants in Rogers et al. (2015). A sample of African American men was recruited from local barbershops and Craigslist postings, and an exploratory factor analysis was conducted. The RGRSS was found to be a 38-item, six-factor scale, with some changes in the theorized factors, now named as follows: giving to others, traditional masculinity and color blind racism, self-definition, African American values, structural oppression, and raising children to think for themselves.

Rogers and colleagues formulation of the racist gender role strain construct highlights the fact that African American men encounter unique experiences of stereotypes and racism. Essed (1991) termed these "every day racism," which is defined as "daily race-related interpersonal slights and systematic re-current practices that instantiate individuals on the basis of race/ethnicity that arise in routines of daily living" (Hammond, Fleming, & Villa Torres, 2016, p. 270). Liu (2016) put it this way: "As scholars we have to continually ask what is it then for men of color to live under dominant masculinity which has as its explicit message, 'Be a man' yet implicitly states, 'You can never be a man like us'" (p. 1).

As a result, African American men have developed a number of adaptations to cope, such as "cool pose" and "John Henryism." The cool pose is "a ritualized form of masculinity that entails behaviors, scripts, physical posturing, impression management, and carefully crafted performances that deliver a single, critical message: pride, strength and control" (Majors & Billson, 1992, p. 4). John Henryism is "a behavioral coping disposition characterized by active effortful coping (e.g., hard work and self-determination (Powell, et al., 2016, p. 270).

It is interesting that several other scales designed to measure Black masculinity using qualitative and quantitative techniques and which emphasize the impact of racism have appeared around the same time as that of Rogers and colleagues. Mincey, Alfonso, and Hackney (2014) developed a culturally sensitive masculinity scale for Black men using qualitative interview and focus group data from undergraduate Black males. The Masculinity Inventory Scale (MIS) items were developed using direct quotes from the qualitative data. Exploratory factor analysis found five subscales: Black masculinity, Primary group, Primary/peer group, Mainstream society, Mainstream society/Black masculinity. Bowleg, del Rio-Gonzalez, Burkholder, Teti, and Tschann (2016) developed qualitatively the Black Men's Experiences Scale (BMES). The BMES assesses Black men's negative experiences with microaggressions and overt discrimination, as well their positive evaluations of what it means to be Black men. First, they conducted individual interviews and focus groups with Black men to develop the BMES. Next, they assessed the BMES with low-income urban Black men. Exploratory factor analysis suggested a 12-item, 3-factor solution, with the subscales Microaggressions, Overt Discrimination and Positives: Black Men. Finally, Schwing, Wong, and Fann (2013) developed and tested the psychometric properties of the 15-item African American Men's Gendered Racism Stress Inventory. Exploratory factor analysis supported a three-factor structure with subscales corresponding to gendered racism stress associated with several stereotypes of African American men: Sports, Absent Fatherhood, and Violence Subscales).

Adolescents' Masculinity Ideologies

Adolescence is a time when gender becomes highly salient and, as a result, concerns about sexuality, gender, and conformity to gender norms become very intense. Only a few scales have been developed to measure the masculinity ideologies of adolescents. First, Pleck, Sonenstein, and Ku (1994a) developed the eight-item Male Role Attitudes Scale to be used with older adolescent boys aged 15 to 19. The chief advantage of the MRAS is its brevity, making it useful for population-based surveys. Its limitations include its low internal consistency[6] and the small number of items, which cover only a small set of the male role norms. Second, Chu, Porche, and Tolman (2005) developed the Adolescent Masculinity Ideology in Relationships Scale (AMIRS), which assesses beliefs about appropriate behavior for boys (aged 12–18) in interpersonal relationships. The AMIRS was developed using adolescent boys' narratives about their experiences of masculinity in their relationships. Limitations of this instrument include its focus on relationships, which recent research suggests is expected more of girls than boys (McDermott et al., 2018), and the fact that it has not been designed to be administered to teenage girls. This is important because, as we have stated, people of all genders have beliefs about how boys should feel, think, and behave.

An adolescent version of the MRNI has been developed, titled the Male Role Norms Inventory–Adolescent (MRNI-A; Brown, 2002). The reading and comprehension levels of the MRNI were adapted to create an instrument developmentally appropriate for use with middle school adolescents. MRNI items were modified to represent adolescent-specific contexts. Also, although they are certainly relevant to the adolescent population, the scale developers opted to not include the Disdain for Sexual Minorities and Nonrelational

---

[6] The coefficient alpha for the MRAS is 0.56, below what is consensually regarded as adequate (0.70), as reported by Pleck et al. (1994a).

Attitudes Toward Sexuality subscales, because they believed that including such scales might create an insurmountable barrier to collecting data from children. Hence the 43-item MRNI-A had five subscales: Aggression, Avoidance of Femininity, Achievement/Status, Restrictive Emotionality, and Self-Reliance. Levant et al. (2008) found that the MRNI-A showed good overall internal consistency for the scale as a whole in samples drawn from the United States and Scotland, but that the reliability of the subscales was inadequate.

Given this limitation, the MRNI-A-revised (MRNI-A-r) was created. It is a 41-item inventory with the same five subscales as the MRNI-A. Levant et al. (2012) conducted an exploratory factor analysis, finding a three-factor structure: (a) Emotionally Detached Dominance, (b) Avoidance of Femininity, and (c) Toughness, which resembles that of the Male Role Norms Scale (Status, Antifeminity, and Toughness). Evidence was found for the internal consistency reliabilities of MRNI-A-r and evidence for validity.

Next, Levant et al. (2016) conducted a confirmatory factor analysis (CFA) of MRNI-A-r with data from middle school boys and girls. They found that a bifactor model best fit the data, similar to the results with MRNI-SF discussed in Chapter 4 of this volume. In this model each item loaded on a general TMI factor and a specific factor corresponding to one of the three hypothesized masculine norms for adolescents. Findings indicate that the MRNI-A-r general factor is a valid and reliable indicator of overall endorsement of TMI in adolescents; however, the specific factors may have different meanings for girls and boys. These findings are consistent with the development of gender schemas, in which adolescence is a time when a differentiated cognitive schema of masculine norms is beginning to form.

Aging Men's Masculinity Ideologies

Levant, Webster, Stanley, and Thompson (2019) developed the Aging Men's Masculinity Ideologies Inventory (AMMII), a measure of the masculinity ideologies relevant to the lives of aging men. To our knowledge, this is the only scale that measures aging men's masculinity ideologies. An exploratory factor analysis revealed a 15-item five-factor scale, which was supported with CFA. The scales are Fatherhood and Family Not Prioritized, Reject Marital Negotiation, Recouple after Widowerhood, Maintain Sex and Vitality, and Retain Patriarchal Authority. An analysis of variance composition through a series of CFA's found that the subscale scores of distinct masculinity ideologies can be used in research, but it would not be advisable to calculate a total scale score to represent a general later-life masculinity ideology. Other analyses indicated that mature and aging women and men share similar beliefs about what is expected of men's later life gender practices. Finding evidence for the validity of four of the AMMII factors supports the use of this short multidimensional scale.

In summary we have learned several things from studies in the intersectional uniqueness paradigm. First, we have fleshed out our picture of African American masculinity ideology. We had seen in the studies discussed in the intergroup paradigm that Black people endorse TMI more strongly that do White and Latin*x* people. We now see in the studies in the intersectional uniqueness paradigm that focus on Black men, that Black men define Black masculinity much more broadly than TMI to include family, community and spiritual dimensions. And, we have learned that Black men's ability to attain the ideals of TMI is impeded by everyday racism and requires some extraordinary adaptations. Second, from studies of adolescents and aging men, we have learned that males must contend with TMI from childhood through old age.

Summary and Conclusions

This chapter highlighted one very important fact—namely, that masculinity endorsement differs across cultures. We learned from the intergroup paradigm research that masculinity endorsement does indeed vary by culture, reflecting differences between cultural groups on their beliefs in gender equality. We learned from studies in the interconstruct paradigm how specific masculine norms may complement or conflict with ethnic and racial group norms, creating acculturative stress when they do conflict. We learned several things from studies in the intersectional uniqueness paradigm. As previously noted, we had seen in the intergroup research that Black people endorse masculinity ideology more strongly that do White and Latinx people. But we now see in the studies in the intersectional uniqueness paradigm that focus on Black men that they define Black masculinity much more broadly than TMI to include family, community, and spiritual dimensions. Finally, from studies of adolescents and aging men, we have learned that males must contend with TMI across the entire lifespan. It just never ends.

We do not know for sure how many variations of masculinity exist, and we could mention only a few of the different masculinities described in the literature. The way that someone might conceptualize masculinity can be influenced by any of their identities (e.g., sexual orientation, race, ethnicity, age). While we have separated each identity we discussed into its own name and meaning, it is important to understand that in terms of men's lived experience, they are anything but divided. Each identity blends in with another, and that unique combination makes a person who they are. For example, a Latino man who identifies as gay might have a different conception of what it means to be a man than a heterosexual Latino man. Alternatively, two men could be similar in age, sexual orientation, race, and ethnicity and still have variations in their own personal performance of masculinity. While the research has placed the different masculinities neatly into boxes, there are individual differences between everyone. A single person can conceptualize masculinity the way that makes the most sense to them. The point of this chapter was to emphasize that there is no "one size fits all" when it comes to masculinity, and that context matters.

9

What Can Be Done

We have spent most of the pages of this book discussing the evidence for masculinity's harmful outcomes, and now we come to the topic of what can be done to ameliorate the situation.

What resources are available to help men who feel that they have no other choice than to be masculine and whose lives (and those around them) are the worse for it? In this chapter, we will examine a number of ways such resources. These include new masculinities, large group awareness training, social marketing and public service announcements, gender neutral parenting (GNP) and involved fathers, academic sources, and psychological services for boys and men.

New Masculinities

The new masculinities include feminist, progressive, permissive, and inclusive masculinities.

Feminist Masculinities

One path is to encourage men to embrace feminism, which in its simplest definition means supporting gender equality. In the global movement of men and women working to achieve gender equality and transform masculinity, the MenEngage Alliance (menengage.org) serves as a hub. Working with the United Nations, governments advancing a male positive, feminist agenda and with hundreds of NGOs in dozens of countries on five continents, it advances an ambitious agenda that promote:

- Ending violence against women and girls
- Preventing child sexual exploitation, sexual abuse and trafficking
- Addressing macro-level policies that perpetuate gender inequalities

- Promoting sexual and reproductive health and rights
- Combating homophobia/transphobia and advocating for LGBTI rights
- Reducing all forms of violence between men and boys
- Supporting men's positive involvement in maternal and child health, as fathers or caregivers
- Increasing HIV and AIDS prevention and treatment

The antisexist or profeminist men's movement has been steadily growing since the late 1970s. Chronicling the movement for the past three decades has been *Voice Male* magazine (voicemalemagazine.org). Edited by Rob Okun, a former executive director of one of the earliest men's centers in North America, the magazine has been described as the *Ms.* magazine of the profeminist men's movement.

An important question that we need to address is, Can feminism help build new standards for being a man? If so, what would that look like? According to Silverstein (2016), that would mean the degendering of society, focusing on gender similarities rather than differences, as Janet Hyde (2005) has advocated. It also means viewing people of any gender as capable of manifesting any human quality. In essence, Silverstein advocates *taking gender out of life's equation*.

How possible is this? It may depend on one's moral orientation. Precopio and Ramsey (2017) investigated whether certain moral orientations contribute to men endorsing feminism. They found that men's feminism was associated with an increased emphasis on the liberal moral concerns of harm and fairness and a decreased emphasis on the conservative moral concerns of ingroup, authority, and purity, even when controlling for political ideology.

A recent article in the *New York Times* (Valenti, 2018) advocated that feminism help boys, saying:

> Feminist ideas can help men—be it the rejection of expectations that men be strong and stoic or ending the silence around male victims of sexual violence. But boys also need the same kind of culture we created for girls. . . . One of feminism's biggest successes was creating an alternative culture for girls and women seeking respite from mainstream constraints. Girls worried about unrealistic beauty standards, for example, can turn to the body positivity movement. . . . But boys and young men who are struggling have no equivalent culture.

Albert Einstein was fond of what he called "thought experiments," which we would like to adapt to this topic for our readers who are men. So guys, imagine that due to a miracle, you are totally free to no longer endorse or conform to masculine norms, with absolutely no penalty, no loss of your "man card," and you can choose any life you wanted. What would you choose? What would you change? I (RL) have used this technique in psychotherapy with my men clients. Some of their responses are as follows: being more fully myself; getting in touch with my feelings; not having to hide my softer, more feminine side; not having to feel ashamed of having emotions other than anger; not having to feel ashamed of needing others; being more fully human; being closer and more intimate with my family and other people in my life; opening up my heart to my children; and being less lonely.

Progressive Masculinities

There is an emerging progressive masculinities movement, which is influenced by feminism and arises from several sources. One source is the nascent sexual violence prevention movement, described in a recent article (Ruiz, 2018). The leadership includes educator Jackson Katz, who founded Mentors in Violence Prevention; sociologist Michael Kimmel, who founded the Center for Men and Masculinities at SUNY Stony Brook; activist and Ted talker Tony Porter, who founded "A Call to Men"; and Michael Kaufman, whose new book, *The Time Has Come*, advocates that the time has come for men to join the gender equality revolution. See also the webpage "How Masculinity Is Evolving" (n.d.).

In response to the #MeToo movement, PettyJohn, Muzzey, Maas, and McCauley (2019) set up the #HowIWillChange Twitter feed, to engage men and boys in the ongoing discussion about sexual violence by asking them to evaluate their role in sustaining rape culture. They collected over 3,000 publicly available tweets containing #HowIWillChange from one day in October 2017. Tweets were analyzed qualitatively and coded into three primary groups of users: committed to dismantle rape culture, indignantly resistant, and hostilely resistant. Actions suggested by users for dismantling rape culture included examining one's own conformity to traditional masculinity, generatively teaching the next generation, calling out abusive men, empathically listening to women's experiences, and promoting egalitarianism. Users indignantly opposed to social change used the rhetoric of "not all men" and promoted benevolently sexist attitudes to assert that men as a group have been unfairly targeted. Users hostile toward the notion of social change attacked perceived weaknesses of men supporting #HowIWillChange; promoted hostile sexist attitudes; made antifeminist, backlash-type statements; and utilized Trump-inspired racist dog whistles and overt racist rhetoric.

Progressive ideas are finding their way into the middle school curriculum. For example, a recent article (Reiner, 2018) reported on a weekly lunchtime boys' group at the Sheridan School, a K–8 private school in Washington, D.C. This pioneering program is teaching boys to question masculine norms, both for their own well-being and as a way to prevent sexual violence. One boy explained the group's purpose to new members as follows: "In here, we get to say stuff we wouldn't normally say in front of other people. And we don't judge each other."

Relatedly, Let Me Run[1] is a wellness program focused on running that encourages boys to develop their psychological, emotional, and social health, in addition to their physical health. Founder Ashley Armistead saw the need for boys to "express their emotions, share their vulnerable side, and develop supportive close relationships." To quote:

> It is our mission to break the "boy code" and allow our boys to develop into the people they are on the inside that is often masked by societal pressures, and Let Me Run is accomplishing just that. A 2016 independent evaluation concluded Let Me Run significantly improves boys' healthy masculinity.

There is also a network of nonprofit groups, including the Institute for Sport and Social Justice, Promundo, Men Can Stop Rape, and The Partnership for Youth, that have created programming and campaigns specifically to help boys and men stop gender violence. They also aim to cultivate a progressive masculinity wherein emotional vulnerability and compassion are virtues, not weaknesses, and it is thus no longer necessary to avoid all things feminine. For example, Promundo's website[2] defines its mission as follows:

> Promundo is a global leader in promoting gender justice and preventing violence by engaging men and boys in partnership with women and girls. We believe that working with men and boys to transform harmful gender norms and unequal power dynamics is a critical part of the solution to achieving gender equality. For the empowerment of women and girls to continue advancing, men and boys must see themselves as allies in the process. Men and boys also benefit when harmful norms are challenged.

For-profit corporations are also stepping up to foster progressive masculinities. There is the Mary Kay Foundation campaign against domestic violence, which attempts to reframe the gender-policing exhortation "Man Up" (Zolla, 2015). According to a 2015 press release[3]:

[1] http://www.letmerun.org/
[2] https://promundoglobal.org/about/
[3] https://3blmedia.com/News/Mary-Kay-Redefining-What-it-Means-Man

Our society defines the phrase "Man up" as being tough and showing no emotion. This Father's Day, global beauty brand Mary Kay, known for enriching women's lives, is asking Dads everywhere to help redefine what it means to "Man Up" by asking young men to lead by example in their attitudes and actions. With one in four women experiencing abuse in their lifetimes, this is part of the Mary Kay's *Don't Look Away* campaign to help prevent and end domestic violence. To learn more or get help visit thehotline.org/manup.

Furthermore, according to Ruiz (2018),

> major brands like Axe, Dove Men+Care, and Getty see the business case for creating more expansive representations of masculinity. Axe, the men's care brand that once gleefully sold consumers sexism in a bottle, launched a campaign last year that rejects macho stereotypes. For the past few years, Dove Men+Care has run ads for Father's Day that focus on men as caregivers. And earlier this year, Getty named "masculinity undone" one of its visual trends for 2018.

Finally, Gillette challenged traditional masculine norms in a new digital ad campaign aimed at men. According to an article in the *Wall Street Journal* (Bruell, 2019),

> the ad, dubbed "We Believe,"[4] opens with audio of news about the current #MeToo movement. A narrator then goes on to dispute the notion that "boys will be boys," asking, "Is this the best a man can get? Is it? We can't hide from it. It has been going on far too long. We can't laugh it off, making the same old excuses." The ad puts a new spin on the brand's 30-year tagline, "The Best A Man Can Get," challenging men to take positive actions, such as stopping other men, and the next generation, from harassing women.

Permissive Masculinities

For several decades there has been a string of prominent athletes and celebrities who have violated the masculine norm of never revealing vulnerability by speaking out about their psychological problems, which has permitted, even encouraged, men to seek mental health care. Most recently NBA star DeMar

[4] https://www.youtube.com/watch?v=koPmuEyP3a0

Rozen openly discussed his depression and Kevin Love likewise discussed his panic attacks. Rozen and Love were traversing the path blazed by earlier athletes such as Terry Bradshaw, Mark McGuire, Warrick Dunn, Alex Rodriguez, Michael Phelps, and many others. A recent website titled Headsupguys.org[5] highlighted male athletes from all over the world who have spoken out about their depression. These athletes included Dwayne "The Rock" Johnson, Joey Votto, Ian Thorpe, Andy Baddeley, Rocky Hatton, John Kirwan, Clarke Carlisle, Dan Carcillo, Greg Stiemsma, Oscar De La Hoya, Shea Emry, Andrew Jensen, David Freese, Larry Sanders, Brandon Marshall, Oliver Bone, Frank Bruno, Jack Green, Michael Yardy, and Rob Krara.[6]

Actors are also getting into the act. Justin Baldoni gave a TEDWomen talk called "Why I'm Done Trying to Be 'Man Enough.'" Terry Crews, an actor and former NFL player, has spoken openly about how masculinity can become like a "cult." So are photographers. Photographer Jessica Amity asked men in Kathmandu for their general thoughts on masculinity and its effect on their lives. Then she asked them to finish this sentence: "It's OK for me to . . ." Wong (2019) wrote an article sharing some of the comments and photos. One man's response exemplifies our thesis proffered in Chapter 2 of this volume that most men come to accept who they are regardless of the traditional masculine norms as follows:

> It's OK for me to be who I am, warts and all. I think 'toxic masculinity' is rooted in men's insecurities. If I were to give advice to my younger self about what it means to be a good man, I think the main thing would be this: Care less about what others think, judge others less, and learn more. Don't worry about maintaining that practiced disheveled look, about how many parties you've been to, or about your experience (or lack thereof) dating girls.

A related trend has been A-list politicians and military leaders violating the no-cry norm by crying openly. Most recently, Joe Biden wept while receiving the Medal of Freedom, but before him there was Bill Clinton, Barack Obama, John Boehner, and General "Storming Norman" Schwarzkopf, the commander of the first Gulf War, who cried openly about losing troops in Iraq.

Finally, men musicians are also jumping into the fray. In recent months, a number of rock and hip-hop artists have released songs that rail against traditional masculinity, some stimulated by suicides of close friends. According to a recent article in the New York Times (Farber, 2019), "the new album by the

---

[5] https://headsupguys.org/22-male-athletes-speaking-depression/
[6] See also: https://mashable.com/2018/05/17/celebrities-mens-mental-health/#ysPPKSj4Biqf

brutalist British band Idles, 'Joy as an Act of Resistance,' uses toxic masculinity as a sustained theme," and "As It Is, a neo-emo band . . . released a single last June, 'The stigma (boys don't cry),' that attacks traditional male restrictions."

Inclusive Masculinities

Developed by Anderson (2005, 2011), inclusive masculinity theory emerged from qualitative research finding more inclusive behaviors of heterosexual men. According to Anderson and McCormack (2018),

> this body of research has shown that many young straight men: reject homophobia; include gay peers in friendship networks; are more emotionally intimate with friends; are physically tactile with other men; recognize bisexuality as a legitimate sexual orientation; embrace activities and artefacts once coded feminine; and eschew violence and bullying. (p. 548)

Large Group Awareness Training

Large group awareness training for men appeared in the national spotlight in the mid-1990s with Robert Bly, Michael Meade, and Sam Keen and others offering "mythopoetic" retreats. These retreats helped some men achieve a reconnection with their emotional lives and their families but were also controversial for the antiwomen views expressed by Bly (1990) in the popular book *Iron John*. Bly strongly advocated for boys to be separated from their mothers at a certain age to live in the world of men, a view that seems to strongly represent the avoid femininity norm of traditional masculinity. While these retreats are no longer available, the ManKind Project (MKP) has been offering similar programs for the past 33 years. MKP has 24 chapters in the United States and 11 regions abroad. It focuses on men's emotional well-being, drawing on Carl Jung's theories of psychotherapy, nonviolent communication, breath work, Native American customs, and male bonding. MKP's retreat is the New Warrior Training Adventure, which has been completed by over 60,000 men: a two-day initiation program that costs almost $700 and includes blindfolded walking tours and cold showers for those who choose to enroll. Some retreats have optional nudity, in an effort to promote healthy body image. After completing the New Warrior Training Adventure, many men join Integration Groups, or I-Groups, where they continue, on a weekly basis with the guidance of a trained peer facilitator, the "work," as it is called in MKP, that was started during those 48 hours (Seligson, 2018).

Social Marketing Campaigns and
Public Service Announcements

Social marketing efforts like the National Institute of Mental Health's "Real Men. Real Depression" campaign can normalize psychological help-seeking by showing a range of men who had been struggling with depression openly acknowledging that they sought psychological help. The website[7] for this campaign states:

> Men are less likely than women to recognize, acknowledge, and seek treatment for depression. In addition, because men may appear to be angry or aggressive instead of sad, their loved ones and even their physicians may not always recognize depression symptoms. To address this concern, the National Institute of Mental Health (NIMH) launched the Real Men. Real Depression. campaign to educate the public about depression in men. The campaign, which ran from 2003 through 2005, became one of the nation's first formal public efforts to raise awareness on the topic. . . . Documentary filmmaker Leslie Wiener captured men speaking candidly about their experiences with depression. Personal accounts from a wide spectrum of men—a retired U.S. Air Force First Sergeant, a firefighter, a writer, a publisher, a national diving champion, a lawyer, a police officer, a student, and others—became the Real Stories of Depression video series. . . . In addition . . . the resources and materials created for the Real Men. Real Depression. campaign included radio and television public service announcements (PSAs), brochures, fact sheets, a web site, and telephone and email hotlines. During the campaign's three-year run, NIMH distributed nearly one million copies of these resources and over 150,000 copies were downloaded from the website. In addition, the campaign's outreach effort generated 14 million hits to the web site and nearly 5,000 emails and phone calls to the information hotlines.

Another example is *Man Up*, developed by King et al. (2018), which is a three-part documentary that examined the link between masculinity, mental health, and suicide for men in Australia. They then conducted an assessment, asking over 300 participants how their views of the term "man up" had changed since watching the documentary/ The men commented on how the documentary prompted them to rethink stereotypes of masculinity.

[7] https://www.nimh.nih.gov/health/topics/men-and-mental-health/men-and-depression/nimhs-real-men-real-depression-campaign.shtml

Social marketing campaigns and public service announcements like these can help men resist the pressure to conform to traditional masculine norms and ultimately improve their lives.

Gender Neutral Parenting and Involved Fathers

Gender stereotyping is taught by parents, as well as teachers, coaches, and peers. The traditional stereotypes have long embedded themselves in parents' minds, influencing their parenting techniques. By using traditional phrases like "Don't cry," "You're OK," and "It's not that bad," parents reinforce the belief that boys are supposed to be emotionally restricted. GNP advocates giving your child opportunities to determine their own gender role identity. It eschews stereotyped roles and allows the child to explore their personalities and abilities instead of force-fitting them into rigid gender roles. Despite the name, GNP is not really neutral at all, but rather it promotes gender diversity as an antidote to restrictive gender roles. GNP advocates exposing your child to a wide variety of gender roles and expressions and then allowing them to choose how they will perform their gender. When Royce and Jessica James found out they were having a daughter, Jessica began to worry about how gender stereotypes would affect their child:

> I remember working at the Boys and Girls Club near our college and seeing the children, watching how they played and how they were able to play based on what they were wearing. And thinking, "Those girls could also be up at the top of that playscape, swinging upside down, if they weren't wearing sandals and sundresses." (Vedantam, 2018)

Jessica and Royce decided they weren't going to let clothing—or gender norms in any form—limit their child's potential. So they said no to dresses and dolls given to them by family members and friends. Jessica said: "We're not going to be getting her baby dolls and Barbies. We want her to have open-ended free play toys."

As a practicing psychologist, I (RL) have had discussions with parents who do not want to raise their boys to conform to traditional masculine standards. This is a reasonable thing to consider, because, after all, children's personalities are quite variable and do not always fit into the gender stereotypes. Girls can be aggressive, tough, independent, and self-reliant, and boys can be sweet and soft and caring and compassionate. Some parents want to allow their children to be who they are and not force them to conform to traditional gender norms. As mentioned previously, this is less of a problem for parents of girls, because girls have much more gender role flexibility than do boys—that is, being a "tomboy" is actually a valued identity for girls. But parents of boys have to realize that they are not the only socialization agents in their sons' lives; quite to the contrary, peers can play an even larger than parents. So I advise such parents to "inoculate" their sons by pointing out, for example,

> In our family we know that everyone gets sad at times and may want to cry, including boys and men, and that is OK in our home. But not everyone agrees, and some people get really mad at boys who cry. So you have to know what you are allowed to do with different people, and we will help you figure that out.

One last consideration regarding parenting concerns involved fathers. A recent article brought to light how a little noticed practice can promote fathers bonding with their children—namely, the bottle-feeding of infants. Popper (2019) wrote about his experiences as a new father. His wife had been having great difficulties lactating, so despite their misgivings informed by the motto "Breast is best," they turned to bottle-feeding. Here is what he had to say about it:

> Those blue plastic boxes of white powder, which at first seemed like a sinful corporate invasion of our sacred family space, introduced an equality and a peace in our home that seemed impossible in those first hellish weeks. Even more unexpectedly, it gave my relationship to my son a depth that I, as a father, would have otherwise missed out on, and that has continued long after he stopped drinking from a bottle.

Academic Sources

The study of gender has long been a core component of the academic social science disciplines of psychology, sociology, and anthropology, as well as some humanities such as English and history, and interdisciplinary programs such as gender studies. In addition there are several professional organizations focused on men and masculinity—the interdisciplinary American Men's Studies Association and the Society for the Psychological Study of Men and Masculinity (SPSMM, Division 51 of the American Psychological Association). These organizations have been very helpful in providing opportunities for Men's Studies to grow and develop. Indeed, the present book could not have been written were it not for the work of SPSMM.

SPSMM members have written text and reference books for undergraduates (e.g., Kilmartin & Smiler, 2015), and graduate students/professionals (e.g.,

Levant & Pollack, 1995; Levant & Wong, 2017). SPSMM sponsors two conferences per year and a journal, the *Psychology of Men and Masculinities* (PMM), which is the focal point for publishing empirical research in this area. Now in its 19th year of publication, it has shown tremendous growth. PMM published two issues a year and 150 pages in the smaller 7×10-inch size when it was inaugurated in 2000 and now publishes four issues per year and 500 pages in the 8½×11-inch size, has a 2018 impact factor of 1.813, and is ranked 28 of 64 social psychology journals. In addition, there are the *Journal of Men's Studies* and *Men and Masculinities*, as well more general journals in the area of sex and gender and specialized journals in men's health.

The field that PMM serves, the psychology of men and masculinities, has also experienced phenomenal growth. The original pioneers of this field (who emerged in the decade from the late 1970s to the late 1980s) spawned several generations of scholars and practitioners, who in turn have generated many other scholars and practitioners, many of whom now hold tenured and tenure-track positions at doctoral programs all across the country and who are now training the next generations of scholars and practitioners. As a result, the literature has grown and developed in many expected and unexpected ways. There are even new psychological scales designed to foster men's freedom from masculinity. One is designed to measure progressive masculinity, which emphasizes gender equality. The scale has four subscales: Attentiveness to Women, Commitment to Household Responsibility, Consideration for Others, and Emancipation From Emotional Restriction and Toughness (Kenkyu, 2017). Another measures men's "stage of change" in regard to masculinity. Stages of change refer to readiness to make needed changes in one's life in psychotherapy, ranging from not even recognizing that there is a problem ("precontemplation") to contemplation, preparation, action, maintenance, and termination. This scale is titled the Critical Awareness of Masculinity Scale. Respondents indicate the degree to which they think men are under pressure to conform to one of eleven specific masculine norms, the degree to which they think it is a problem, and their desire to resist or change the norm (Addis & Stewart, 2019).

Psychological Services for Boys and Men

SPSMM has also been an important source for developing new perspectives on men's mental health and designing new techniques for psychotherapy with men. A task force headed by Frederick Rabinowitz at the University of the Redlands in California spent 13 years developing and refining a set of *Guidelines for Psychological Practice With Boys and Men*, which has recently been adopted by the American Psychological Association and have been published (American Psychological Association, Boys and Men Guidelines Group, 2018). The

American Psychological Association had published a similar set of guidelines for girls and women in 2007. For a number of years, SPSMM ran the biannual Psychotherapy with Men conferences, in which new experimental therapeutic work with men was presented and which were attended by hundreds of therapists. Furthermore, SPSMM members have produced a large number of books on psychotherapy with men (Andronico, 1996; Brooks, 1998, 2010; Englar-Carlson & Stevens, 2006; Good & Brooks, 2005; Kiselica, Englar-Carlson, & Horne, 2008; Oren & Oren, 2010; Rabinowitz & Cochran, 2002; Shepard & Harway, 2012; Sweet, 2012; Wexler, 2009). In addition, SPSMM members have produced several self-help books for men (Adams, n.d.; Levant & Kopecky, 1995). A notable example is *Building a Better Man*, a self-help book and accompanying workshops (Seymour, Smith, & Torres, 2014). Finally, for the reader who would like more information on available programming to help men curb violence and substance abuse, there is the chapter by Liang, Molenaar, Herman, and Rivera (2017).

Psychoeducational Programs for Men

Several programs have been developed for men as adjuncts to psychotherapy that rely on psychological educational techniques. One such program is titled the Gender Role Journey Workshop, designed to help people examine how their gender role socialization and sexism have affected their lives. According to O'Neil (1996), the workshop is designed to help participants progress through three stages: (a) accepting traditional gender roles; (b) gender role ambivalence, fear, anger, and confusion; and (c) personal and professional activism. Another program developed as an adjunct to psychotherapy with alexithymic men to increase their emotional self-awareness is titled alexithymia reduction treatment (ART). According to Levant (1998), ART has five steps, which will be described in the following case study.

Case Study

To give the reader an idea of how these new therapies for men work, we present a brief case study of a man with alexithymia treated by RL using ART (Levant, 2000), which he developed (Levant, 1998).

Craig, a 40-year-old successful stockbroker, called me (RL) for an appointment because he "felt nothing" about the fact that he and his wife of 18 years were expecting their first child. The first-born son of a rural family, responsibility was his middle name. His sister had a disabled child whom he financially supported. Apart from the fact that his wife was pregnant and he thought he "should" feel something about that, Craig did not find it particularly odd that he "felt nothing." He usually felt nothing. The last time he cried was when his dog was killed by a car. That was 10 years ago.

I worked with Craig for several weeks using the psychoeducational program that I have developed to help men increase their emotional self-awareness and overcome normative alexithymia, now called ART (Levant, 1997b, 1998; Levant & Kopecky, 1995). ART helps men through three major tasks: developing a vocabulary for emotions, particularly the vulnerable and caring-connection emotions; learning to read the emotions of other people through observing their facial expressions and tone of voice; and learning to read their own emotions and put them into words. The essential tool for this task is a formal record, the "emotional response log," which he keeps for the duration of therapy. Each entry will have three parts:

- The feeling, bodily sensation, or sign of stress that he first becomes aware of. (For many men, this will be the undifferentiated "buzz" of emotional arousal.)
- The context—social situation, conversation, event, or circumstance—in which it occurred. Who is doing what to whom, and how does it affect him?
- The identified emotion. I suggest that he go through his vocabulary list to figure out the words that best describe the experience that he is having.

Craig worked hard during this period and became more able to identify his emotions and put them into words.

Craig said at the outset that he thought that a lot of his problems had to do with his father. His father was 11 years older than his mother, was 38 when Craig was born, and had died of a heart attack 13 years ago. Craig believed that his father had a great life as an Air Force officer during World War II—a life that he had to leave behind when he married and started a family and one that he seemed to miss greatly throughout Craig's childhood. Because of his father's self-absorption and detachment, Craig was always unsure of his father's feelings about him, and yet he yearned to get closer. For example, Craig's lifelong hobby was participating in Scottish rites and learning about his Scottish ancestry, an activity in which he had earlier hoped he could involve his father. The first time I saw Craig display emotions openly was when he spoke of how he had always wanted to see his Dad in a kilt, carrying a set of bagpipes.

As therapy progressed, Craig's initial detachment about his father turned to curiosity. Craig discovered he had many questions he wanted to ask his father, so we constructed a therapeutic ritual in which he would write down the questions that he had for his father on 3×5-inch cards. I also suggested digging out old family photos to stimulate his memories. His initial response to these tasks was to get very angry that his father "just wasn't there." He later talked of how, when his father needed him after his first heart attack, he decided he was too busy to visit. In describing this event, he said "It's a family curse. I come from a long line of uncaring fathers".

The therapy deepened on a trip to see his mother, during which he visited his father's grave. He described the experience as "raw emotion." His sadness poured out of him, as he stood alone at his father's headstone, reading though his cards filled with unanswered questions.

He was later able to locate an old friend of his father, Henry, who remembered the day Craig was born. Henry said that that was the only time he saw Craig's father cry. We can never know how accurate Henry's recollection is, but that is not the point. Craig was able to use this information to be able to feel for the first time in his life that maybe his father really did care about him after all. With this shift, Craig then was able to begin to address a lifelong sense of shame, which stemmed in no small measure from his relationship with his father.

Having made progress in addressing his sense of shame and recapturing his ability to tune into and verbalize his emotional life, Craig began to experience some strong feelings about his expectant fatherhood—fear, worry, and anxiety. He began to worry about whether the baby was going to be all right, given his wife's age (40 also). He also investigated some obscure genetic diseases that ran in families of Scottish descent. I encouraged him to address his worries directly, by attending one of his wife's visits to the obstetrician. He did so and was reassured about the baby's health and also heard the baby's heartbeat. His fear then turned to joy and excitement. We terminated 1 month before the baby was due. I got a postcard from him two months later "Ron, the baby was 2 weeks late. But he's a big guy, 8 lbs. 13 oz. And he definitely looks Scottish."

Summary and Conclusions

When we were first beginning to conceptualize this book, we decided to include alternatives for men who might be looking to change their way of being a man. In this chapter, we covered a number of different ideas, some of which are not widely known. We began by describing new and different ways of conceiving masculinity, including feminist, progressive, and permissive masculinities. These new views of masculinity paved the way for a new type of social marketing that aspires to enlighten people about traditional gender roles. Finally, we discussed concrete options that men might use to help influence change such as large group programs and psychological services. Importantly, we suggested an alternative to traditional gender role socializing through GNP which allows young boys to decide early on how they want to think, feel, and behave, paving the way for inner security and individualized values. We also noted a little-known way to promote father involvement—namely, bottle-feeding. Decades of research on the psychology of gender has helped to create many of these new definitions of masculinity and interventions for men that you have read about in this chapter. This research on masculinity will no doubt continue to develop and influence future change. While not always conveniently advertised, information and resources on men and masculinity are available and will continue to grow.

We ended this chapter with a case example of the course of psychotherapy of a man who was experiencing a not-uncommon struggle among men. Please consider that case example. Did you relate at all to Craig's struggle? What stood out to you? Craig described his "family curse" of coming from a long line of uncaring fathers. Craig began to recognize how his aloof and distant father might have affected him, resulting in him not wanting to follow those same footsteps with his own children. This case study painted a realistic but painful picture about where many men are today with their fathers and becoming fathers themselves. Ultimately, it was through therapy that Craig began to feel safe and capable enough to face his feelings. Other men might feel unhappy with how things are in their lives, yet they might feel that they have no options or that no one understands their concerns. We want to drive home the point that there are options and that one is never alone in his struggle. A clear change is on the horizon for men, a change that allows for many different conceptualizations of masculinity and that embraces the fact that men are human beings first, with emotions and weaknesses as well as strengths. Men can love and be loved, cry, experience trauma, and seek help. Most important, men can fail to attain masculine ideals and still be men.

CODA

This book was not easy to write. It was likely not easy to read at times. We realize that there were some messages that were probably difficult to receive and that some readers may have been challenged by the evidence that we marshalled. A colleague best expressed our position on this point, so in the following passage, we adopt his statement as our own: "[Our] intent is not to attack any man for ascribing to qualities that give his life meaning and value, but rather to open some men up to new and flexible patterns of behavior" (Isoma, 2019). However, each of us, with our very different biographies, believe that it is very important to have laid out the case that we made. For me (RL), it was an opportunity to synthesize a career's worth of work and to see what it all added up to. We want to close by first summarizing the main points of this book, the headlines as it were, as a set of bullet points.

1. Sex (male) is not the same thing as gender (masculinity), which is socially constructed.
2. Masculinity can be measured and studied using various masculinity scales or measures (i.e., Male Role Norms Inventory, Conformity to Masculine Norms Inventory, Gender Role Conflict Scale, Masculine Gender Role Stress Scale, Male Role Norms Scale).
3. Masculinity is problematic because
   a. Most boys feel obliged to conform to masculine norms.
   b. Masculinity otherizes women and racial, ethnic, sexual, and gender minority men.
   c. Masculinity is associated with broad range of harmful outcomes for the men, their partners, families, and society-at-large.
4. The harmful outcomes are probably accounted for by the extreme high scorers who endorse or conform rigidly to traditional masculine norms.

5. There are aspects of masculinity which are positive, and some masculinity scales are associated with some beneficial outcomes.
   a. It is very important to investigate and discover what aspects of the person and/or situation accounts for these positive outcomes.
6. Masculinity negatively affects men's families and society at large through its documented role in these problems:
   a. School and other mass shootings.
   b. Police violence against unarmed Black boys and men.
   c. Hate crimes against marginalized groups.
   d. Intimate partner violence perpetrated by men.
   e. Sexual violence perpetrated by men.
7. Masculinity negatively affects boys and men themselves in these documented ways:
   a. Exacerbates working class men's economic difficulties.
   b. Encourages men to take risks with their physical health, affecting men's morbidity and mortality.
   c. Creates strain, stress, and conflict, affecting boys and men's mental health, while also making them reluctant to seek psychological help.
   d. Impairs men's ability to recover, heal, and grow from psychological trauma resulting from intimate partner or sexual violence.
8. Gender (masculinity) intersects with other dimensions of a person's identity, such as race/ethnicity, age/life stage, and sexual orientation, creating variations in masculinity (termed masculinities). These intersections have been studied in three main ways:
   a. Comparing different groups on their scores on masculinity scales, which might reflect differences between groups on their beliefs regarding gender equality.
   b. Looking at the differential relationships between scores on masculinity scales and outcomes (such as alexithymia) that might reflect masculinity cultural incongruence or congruence.
   c. Studying the specific form of masculinity in various groups, such as those defined by the intersection of gender and race, or gender and age.
9. There are a growing number of resources to help men and those who love them evolve new, more flexible, inclusive, and egalitarian ways of being a man in the world. These include new masculinities, large-group awareness training programs, social marketing and public service announcements, gender-neutral parenting, promoting father involvement, academic sources creating new knowledge, and psychological services for boys and men.

Next, we want to reflect on where we think we need to go from here. We posited that the harmful effects of masculinity are likely due to the extreme high scorers on masculinity scales—that is, those who most strongly and rigidly endorse or conform to traditional masculine norms or experience gender role conflict or stress. While there are some gaps to fill in this area, this notion seems to be largely supported by the data we have at present. However, we are not yet able to answer with any precision the bigger question of why a small percentage of boys and men commit violence while the vast majority of boys and men do not. How do traditional masculinity ideology, conformity to masculine norms, and gender role conflict and stress interact with the personality and individual difference variables as well as aspects of the situational context in such a way that lead boys and men to do these horrible things. Answering this question is a most urgent task for future research.

Finally, we want to say that it is our hope that this book, by providing an evidence-based analysis of the topic, will foster greater consideration of the role of masculinity in these serious contemporary social problems and stimulate conversations on this topic between researchers, educators, policymakers, legislators, journalists, bloggers, parents, religious leaders, and coaches.

APPENDIX

Table 2.1. **Men's Mean Scores and Standard Deviations on the Male Role Norms Inventory–Revised**

	Mean Score	Standard Deviation
MRNI-R: Total Scale	3.88	1.07
Restrictive Emotionality	3.19	1.18
Self-Reliance Through Mechanical Skills	4.76	1.34
Negativity Toward Sexual Minorities	3.64	1.57
Avoidance of Femininity	4.17	1.32
Importance of Sex	3.80	1.56
Toughness	4.92	1.14
Dominance	3.44	1.28

Note: MRNI-R, Male Role Norms Inventory–Revised

Source: Levant et al., 2010.

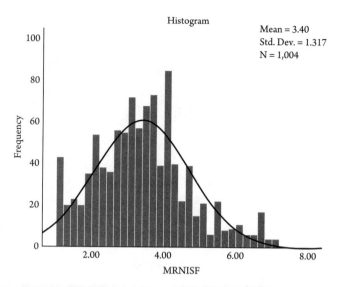

Figure 2.1. Histogram of men's scores on the Male Role Norms Inventory-Short Form. Data files, University of Akron Gender Research Team Laboratory.

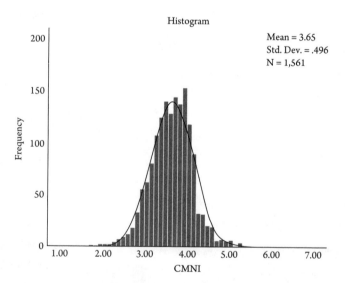

Figure 2.2. Histogram of men's scores on the Conformity to Masculine Norms Inventory. Data files, University of Akron Gender Research Team Laboratory.

Table 4.1. **Factor Loadings and Intercorrelations from Single-Group Confirmatory Factor Analysis of the MRNI-SF Using the Bifactor Model**

| | General and Specific Factors | | | | | | | |
Scale and Item	TM	F1	F2	F3	F4	F5	F6	F7
F1: Restrictive Emotionality (RE)								
38. A man should never admit when others hurt his feelings.	0.51	0.66						
41. Men should be detached in emotionally charged situations.	0.43	0.63						
53. Men should not be too quick to tell others that they care about them.	0.52	0.53						
F2: Self-Reliance through Mechanical Skills (SR)								
13. Men should have home improvement skills.	0.48		0.79					
14. Men should be able to fix most things around the house.	0.53		0.74					
36. A man should know how to repair his car if it should break down.	0.42		0.48					
F3: Negativity toward Sexual Minorities (NT)								
1. Homosexuals should never marry.	0.51			0.59				
8. All homosexual bars should be closed down.	0.56			0.69				

(continued)

Table 4.1. **Continued**

Scale and Item	General and Specific Factors							
	TM	F1	F2	F3	F4	F5	F6	F7
25. Homosexuals should never kiss in public.	0.68			0.47				
F4: Avoidance of Femininity (AF)								
7. Men should watch football games instead of soap operas.	0.70				0.35			
15. A man should prefer watching action movies to reading romantic novels.	0.67				0.17			
19. Boys should prefer to play with trucks rather than dolls.	0.83				0.68			
F5: Importance of Sex (IS)								
16. Men should always like to have sex.	0.58					0.49		
20. A man should not turn down sex.	0.51					0.55		
43. A man should always be ready for sex.	0.56					0.63		
F6: Dominance (Do)								
2. The President of the US should always be a man.	0.52						0.60	
3. Men should be the leader in any group.	0.44						0.85	
21. A man should always be the boss.	0.56						0.58	

(continued)

Table 4.1. **Continued**

Scale and Item	General and Specific Factors							
	TM	F1	F2	F3	F4	F5	F6	F7
F7: Toughness								
42. It is important for a man to take risks, even if he might get hurt.	0.44							0.42
45. When the going gets tough, men should get tough.	0.59							0.49
48. I think a young man should try to be physically tough, even if he's not big.	0.61							0.46
Factor Intercorrelations								
F1: Restrictive Emotionality		—	– 0.06	0.24*	0.18	0.39*	0.49*	0.34*
F2: Self-Reliance through Mechanical Skills			—	–0.15	0.34	0.17	–0.05	0.40*
F3: Negativity Toward Sexual Minorities				—	0.02	–0.19	0.45*	–0.18
F4: Avoidance of Femininity					—	0.10	0.09	0.20
F5: Importance of Sex						—	0.27*	0.48*
F6: Dominance							—	0.13
F7: Toughness								—

Note: Item numbers refer to the number of the item in the MRNI-R. Standardized factor loadings are reported. MRNI-SF = Male Role Norms Inventory–Short Form. MRNI-R = Male Role Norms Inventory–Revised. TM = general traditional masculinity ideology factor. All factor loadings are statistically significant at $p < 0.05$. All factor intercorrelations marked with an asterisk are statistically significant at $p < 0.05$. Copyright, American Psychological Association. Reprinted by permission.

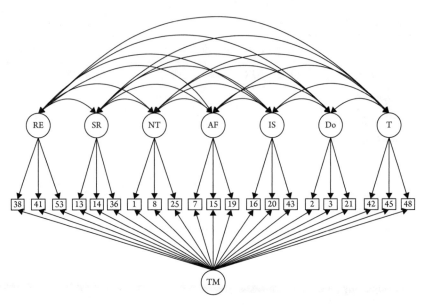

Figure 4.1. The MRNI-SF bifactor model. The small boxes represent the individual items and are numbered to correspond to the item number in Table 4.1. The circles represent the general and specific factors, and their abbreviated labels are defined in Table 4.1. Copyright, American Psychological Association. Reprinted by permission.

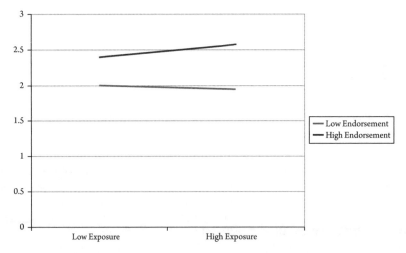

Figure 5.1. Moderation of the Relationship between Exposure to Violent Videogames (X Axis) and Aggression (Y Axis) by the Endorsement of Traditional Masculinity Ideology (Thomas & Levant, 2011).

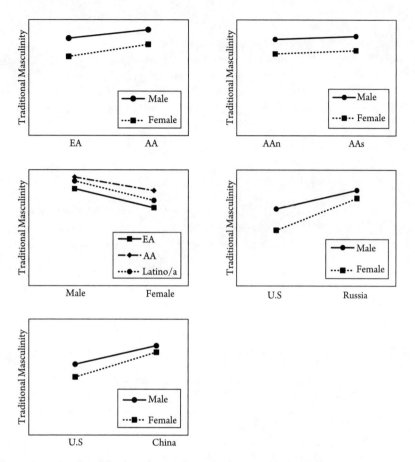

Figure 8.1. Graphical display of research results from studies comparing men and women of different ethnicities, races, geographic regions and nationalities on MRNI total traditional scores. M = male, F = female, EA = European American, AA = African American, AAn = African American residing the U.S. North, AAs = African American residing the U.S. South.

ABOUT THE AUTHORS

Ronald F. Levant, EdD, ABPP, is Professor Emeritus of Psychology, the University of Akron. Dr. Levant earned his bachelors in psychology from the University of California, Berkeley, and his doctorate in Clinical Psychology and Public Practice from Harvard University. He served on the faculty of Boston University for 13 years, where he directed the nationally prominent Fatherhood Project, an innovative community outreach program that offered preventive psychological services to men and their families. Following a brief stint at Rutgers University with a joint appointment in the Graduate Schools of Education and Applied and Professional Psychology, he served for seven years on the faculty of Harvard Medical School at The Cambridge Hospital and then for eight years as Dean and Professor, Center for Psychological Studies, Nova Southeastern University. At the University of Akron, he served for four years as Dean of the College of Arts and Sciences and nine additional years as Professor of Psychology. Dr. Levant has authored, co-authored, edited, or co-edited 19 books and 250 peer-refereed journal articles and book chapters in family and gender psychology and in advancing professional practice.

Dr. Levant has been one of the leading pioneers of the field of the psychology of men and masculinities. He played a key role in the late 1980s and early 1990s in envisioning and developing this new field, serving as the co-founder, co-chair, and the first President of the Society for the Psychological Study of Men and Masculinities (APA Division 51). He co-edited *A New Psychology of Men* (Basic Books, 1995), which has been cited as the most salient publication of the fledgling field. It served as the standard graduate text and professional reference book for over 20 years. Dr. Levant served two terms as Editor of the APA journal *Psychology of Men and Masculinity*.

Dr. Levant has contributed to the development of the Gender Role Strain Paradigm, the major theoretical perspective in the psychology of men and masculinities. He has developed and evaluated 15 scales designed to assess a variety of gender constructs, the most prominent of which is the Male Role Norms Inventory (MRNI), including the Revised, Short, Very Brief, Adolescent, and Adolescent Revised versions. Dr. Levant's signature contribution has been in establishing the empirical foundation for the normative male alexithymia hypothesis. In addition, Levant developed alexithymia reduction treatment (ART), a brief psychoeducational intervention designed to remediate normative male alexithymia to prepare men to engage more fully in psychotherapy. ART is designed as an adjunctive treatment that can be administered prior to, or concurrently with, standard care. Finally, Dr. Levant developed a leadership role in the American Psychological Association (APA), serving as the 2005 president. Further information on his work is at his website: www.DrRonaldLevant.com.

Personal Statement: How I Got Involved in the Psychology of Men and Masculinities

It is often said that psychological research is "me-search," and that is true in my case. Let me explain how I became involved in the psychology of men and masculinities. In the mid-1970s, I was a young assistant professor in counseling psychology at Boston University, who held himself out to the world as an expert in the family. I taught the doctoral sequence in family psychology and conducted research on prevention-oriented programs for parents. During this time, I was also struggling on a personal level with the role of a divorced, semi-custodial father. I visited my daughter on the weekends, and she lived with me during the summers. I have to say at the outset that I had some trepidation about being an involved father in the first place. It was hard to imagine myself as a father. I did not have much to draw on in my memories of my own father, whose idea of spending time with his boys always involved work, like having my brother and I mow the lawn while he supervised.

In any event, these extended 12-week visits with my daughter did not go smoothly. I was not adept at understanding her needs nor in managing her behavior. For what seemed like the longest time I lived with a sense of fraudulence. My inner thoughts at the time went something like this; "Who do you think you are, pretending to be an expert on parenting, when you are struggling in your own life as father?" The shame I felt about my role as a father was intensified because of my unresolved feelings about my own father. Not yet having had the experience of exonerating him for the ways that I felt he failed me, I was unremittingly hard on myself for the ways that I felt that I was failing my daughter. And like most men, I kept my sense of inadequacy to myself and did not share it with anyone, for fear of violating the male code of self-reliance and invulnerability.

Thus, I deprived myself of the experience of learning that maybe other fathers may be struggling with this role.

In the late 1970s, I saw the film, *Kramer vs. Kramer*, which resulted in a major epiphany in my life. I saw myself in the Mr. Kramer character portrayed by Dustin Hoffman, and instead of continuing to think I was just a struggling father and all the other guys were doing fine, I began to wonder if this wasn't more of a broader phenomenon affecting many fathers. Fathers then were starting to take on roles vastly different from that of their own fathers, and for which they had received little, if any, preparation. I asked the question of what resources existed for fathers like myself who wanted to be fully involved, effective parents of their children. The answer was, Nothing. A review of the major literature reviews on parent education available at the time (Loiselle, 1980) revealed that none of the studies indicated whether the parent groups included fathers. Echoing Michael Lamb (1979), I concluded that the father was the forgotten parent and that parent education was synonymous with mother education.

This was for me a disjunctive event. I no longer considered myself a student of parenting and the family. I was now interested in fathering and the roles of men in families. This lead to the founding of the Boston University Fatherhood Project in the early 1980s, which was a research, service, and training program focusing on enhancing fathers' involvement in the care of their children. I (with the help of doctoral students Greg Doyle, Wendy Nelson, Joel Kanigsburg, Joe Rabinovitz, and Liz Tarshis) turned to the task of designing psycho-educational parenting programs for men (Levant & Kelly, 1989). That, of course, was the proverbial fork in the road that opened up my subsequent career involvement in fathering and ultimately in the new psychology of men and the new psychotherapy for men. From the early 1980s to the 1990s my professional work with men and my own development as a man were increasingly intertwined. While working on overcoming my own sense of shame for perceived personal failings, I became increasingly aware of the role that shame plays in most men's lives, locked into their hearts by the harsh injunctions of the male code.

Shana Pryor, MA, is a graduate student at the University of Akron working toward her PhD in Counseling Psychology. She obtained her master's degree from the same institution in 2018. During that time she was the lab manager for Dr. Ronald Levant's Gender Research Team from 2016 to 2018, coordinating various data collection efforts, helping undergraduate student research assistants with their graduate school aspirations and facilitating discussions about gender. She has worked with the Rape Crisis Centers of Medina and Summit counties and was the first undergraduate to be in the student organization, Defined Lines, where she worked to abolish rape culture on college campuses. She has

presented at conferences where she has talked about the need for more attention to male survivors of sexual trauma and just recently completed her master's
thesis on how traditional masculinity negatively affects how men reacted to and
grew from sexually coercive experiences. She plans to continue to advocate for
male survivors of sexual trauma and interpersonal violence and hopes to work
even more with this the population in the future.

REFERENCES

Abbey, A., Jacques, T. A. J., & LeBreton, J. M. (2011). Risk factors for sexual aggression in young men: An expansion of the confluence model. *Aggressive Behavior, 37*, 450–464. https://doi-org.ezproxy.uakron.edu:2443/10.1002/ab.20399

Abrams, A. (2016, November 7). See how many men there are for each woman in U.S. government. *Time.* Retrieved from http://time.com/4556917/presidential-election-2016-women-government/

Addis, M. E. (2008). Gender and depression in men. *Clinical Psychology: Science and Practice, 15*, 153–168. https://doi.org/10.1111/j.1468-2850.2008.00125.x

Addis, M. E., & Hoffman, E. (2017). Men's depression and help-seeking through the lens of gender. In R. F. Levant & Y. J. Wong (Eds.), *The psychology of men and masculinities* (pp. 171–196). Washington, DC: American Psychological Association.

Addis, M. E., & Stewart, A. (2019, August). Measuring change in traditional masculinity ideology: Psychometric evaluation of the critical awareness of masculinity scale. In R. F. Levant (Chair). *Recent advances in scale development in the psychology of men and masculinities.* Symposium conducted at the meeting of the American Psychological Association, Denver, Colorado.

Alleyne-Green, B., Grinnell-Davis, C., Clark, T. T., & Cryer-Coupet, Q. R. (2015). The role of fathers in reducing dating violence victimization and sexual risk behaviors among a national sample of Black adolescents. *Children and Youth Services Review, 55*, 5548–5555. doi:10.1016/j.childyouth.2015.04.005

Allport, G. W. (1954). *The nature of prejudice.* Cambridge, MA: Perseus Books.

American Cancer Society. (2015). Incidence rates, 2011–2015. Retrieved from https://cancerstatisticscenter.cancer.org/?_ga=2.87881752.1096602244.1548529506-724853190.1548529506#!/data-analysis/IncRate

American Psychiatric Association. (2013). *Diagnostic and statistical manual of mental disorders* (5th ed.). Arlington, VA: Author. http://dx.doi.org/10.1176/appi.books.9780890425596

American Psychological Association. (2013). Gun violence: Prediction, prevention, and policy. Retrieved from http://www.apa.org/pubs/info/reports/gun-violence-prevention.aspx

American Psychological Association, Boys and Men Guidelines Group. (2018). APA guidelines for psychological practice with boys and men. Retrieved from http://www.apa.org/about/policy/psychological-practice

Anderson, C. A., & Anderson, K. B. (2008). Men who target women: Specificity of target, generality of aggressive behavior. *Aggressive Behavior, 34*, 605–622. https://doi-org.ezproxy.uakron.edu:2443/10.1002/ab.20274

Anderson, E. (2005). Orthodox and inclusive masculinity: Competing masculinities among heterosexual men in a feminized terrain. *Sociological Perspectives, 48,* 337–355. https://doi.org/10.1525/sop.2005.48.3.337

Anderson, E. (2011). Updating the outcome: Gay athletes, straight teams, and coming out in educationally based sport teams. *Gender & Society, 25,* 250–268. https://doi.org/10.1177/0891243210396872

Anderson, E., & McCormack, M. (2018). Inclusive masculinity theory: Overview, reflection and refinement. *Journal of Gender Studies, 27,* 547–561. https://doi.org/10.1080/09589236.2016.1245605

Anderson, K. L., & Umberson, D. (2001). Gendering violence: Masculinity and power in men's accounts of domestic violence. *Gender & Society, 15,* 358–380. doi:10.1177/089124301015003003. Retrieved from http://journals.sagepub.com/doi/10.1177/08912 4301015003003#articleCitationDownloadContainer

Andronico, M. (Ed.). (1996). *Men in groups: Insights, interventions, & psychoeducational work.* Washington, DC: American Psychological Association.

Aosved, A. C., Long, P. J., & Voller, E. K. (2011). Sexual revictimization and adjustment in college men. *Psychology of Men & Masculinity, 12,* 285–296. doi:10.1037/a0020828

Appiah, K. A. (2018, December 16). Do I have to repay a loan to an ex-lover? *The New York Times Sunday Magazine,* p. 24. Retrieved from https://www.nytimes.com/2018/12/11/magazine/do-i-have-to-repay-a-loan-to-an-ex-lover.html

Arciniega, G. M., Anderson, T. C., Tovar-Blank, Z. G., & Tracey, T. J. (2008). Toward a fuller conception of machismo: Development of a traditional machismo and caballerismo scale. *Journal of Counseling Psychology, 55,* 19–33. doi:10.1037/0022-0167.55.1.19

Astor, M., & Russell, K. (2018, December 15). New state gun control laws surge. *New York Times,* A19.

Autor, D., Dorn, D., & Hanson, G. (2018, December). *When work disappears: Manufacturing decline and the falling marriage market value of young men.* Unpublished manuscript. Retrieved from https://economics.mit.edu/files/12736

Baer, J. L., Kohut, T., & Fisher, W. A. (2015). Is pornography use associated with anti-woman sexual aggression? Re-examining the confluence model with third variable considerations. *Canadian Journal of Human Sexuality, 24,* 160–173. https://doi-org.ezproxy.uakron.edu:2443/10.3138/cjhs.242-A6

Bagby, R. M., Parker, J. D., & Taylor, G. J. (1994). The twenty-item Toronto Alexithymia Scale: 1. Item selection and cross validation of the factor structure. *Journal of Psychosomatic Research, 38,* 23–32. doi:10.1016/0022-3999(94)90005-1

Balsam, K. F., Rothblum, E. D., & Beauchaine, T. P. (2005). Victimization over the life span: A comparison of lesbian, gay, bisexual, and heterosexual siblings. *Journal of Consulting and Clinical Psychology, 73,* 477–487. https://doi.org/10.1037/0022-006X.73.3.477

Bandura, A., Ross, D., & Ross, S. (1961). Transmission of aggression through imitation of aggressive models. *Journal of Abnormal and Social Psychology, 63,* 187–197.

Barnett, R. C. (2008). On multiple roles: Past, present, and future. In K. Korabik, D. Lero, & D. L. Whitehead.(Eds.), *Handbook of work–family integration* (pp. 75–93). San Diego, CA: Academic Press.

Barron, J. M., Struckman-Johnson, C., Quevillon, R., & Banka, S. R. (2008). Heterosexual men's attitudes toward gay men: A hierarchical model including masculinity, openness, and theoretical explanations. *Psychology of Men & Masculinity, 9,* 154–166. https://doi-org.ezproxy.uakron.edu:2443/10.1037/1524-9220.9.3.154

Bates, E. A., Kaye, L. K., Pennington, C. R., & Hamlin, I. (2019). What about the male victims? Exploring the impact of gender stereotyping on implicit attitudes and behavioural intentions associated with intimate partner violence. *Sex Roles, 81,* 34–43. doi:10.1007/S11199-019-01029-9

Becker, J. B., & Hu, M. (2007). Sex differences in drug abuse. *Frontiers in neuroendocrinology, 29,* 36–47. https://doi.org/10.1016/j.yfrne.2007.07.003

Berger, J. L., Addis, M. E., Green, J. D., Mackowiak, C., & Goldberg, V. (2013). Men's reactions to mental health labels, forms of help-seeking, and sources of help-seeking advice. *Psychology of Men & Masculinity, 14,* 433–443. https://doi-org.ezproxy.uakron.edu:2443/10.1037/a0030175

Berger, J. L., Douglas, E. M., & Hines, D. A. (2016). The mental health of male victims and their children affected by legal and administrative partner aggression. *Aggressive Behavior, 42,* 346–361. https://doi.org/10.1002/ab.21630

Berke, D. S., Sloan, C. A., Parrott, D., & Zeichner, A. (2012). Effects of female gender role and gender norm conformity on aggression in men: Does positive masculinity reduce the risk? *Psychology of Men & Masculinity, 13,* 367–378. https://doi-org.ezproxy.uakron.edu:2443/10.1037/a0026525

Berke, D. S., Wilson, L., Mouilso, E., Speir, Z., & Zeichner, A. (2015). Isolating the gendered component of men's physical aggression. *Sex Roles, 72,* 509–520. https://doi-org.ezproxy.uakron.edu:2443/10.1007/s11199-015-0488-7

Black, M. (2018, February 21). The boys are not all right. *The New York Times.* Retrieved from https://www.nytimes.com/2018/02/21/opinion/boys-violence-shootings-guns.html?action=click&contentCollection=Opinion&module=Trending&version=Full&region=Marginalia&pgtype=article

Blosnich, J. R., & Bossarte, R. M. (2009). Comparisons of intimate partner violence among partners in same-sex and opposite-sex relationships in the United States. *American Journal of Public Health, 99,* 2182–2184. https://doi.org/10.2105/AJPH.2008.139535

Blume, O. (2018, December 4). Incels: The dangerous new wave of women-haters. *Next Tribe.* Retrieved from https://nexttribe.com/the-incel-movement/?fbclid=IwAR2gRi9-EJlT-TEvZs9tfiVeDkBHeTP42FJ_UegozZuPfwuUD6heQE4KPpw

Bly, R. (1990). *Iron John: A book about men.* Reading, MA: Addison Wesley.

Bohan, J. S. (1997). Regarding gender: Essentialism, constructionism, and feminist psychology. In M. M. Gergen & S. N. Davis (Eds.), *Toward a new psychology of gender* (pp. 31–47). New York, NY: Routledge.

Borgogna, N. C., McDermott, R. C., & Browning, B. R., Beach, J. D., & Aita, S. L. (2019). How does traditional masculinity relate to men and women's problematic pornography viewing? *Sex Roles, 80*(11–12), 693–706. https://doi.org/10.1007/s11199-018-0967-8

Bosson, J. K., & Vandello, J. A. (2011). Precarious manhood and its links to action and aggression. *Current Directions in Psychological Science, 20,* 82–86. https://doi-org.ezproxy.uakron.edu:2443/10.1177/0963721411402669

Boudewyn, A., & Liem, J. (1995). Childhood sexual abuse as a precursor to depression and self-destructive behavior in adulthood. *Journal of Traumatic Stress, 8,* 445–459. doi:10.1002/jts.2490080307

Bowleg, L. (2012). The problem with the phrase women and minorities: Intersectionality—an important theoretical framework for public health. *American Journal of Public Health, 102,* 1267–1273. doi:10.2105/AJPH.2012.300750

Bowleg, L., English, D., Del Rio-Gonzalez, A. M., Burkholder, G. J., Teti, M., & Tschann, J. M. (2016). Measuring the pros and cons of what it means to be a Black man: Development and validation of the Black Men's Experiences Scale (BMES). *Psychology of Men & Masculinity, 17,* 177–188. https://doi.org/10.1037/men0000026

Brannon, R., & Juni, S. (1984). A scale for measuring attitudes about masculinity. *Psychological Documents, 14* (University Microfilms No. 2612).

Brayboy Jackson, P., & Williams, D. R. (2006). The intersection of race, gender and SES: Health paradoxes. In A. J. Shultz & J. Mullings (Eds.), *Gender, race, class and health: Intersectional perspectives* (pp. 131–162). San Francisco, CA: Jossey Bass.

Bridges, T., & Pascoe, C. J. (2014). Hybrid masculinities: New directions in the sociology of men and masculinities. *Sociology Compass, 8,* 246–258. https://doi.org/10.1111/soc4.12134

Brislin, R. (1970). Back translation for cross-cultural research. *Journal of cross-cultural psychology, 1,* 185–216. https://doi.org/10.1177/135910457000100301

Brooks, G. R. (1998). *A new psychotherapy for traditional men.* San Francisco, CA: Jossey Bass.

Brooks, G. R. (2010). *Beyond the crisis of masculinity: A transtheoretical model for male-friendly therapy.* Washington, DC: American Psychological Association.

Brown, J. (2002). *Statistical analysis of a measure of adolescent gender ideology, the Male Role Norms Inventory-Adolescent: A pilot study.* Unpublished doctoral directed study, Nova Southeastern University, Davie, FL.

Brown, R. P., Baughman, K., & Carvallo, M. (2018). Culture, masculine honor, and violence toward women. *Personality and Social Psychology Bulletin, 44,* 538–549. https://doi.org/10.1177/0146167217744195

Bruell, A. (2019, January 14). P&G challenges men to shave their 'toxic masculinity' in Gillette ad. *Wall Street Journal.* Retrieved from https://www.wsj.com/articles/p-g-challenges-men-to-shave-their-toxic-masculinity-in-gillette-ad-11547467200

Bureau of Justice Statistics. (2008). *National Crime Victimization Survey: Criminal victimization in the United States, 2006 statistical tables* (NCJ 223436). Retrieved from http://www.bjs.gov/content/pub/pdf/cvus06.pdf

Burns, S. M., & Mahalik, J. R. (2008). Treatment type and emotional control as predictors of men's self-assessed physical well-being following treatment for prostate cancer. *Psychology of Men & Masculinity, 9,* 55–66. https://doi-org.ezproxy.uakron.edu:2443/10.1037/1524-9220.9.2.55

Buck, R. (1977). Non-verbal communication of affect in preschool children: Relationships with personality and skin conductance. *Journal of Personality and Social Psychology, 35,* 225–236. https://doi.org/10.1037/0022-3514.35.4.225

Bushman, B. (2002). Does venting anger feed or extinguish the flame? Catharsis, rumination, distraction, anger and aggressive responding. *Personality and Social Psychology Bulletin, 28,* 724–731. https://doi.org/10.1177/0146167202289002

Bushman, B. J., Bonacci, A. M., van Dijk, M., & Baumeister, R. F. (2003). Narcissism, sexual refusal, and aggression: Testing a narcissistic reactance model of sexual coercion. *Journal of Personality and Social Psychology, 84,* 1027–1040. http://dx.doi.org/10.1037/0022-3514.84.5.1027

Butler, J. (1990). *Gender trouble.* New York, NY: Routledge.

Calton, J. M., Heesacker, M., & Perrin, P. B. (2014). The elusiveness of progressive masculinity: Gender differences in conceptualizations of nontraditional gender roles. *Journal of Gender and Power, 2,* 37–58.

Carley, M. (2018, October 20). Masculinity: Healthy vs. toxic. *The Good Men Project.* Retrieved from https://goodmenproject.com/ethics-values/masculinity-healthy-vs-toxic-dg/

Caron, C. (2019, January 10). Two North Carolina women charged with sexually assaulting transgender woman in bar. *New York Times.* Retrieved from https://www.nytimes.com/2019/01/10/us/transgender-woman-sexual-assault-nc.html

Carlsen, A., Salam, M., Cain Miller, C., Lu, D., Ngu, A., Patel, J. K., & Wichter, Z. (2018, October 23). #MeToo brought down 201 powerful men. Nearly half of their replacements Are women. *New York Times.* Retrieved from https://www.nytimes.com/interactive/2018/10/23/us/metoo-replacements.html?nl=top-stories&nlid=46999675ries&ref=cta

Carr, J. L., & VanDeusen, K. M. (2004). Risk factors for male sexual aggression on college campuses. *Journal of Family Violence, 19,* 279–289. https://doi-org.ezproxy.uakron.edu:2443/10.1023/B:JOFV.0000042078.55308.4d

Carvalho, A. F., Lewis, R. J., Derlega, V. J., Winstead, B. A., & Viggiano, C. (2011). Internalized sexual minority stressors and same-sex intimate partner violence. *Journal of Family Violence, 26,* 501–509. https://doi.org/10.1007/s10896-011-9384-2

Center for American Women and Politics. (2018). In 2018, 1,875, or 25.4% of the 7,383 state legislators in the United States are women. Retrieved from http://www.cawp.rutgers.edu/data_element/data_page_archive/188

Centers for Disease Control and Prevention. (2013, August 23). Injury prevention & control: Data & statistics (WISQARS™). Retrieved from http://www.cdc.gov/injury/wisqars/index.html

Centers for Disease Control and Prevention. (2015). Leading causes of death by age group, all males–United States. Retrieved from https://www.cdc.gov/healthequity/lcod/men/2015/all-males/index.htm

Centers for Disease Control and Prevention. (2016). Data & statistics fatal injury. Retrieved from https://afsp.org/about-suicide/suicide-statistics/

Centers for Disease Control and Prevention. (2018). Intimate partner violence: Definitions. Retrieved from https://www.cdc.gov/violenceprevention/intimatepartnerviolence/definitions.html

Centers for Disease Control and Prevention. (n.d.). *What is sexual violence?* Retrieved from https://www.cdc.gov/violenceprevention/sexualviolence/definitions.html

Chicago Tribune Staff. (2019, September). #MeToo: A timeline of events. *Chicago Tribune.* Retrieved from https://www.chicagotribune.com/lifestyles/ct-me-too-timeline-20171208-htmlstory.html

Chu, J. Y., Porche, M. V., & Tolman, D. L. (2005). The Adolescent Masculinity Ideology in Relationships Scale: Development and validation of a new measure for boys. *Men and Masculinities, 8,* 93–115. https://doi.org/10.1177/1097184X03257453

Cleary, T. (2016, June 6). Judge Aaron Persky: 5 fast facts you need to know. *Heavy News.* Retrieved from http://heavy.com/news/2016/06/aaron-persky-brock-turner-judge-stanford-recall-petition-election-photos-sentence

Cochran, S. V. (2010). Emergence and development of the psychology of men and masculinity. In J. C. Chrisler & D. R. McCreary (Eds.), *Handbook of gender research in psychology: Vol. 1, Gender research in general and experimental psychology* (pp. 43–58). New York: Springer.

Cohen, R., & Vedantam, S. (2018, March 19). Guys, we have a problem: How American masculinity creates lonely men. *The Hidden Brain.* Retrieved from https://www.npr.org/2018/03/19/594719471/guys-we-have-a-problem-how-american-masculinity-creates-lonely-men

Cole, E. R. (2009). Intersectionality and research in psychology. *American Psychologist, 64,* 170–180. https://doi.org/10.1037/a0014564

Connell, R. W., & Messerschmidt, J. W. (2005). Hegemonic masculinity: Rethinking the concept. *Gender & Society, 19,* 829–859. https://doi.org/10.1177/0891243205278639

Cooper, F. R. (2016, July 19). America's police culture has a masculinity problem. *The Conversation.* Retrieved from http://theconversation.com/americas-police-culture-has-a-masculinity-problem-62666

Courtenay, W. H. (2000a). Behavioral factors associated with disease, injury, and death among men: Evidence and implications for prevention. *Journal of Men's Studies, 9,* 81–142. https://doi.org/10.3149/jms.0901.81

Courtenay, W. H. (2000b). Endangering health: A social constructionist examination of men's health beliefs and behaviors. *Psychology of Men and Masculinity, 1,* 4–15. https://doi.org/10.1037/1524-9220.1.1.4

Creighton, G., & Oliffe, J. L. (2010). Theorising masculinities and men's health: A brief history with a view to practice. *Health Sociology Review, 19,* 409–418. https://doi.org/10.5172/hesr.2010.19.4.409

Crenshaw, K. (1991). Mapping the margins: Intersectionality, identity politics, and violence against women of color. *Stanford Law Review, 43,* 1241–1299.

Daniel-Ulloa, J., Sun, C., & Rhodes, S. D. (2017). The intersection between masculinity and health among rural immigrant Latino men. *International Journal of Men's Health, 16,* 84–95.

De La Mora, S. (2006). *Cinemachismo: Masculinities and sexuality in Mexican film.* Austin, TX: University of Texas Press.

Deaux, K. (1984). From individual differences to social categories: Analysis of a decade's research on gender. *American Psychologist, 39,* 105–116. https://doi.org/10.1037/0003-066X.39.2.105

Dobash, R. P., & Dobash, R. E. (2004). Women's violence to men in intimate relationships: Working on a puzzle. *British Journal of Criminology, 44,* 324–349. https://doi.org/10.1093/bjc/azh026

Domingue, B. W., Cislaghi, B., Nagata, J. M., Shakya, H. B., Weber, A. M., Boardman, J. D., Darmstadt, G. L., & Harris, K. M. (2019). Implications of gendered behaviour and contexts for social mobility in the USA: a nationally representative observational study. *The Lancet/ Planetary Health, 3*, e420–428.

Douglas, S. J. (2017, August). The antidote to toxic masculinity. Questia Magazine. Retrieved from https://www.questia.com/magazine/1P4-1923046380/the-antidote-to-toxic-masculinity

Easton, S. D., Coohey, C., Rhodes, A. M., & Moorthy, M. V. (2013). Posttraumatic growth among men with histories of child sexual abuse. *Child Maltreatment, 18*, 211–220. doi:10.1177/1077559513503037

Easton, S. D., Renner, L. M., & O'Leary, P. (2013). Suicide attempts among men with histories of child sexual abuse: Examining abuse severity, mental health, and masculine norms. *Child Abuse & Neglect, 37*, 380–387. https://doi.org/10.1016/j.chiabu.2012.11.007

Easton, S. D., Saltzman, L. Y., & Willis, D. G. (2014). "Would you tell under circumstances like that?" Barriers to disclosure of child sexual abuse for men. *Psychology of Men & Masculinity, 15*, 460–469. https://doi-org.ezproxy.uakron.edu:2443/10.1037/a0034223

Eisenberg, N., & Lennon, R. (1983). Sex differences in empathy and related capacities. *Psychological Bulletin, 94*, 100–131. https://doi.org/10.1037/0033-2909.94.1.100

Eisler, R. M., & Skidmore, J. R. (1987). Masculine gender role stress: Scale development and component factors in the appraisal of stressful situations. *Behavior Modification, 11*, 123–136. https://doi.org/10.1177/01454455870112001

Endendijk, J. J., Groeneveld, M. G., van der Pol, L. D., van Berkel, S. R., Hallers-Haalboom, E. T., Mesman, J., & Bakermans-Kranenburg, M. J. (2014). Boys don't play with dolls: Mothers' and fathers' gender talk during picture book reading. *Parenting: Science and Practice, 14*, 141–161. doi:10.1080/15295192.2014.972753

Englar-Carlson, M., & Stevens, M. A. (2006). *In the room with men: A casebook of therapeutic change.* Washington, DC: APA Books

Epps, B. (2018, February 16). America's gun violence problem is a symptom of toxic masculinity. *Them.* Retrieved from https://www.them.us/story/beyond-gun-control-we-need-to-end-toxic-masculinity

Epstein, M., & Ward, L. M. (2011). Exploring parent-adolescent communication about gender: Results from adolescent and emerging adult samples. *Sex Roles, 65*, 108–118. doi:10.1007/s11199-011-9975-7

Essed, P. (1991). *Understanding everyday racism: An interdisciplinary theory.* Thousand Oaks, CA: SAGE.

Evans, T. (1994). Spiritual purity. In *Seven promises of a promise keeper* (pp. 73–100). Colorado Springs, CO: Focus on the Family.

Fagot, B. I., & Hagan, R. (1991). Observations of parent reactions to sex-stereotyped behaviors: Age and sex effects. *Child Development, 62*, 617–628. doi:10.2307/1131135

Faludi, S. (1999). *Stiffed: The betrayal of the American man.* New York, NY: Harper Collins.

Farber, J. (2019, January 11). The new angry young men: Rockers who rail against "toxic masculinity." *The New York Times.* Retrieved from https://www.nytimes.com/2019/01/11/style/rock-masculinity-men-emotions.html

Fausto-Sterling, A. (2000). *Sexing the body.* New York, NY: Basic Books.

Feder, J., Levant, R. F., & Dean, J. (2007). Boys and violence: A gender informed analysis. *Professional Psychology: Research and Practice, 38*, 385–391. https://doi.org/10.1037/0735-7028.38.4.385

Federal Bureau of Investigation. (2007). Crime in the United States, 2007. Retrieved from http://www2.fbi.gov/ucr/cius2007

Federal Bureau of Investigation. (2017). About hate crime statistics, 2017. Retrieved from https://ucr.fbi.gov/hate-crime/2017/hate-crime

Felmlee, D., Sweet, E., & Sinclair, H. C. (2012). Gender rules: Same-and cross-gender friendship norms. *Sex Roles, 66*, 518–529. https://doi.org/10.1007/s11199-011-0109-z

Finneran, C., & Stephenson, R. (2013). Intimate partner violence among men who have sex with men: A systematic review. *Trauma, Violence, & Abuse, 14,* 168–185. https://doi.org/10.1177/1524838012470034

Finley, G. E., & Schwartz, S. J. (2004). The Father Involvement and Nurturant Fathering Scales: Retrospective measures for adolescent and adult children. *Educational and Psychological Measurement, 64,* 143–164. https://doi.org/10.1177/0013164403258453

Finley, G. E., & Schwartz, S. J. (2007). Father involvement and long-term young adult outcomes: The differential contributions of divorce and gender. *Family Court Review, 45,* 573–587 https://doi.org/10.1111/j.1744-1617.2007.00172.x.

Florida, R. (2018, February 14). The real cause of the opioid crisis. *City Lab.* Retrieved from https://www.citylab.com/life/2018/02/the-real-cause-of-the-opioid-crisis/553118/

Fortin, J. (2018, December 13). How "Baby, it's cold outside" went from parlor act to problematic. *New York Times.* Retrieved from https://www.nytimes.com/2018/12/13/arts/music/baby-its-cold-outside-history-facts.html

Fortin, J. (2019, January 10). Traditional masculinity can hurt boys, say new A.P.A. guidelines. *New York Times.* Retrieved from https://www.nytimes.com/2019/01/10/science/apa-traditional-masculinity-harmful.html

Freeland, R., Goldenberg, T., & Stephenson, R. (2018). Perceptions of informal and formal coping strategies for intimate partner violence among gay and bisexual men. *American Journal of Men's Health, 12,* 302–312. https://doi-org.ezproxy.uakron.edu:2443/10.1177/1557988316631965

Gage, N. A., & Lease, S. (2018). An exploration of the link between masculinity and endorsement of IPV myths in American men. *Journal of Interpersonal Violence.* [Published online first] https://doi.org/10.1177/0886260518818430

Gallagher, K. E., & Parrott, D. J. (2011). What accounts for men's hostile attitudes toward women?: The influence of hegemonic male role norms and masculine gender role stress. *Violence Against Women, 17,* 568–583. https://doi.org/10.1177/1077801211407296

Galuska, D. A., Serdula, M., Pamuk, E., Siegal, P. Z., & Byers, T. (1996). Trends in overweight among U.S. adults from 1987 to 1993: A multistate telephone survey. *American Journal of Public Health, 86,* 1729–1735. https://doi.org/10.2105/AJPH.86.12.1729

Garfield, C. F., Isacco, A., & Rogers, T. E. (2008). A review of men's health and masculinity. *American Journal of Lifestyle Medicine, 2,* 474–487. https://doi.org/10.1177/1559827608323213

Gbadamosi, N. (2018, 12/21). The all-male group tackling toxic masculinity. *CNN.* Retrieved from https://www.cnn.com/2018/12/21/health/south-africa-male-group-toxic-masculinity-intl/index.html

Gebhard, K. T., Cattaneo, L. B., Tangney, J. P., Hargrove, S., & Shor, R. (2019). Threatened-masculinity shame-related responses among straight men: Measurement and relationship to aggression. *Psychology of Men & Masculinity, 20*(3), 429–444. http://dx.doi.org/10.1037/men0000177

Gerdes, Z. T. (2018). Stuck in the present: Gaps in the theoretical past and applied future of the psychology of men and masculinities. *Psychology from the Margins, 1.* Retrieved from http://ideaexchange.uakron.edu/psychologyfromthemargins/vol1/iss1/1

Gerdes, Z. T., Alto, K. M., Jadaszewski, S., D'Auria, F., & Levant, R. F. (2017). A content analysis of research on masculinity ideologies using all forms of the Male Role Norms Inventory (MRNI). *Psychology of Men & Masculinity, 19,* 584–599. https://doi.org/10.1037/men0000134

Gerdes, Z., & Levant, R. (2018). Complex relationships among masculine norms and health/well-being Outcomes: Correlation patterns of the Conformity to Masculine Norms Inventory subscales. *American Journal of Men's Health, 12,* 229–240. https://doi.org/10.1177/1557988317745910

Giridharadas, A. (2018, September 2). What is identity? *New York Times Book Review,* 1, 13. Retrieved from https://www.nytimes.com/2018/08/27/books/review/francis-fukuyama-identity-kwame-anthony-appiah-the-lies-that-bind.html#

Goldberg, N. G., & Meyer, I. H. (2013). Sexual orientation disparities in history of intimate partner violence: Results from the California health interview survey. *Journal of Interpersonal Violence, 28*, 1109–1118. https://doiorg.ezproxy.uakron.edu:2443/10.1177/0886260512459384

Good, G. E., & Brooks, G. R. (Eds.) (2005). *A new handbook of counseling and psychotherapy with men.* San Francisco, CA: Jossey Bass.

Goodwin, J. S., Kuo, Y., Brown, D., Juurlink, D., & Raji, M. (2018). Association of chronic opioid use with presidential voting patterns in US counties in 2016. *JAMA Network Open, 1*. https://doi.org/10.1001/jamanetworkopen.2018.0450

Gough, B. (2013). The psychology of men's health: Maximizing masculine capital. *Health Psychology, 32*, 1–4. https://doi-org.ezproxy.uakron.edu:2443/10.1037/a0030424

Gough, B., & Robertson, S. (2017). A review of research on men's health. In R. F. Levant & Y. J. Wong (Eds.), *The psychology of men and masculinities* (pp. 197–227). Washington, DC: American Psychological Association.

Greene, P. L., & Davis, K. C. (2011). Latent profiles of risk among a community sample of men: Implications for sexual aggression. *Journal of Interpersonal Violence, 26*, 1463–1477. https://doi.org/10.1177/0886260510369138

Greenwood, G. L., Relf, M. V., Huang, B, Pollack, L. M, Canchola, J. A., & Catania, J. A. (2002). Battering victimization among a probability-based sample of men who have sex with men. *American Journal of Public Health, 92*, 1964–1969 https://doi.org/10.2105/AJPH.92.12.1964

Griffith, D. M., & Thorpe, R. J. (2016). Men's physical health and health behaviors. In Y. J. Wong & S. R Wester (Eds.), *APA handbook on men and masculinities* (pp. 709–730). Washington, DC: American Psychological Association.

Griffiths, S., Mond, J. M., Murray, S. B., & Touyz, S. (2015). Positive beliefs about anorexia nervosa and muscle dysmorphia are associated with eating disorder symptomatology. *Australian and New Zealand Journal of Psychiatry, 49*, 812–820. https://doi-org.ezproxy.uakron.edu:2443/10.1177/0004867415572412

Guthrie, R. V. (2004). *Even the rat was white: A historical view of psychology* (2nd Ed.). New York: Allyn & Bacon.

Hall, G. C. N., DeGarmo, D. S., Eap, S., Teten, A. L., & Sue, S. (2006). Initiation, desistance, and persistence of men's sexual coercion. *Journal of Consulting and Clinical Psychology, 74*, 732–742. https://doi-org.ezproxy.uakron.edu:2443/10.1037/0022-006X.74.4.732

Hamilton, C. J., & Mahalik, J. R. (2009). Minority stress, masculinity, and social norms predicting gay men's health risk behaviors. *Journal of Counseling Psychology, 56*, 132–141. https://doi.org/10.1037/a0014440

Hammer, J. H., Heath, P. J., & Vogel, D. L. (2018). Fate of the total score: Dimensionality of the Conformity to Masculine Norms Inventory-46 (CMNI-46). *Psychology of Men & Masculinity, 19*(4), 645–651. http://dx.doi.org/10.1037/men0000147

Hammond, W. P., Fleming, P. J., & Villa Torres, L. (2016). Everyday racism as a threat to the masculine social self: Framing investigations of African American health disparities. In Y. J. Wong & S. R Wester (Eds.), *APA handbook on men and masculinities* (pp. 259–283). Washington, DC: American Psychological Association.

Hammond, W. P., & Mattis, J. S. (2005). Being a man about it: Manhood meaning among African American men. *Psychology of Men & Masculinity, 6*, 114. https://doi.org/10.1037/1524-9220.6.2.114

Harrington, E. F., Crowther, J. H., & Shipherd, J. C. (2010). Trauma, binge eating, and the "Strong Black Woman." *Journal of Consulting & Clinical Psychology, 78*, 469–479. https://doi.org/10.1037/a0019174

Harrison, J. (1978). Warning: The male sex role may be dangerous to your health. *Journal of Social Issues, 34*, 65–86.

Hermann, C., Liang, C. T. H., & DeSipio, B. E. (2018). Exploring sexual consent and hostile masculine norms using the theory of planned behavior. *Psychology of Men & Masculinity, 19*, 491–499. https://doi.org/10.1037/men0000127

Hines, D. A., Brown, J., & Dunning, E. (2007). Characteristics of callers to the domestic abuse helpline for men. *Journal of Family Violence, 22,* 63–72. https://doi-org.ezproxy.uakron.edu:2443/10.1007/s10896-006-9052-0

Hines, D. A., Douglas, E. M., & Berger, J. L. (2014). The measurement of legal/administrative aggression with intimate relationships. *Aggressive Behavior, 41,* 295–309. https://doi.org/10.1002/ab.21540

Hong, J., Cho, H., Allen-Meares, P., & Espelage, D. (2011). The social ecology of the Columbine High School shootings. *Children and Youth Services Review, 33,* 861–868. 10.1016/j.childyouth.2010.12.005.

How masculinity is evolving. (n.d.). *TED.* Retrieved from https://www.ted.com/playlists/404/how_masculinity_is_evolving

Huisman, K., Martinez, J., & Wilson, C. (2005). Training police officers on domestic violence and racism: Challenges and strategies. *Violence Against Women, 11,* 792–821. https://doi-org.ezproxy.uakron.edu:2443/10.1177/1077801205276110

Hunter, A. G., & Davis, J. E. (1992). Constructing gender: An exploration of Afro-American men's conceptualization of manhood. *Gender & Society, 6,* 464–479. https://doi.org/10.1177/089124392006003007

Hunter, A. G., & Davis, J. E. (1994). Hidden voices of Black men: Meaning, structure, and complexity of manhood. *Journal of Black Studies, 25,* 20–40. https://doi.org/10.1177/002193479402500102

Hyde, J. S. (2005). The gender similarities hypothesis. *American Psychologist, 60,* 581–592. https://doi.org/10.1037/0003-066X.60.6.581

Isoma, Z. (2019, February 22). The evolving possibilities of manhood [blogpost]. *Lyra.* Retrieved from https://www.lyrahealth.com/blog/the-evolving-possibilities-of-manhood/

Iwamoto, D. K., Corbin, W., Lejuez, C., & MacPherson, L.(2013). College men and alcohol use: Positive alcohol expectancies as a mediator between distinct masculine norms and alcohol use. *Psychology of Men & Masculinity, 15,* 29–39. https://doi.org/10.1037/a0031594

Jackson, J. S., & Knight, K. M. (2006). Race and self-regulatory health behaviors: The role of the stress response and the HPA axis. In K. W. Schaie, & L. L. Carstensten (Eds.), *Social structure, aging, and self-regulation in the elderly* (pp. 189–240). New York, NY: Springer.

Jackson, J. S., Knight, K. M., & Rafferty, J. A. (2010). Race and unhealthy behaviors: Chronic stress, the HPA axis, and physical and mental health disparities over the life course. *American Journal of Public Health, 100,* 933–939. http://dx.doi.org/10.2105/AJPH.2008.143446

Jakupcak, M., Lisak, D., & Roemer, L. (2002). The role of masculine ideology and masculine gender role stress in men's perpetration of relationship violence. *Psychology of Men and Masculinity, 3,* 97–106. https://doi.org/10.1037/1524-9220.3.2.97

Jolly, J. (2014, November 18). Is violence more common in same-sex relationships? *BBC News.* Retrieved from https://www.bbc.com/news/magazine-29994648

Jones, C. (2018, October 9). When will MeToo become WeToo? Some say voices of Black women, working class left out. *USA Today.* Retrieved from https://www.usatoday.com/story/money/2018/10/05/metoo-movement-lacks-diversity-blacks-working-class-sexual-harassment/1443105002/

Jones, T. (2018, July 6). What Nelson Mandela lost. *New York Times.* Retrieved from https://www.nytimes.com/2018/07/06/opinion/sunday/nelson-mandela-tayari-jones-prison-letters.html

Johnson, M. P. (1995). Patriarchal terrorism and common couple violence: Two forms of violence against women. *Journal of Marriage and the Family, 57,* 283–294. https://doi.org/10.2307/353683

Jozkowski, K. N., & Wiersma-Mosley, J. D. (2017). The Greek system: How gender inequality and class privilege perpetuate rape culture. *Family Relations: An Interdisciplinary Journal of Applied Family Studies, 66,* 89–103. doi:10.1111/fare.12229

Katz, J. (n.d.). Violence against women—it's a men's issue. *Ted Talk.* Retrieved from https://www.ted.com/talks/jackson_katz_violence_against_women_it_s_a_men_s_issue/transcript?language=en

Kavanagh, S., & Graham, M. (2019). How gender inequity impacts on men's health: An exploration of theoretical pathways. *International Journal of Men's Social and Community Health, 2,* e11–e21. https://doi.org/10.22374/ijmsch.v2i1.5

Keneally, M. (2019, January 7) Domestic violence plays a role in many mass shootings, but receives less attention: Experts. *ABC News.* Retrieved from https://abcnews.go.com/US/domestic-violence-plays-role-mass-shootings-receives-attention/story?id=59418186

Kenkyu, S. (2017). Development of the new male roles scale: Reliability and validity. *Japanese Journal of Psychology, 88,* 251–259. https:doi.org/10.4992/jjpsy88.16210

Kessler, R. C., Berglund, P., Demler, O., Jin, R., Koretz, D., Merikangas, K. R.,... Wang, P. S. (2003). The epidemiology of major depressive disorder: Results from the National Comorbidity Survey Replication (NCS-R). *Journal of the American Medical Association, 289,* 3095–3105. https://doi.org/10.1001/jama.289.23.3095

Kia-Keating, M., Grossman, F. K., Sorsoli, L., & Epstein, M. (2005). Containing and resisting masculinity: Narratives of renegotiation among resilient male survivors of childhood sexual abuse. *Psychology of Men & Masculinity, 6,* 169–185. https://doi.org/10.1037/1524-9220.6.3.169

Kiesel, L. (2018, January 17). Don't blame mental illness for mass shootings; Blame men. *Politico Magazine.* Retrieved from https://www.politico.com/magazine/story/2018/01/17/gun-violence-masculinity-216321

Kilmartin, C., & McDermott, R. C. (2016). Violence and masculinities. In Y. J. Wong & S. R Wester (Eds.), *APA handbook on men and masculinities* (pp. 615–636). Washington, DC: American Psychological Association.

Kilmartin, C., & Smiler, A. P. (2015). *The masculine self* (5th ed.). Cornwall-on-the Hudson, NY: Sloan.

Kim, B. S., Atkinson, D. R., & Umemoto, D. (2001). Asian cultural values and the counseling process: Current knowledge and directions for future research. *Counseling Psychologist, 29,* 570–603.

Kimmel, M. S. (1987). The contemporary "crisis" of masculinity in historical perspective. In H. Brod (Ed.), *The making of masculinities: The new men's studies* (pp. 121–153). Boston, MA; Unwin Hyman.

Kimmel, M. (2013). *Angry White men: American masculinity and the end of an era.* New York, NY: Nation Books.

King, K., Schlichthorst, M., Keogh, L., Reifels, L., Spittall, M. J., Phelps, A., & Pirkis, J. (2018). Can watching a television documentary change the way men view masculinity? *Journal of Men's Studies, 27*(3), 287–306. https://doi.org/10.1177/1060826518815909

Kiselica, M. S., & Englar-Carlson, M. (2010). Identifying, affirming, and building upon male strengths: The positive psychology/positive masculinity model of psychotherapy with boys and men. *Psychotherapy Theory, Research, Practice, Training, 47,* 276–287.

Kiselica, M. S., Englar-Carlson, M., & Horne, A. M. (2008). (Eds.), *Counseling troubled boys: A guidebook for professionals.* New York, NY: Routledge.

Klein, A. (2018, June 30). What men say about #MeToo in therapy. *New York Times.* Retrieved from https://www.nytimes.com/2018/06/30/opinion/sunday/men-metoo-therapy-masculinity.html

Knapton, S. (2014, March 6). Educated and well paid women "more likely to suffer domestic abuse." *The Telegraph.* Retrieved from http://kjonnsforskning.no/en/2015/09/higher-status-ones-partner-makes-both-men-and-women-vulnerable-intimate-partner-violence

Kochanek, K. D., Murphy, S. L., Xu, J., & Arias, E. (2017, December). *Mortality in the United States* (2016 NCHS Data Brief No. 293). Retrieved from https://www.cdc.gov/nchs/products/databriefs/db293.htm

Koeze, E., & Barry-Jester, A. M. (2018, June 20). What do men think it means to be a man? *Five Thirty Eight.* Retrieved from https://fivethirtyeight.com/features/what-do-men-think-it-means-to-be-a-man/

Kohn, D. (2002, October 31). The gender gap: Boys lagging. *60 Minutes*. Retrieved from https://www.cbsnews.com/news/the-gender-gap-boys-lagging/

Koss, M. P., Gidycz, C. A., & Wisniewski, N. (1987). The scope of rape: Incidence and prevalence of sexual aggression and victimization in a national sample of higher education students. *Journal of Consulting and Clinical Psychology, 55*, 162–170. http://dx.doi.org/10.1037/0022-006X.55.2.162

Kraemer, S. (2000). The fragile male. *British Medical Journal, 321*, 1609–1612.

Krahe, B., Reimer, T., Scheinberger-Olwig, R., & Fritsche, I. (1999). Measuring sexual aggression: The reliability of the Sexual Experiences Survey in a German sample. *Journal of Interpersonal Violence, 14*, 91–100. https://doi.org/10.1177/088626099014001006

Kuhlberg, J. A., Peña, J. B., & Zayas, L. H. (2010). Familism, parent adolescent conflict, self-esteem, internalizing behaviors, and suicide attempts among adolescent Latinas. *Child Psychiatry and Human Development, 41*, 425–440. https://doi.org/10.1007/s10578-010-0179-0

Kupers, T. A. (2005). Toxic masculinity as a barrier to mental health treatment in prison. *Journal of Clinical Psychology, 61*, 713–724. https://doi.org/10.1002/jclp.20105

Kussin-Shoptaw, A. L., Fletcher, J. B., & Reback, C. J. (2017). Physical and/or sexual abuse is associated with increased psychological and emotional distress among transgender women. *LGBT Health, 4*, 268–274. https://doi.org/10.1089/lgbt.2016.0186

Lamb, M. E. (1979). Paternal influences and the father's role: A personal perspective. *American Psychologist, 43*, 938–943. https://doi.org/10.1037/0003-066X.34.10.938

Langman, P. (2009). Rampage school shooters: A typology. *Aggression and Violent Behavior, 14*, 79–86. https://doi.org/10.1016/j.avb.2008.10.003

LeBreton, J. M., Baysinger, M. A., Abbey, A., & Jacques-Tiura, A. J. (2013). The relative importance of psychopathy-related traits in predicting impersonal sex and hostile masculinity. *Personality and Individual Differences, 55*, 817–822. https://doi-org.ezproxy.uakron.edu:2443/10.1016/j.paid.2013.07.009

Leone, R. M., Parrott, D. J., Swartout, K. M., & Tharp, A. T. (2016). Masculinity and bystander attitudes: Moderating effects of masculine gender role stress. *Psychology of Violence, 6*, 82–90. https://doi.org/10.1037/a0038926

Levant, R. F. (1992). Toward the reconstruction of masculinity. *Journal of Family Psychology, 5*, 379–402. https://doi.org/10.1037/0893-3200.5.3-4.379

Levant, R. F. (1996). The new psychology of men. *Professional Psychology, 27*, 259–265.

Levant, R. F. (1997a). The masculinity crisis. *Journal of Men's Studies, 5*, 221–231. https://doi.org/10.1177/106082659700500302

Levant, R. F. (1997b). *Men and emotions: A psychoeducational approach.* The Assessment and Treatment of Psychological Disorders Video Series. Hicksville, NY: Newbridge Communications.

Levant, R. F. (1997c). Nonrelational sexuality in men. In R. F. Levant & G. Brooks (Eds.), *Men and sex: New psychological perspectives* (pp. 9–27) New York, NY: Wiley.

Levant, R. F. (1998). Desperately seeking language: Understanding, assessing and treating normative male alexithymia. In W. Pollack & R. F. Levant (Eds.), *New psychotherapy for men* (pp. 35–56). New York, NY: Wiley.

Levant, R. F. (2000). A quarter century of psychotherapy. In J. Shay & J. Wheelis (Eds.), *Odysseys in psychotherapy* (pp. 187–208). New York, NY: Irvington Press.

Levant, R. F. (2011). Research in the psychology of men and masculinity using the Gender Role Strain Paradigm as a framework. *American Psychologist, 66*, 762–776. https://doi.org/10.1037/a0025034

Levant, R. F., Cuthbert, A. C., Richmond, K., Sellers, A., Matveev, A., Matina, O., & Soklovsky, M. (2003). Masculinity ideology among Russian and U.S. young men and women and its relationship to unhealthy lifestyle habits among young Russian men. *Psychology of Men and Masculinity, 4*, 26–36. https://doi.org/10.1037/1524-9220.4.1.26

Levant, R. F., Gerdes, Z., Alto, K., Jadaszewski, S., & McDermott, R. (August, 2016). "Not my father's son:" Relationships between fathers' expectations, involvement, parenting quality, and son's masculinity ideology and wellbeing. In R. F. Levant (Chair), *Recent Research in the Gender Role Strain Paradigm Using Advanced Methods*. A symposium presented at the annual convention, American Psychological Association, Denver, CO.

Levant, R. F., Good, G. E., Cook, S., O'Neil, J., Smalley, K. B., Owen, K. A., & Richmond, K. (2006). Validation of the Normative Male Alexithymia Scale: Measurement of a gender-linked syndrome. *Psychology of Men and Masculinity, 7*, 212–224. https://doi.org/10.1037/1524-9220.7.4.212

Levant, R. F., Graef, S. T., Smalley, K. B., Williams, C., & McMillan, N. (2008). The evaluation of the Male Role Norms Inventory-Adolescent (MRNI-A). *Thymos: Journal of Boyhood Studies, 2*, 46–59.

Levant, R. F., Hall, R. J., & Rankin. T. J. (2013). Male Role Norms Inventory-Short Form (MRNI-SF): Development, confirmatory factor analytic investigation of structure, and measurement invariance across gender. *Journal of Counseling Psychology, 60*, 228–238. https://doi.org/10.1037/a0031545

Levant, R. F., Hall, R. J., Williams, C., & Hasan, N. T. (2009). Gender differences in alexithymia: A meta-analysis. *Psychology of Men and Masculinity, 10*, 190–203. https://doi.org/10.1037/a0015652

Levant, R. F., Hirsch, L., Celentano, E., Cozza, T., Hill, S., MacEachern, M. . . . Schnedeker, J. (1992). The male role: An investigation of contemporary norms. *Journal of Mental Health Counseling, 14*, 325–337.

Levant, R.F, Jadaszewski, S., Alto, K., Richmond. K., Pardo, S., Keo-Meier, C., & Gerdes, Z. T. (2019). Moderation and mediation of the relationships between masculinity ideology and health status. *Health Psychology, 38*, 162–171. https://doi.org/10.1037/hea0000709

Levant, R. F., & Kelly, J. (1989). *Between father and child*. New York, NY: Viking.

Levant, R. F., & Kopecky, G. (1995). *Masculinity reconstructed: Changing the rules of manhood—at work, in relationships, and in family life*. New York, NY: Dutton.

Levant, R. F., & Majors, R. (1997). An investigation into variations in the construction of the male gender role among young African-American and European-American women and men. *Journal of Gender, Culture and Health, 2*, 33–43.

Levant, R. F., Majors, R., & Kelley, M. (1998). Masculinity ideology among young African-American and European-American women and men in different regions of the United States. *Cultural Diversity and Mental Health, 4*, 227–236. https://doi.org/10.1037/10999809.4.3.227

Levant, R. F., McDermott, R., Hewitt, A., Alto, K., & Harris, K. (2016). Confirmatory factor analytic investigation of variance composition, gender invariance, and validity of the Male Role Norms Inventory-Adolescent-revised (MRNI-A-r). *Journal of Counseling Psychology, 63*, 543–556. http://dx.doi.org/10.1037/cou0000163

Levant, R. F., Parent, M. C., McCurdy, E. R, & Bradstreet, T. C. (2015). Moderated mediation and health outcomes of the relationships between masculinity ideology, outcome expectations, and energy drink use. *Health Psychology, 34*, 110–1106. https://doi.org/10.1037/hea0000214

Levant, R. F., & Pollack, W. S. (1995). (Eds.) *A new psychology of men*. New York, NY: Basic Books.

Levant, R. F., Rankin, T. J., Williams, C., Hasan, N. T., Smalley, K. B. (2010). Evaluation of the factor structure and construct validity of the Male Role Norms Inventory-Revised (MRNI-R). *Psychology of Men and Masculinity, 11*, 25–37. https://doi.org/10.1037/a0017637

Levant, R. F., & Richmond, K. (2007). A review of research on masculinity ideologies using the Male Role Norms Inventory. *Journal of Men's Studies, 15*, 130–146. https://doi.org/10.3149/jms.1502.130

Levant, R. F., & Richmond, K. (2016). The gender role strain paradigm and masculinity ideologies. In Y. J. Wong & S. R. Wester (Eds.), *APA Handbook on Men and Masculinities* (pp. 23–49). Washington, DC: American Psychological Association.

Levant, R. F., Rogers, B. K., Cruickshank, B., Kurtz, B. A., Rankin, T. J., Williams, C. M., & Colbow, A, (2012). Exploratory factor analysis and construct validity of the Male Role Norms

Inventory-Adolescent-revised (MRNI-A-r). *Psychology of Men and Masculinity, 13,* 354–366. https://doi.org/10.1037/a0029102

Levant, R. F., Webster, B. M., Stanley, J. T., & Thompson, E. (2019, March 7). The Aging Adults Masculinity Ideologies Inventory (AAMII): Dimensionality, variance composition, measurement invariance by gender, and validity. *Psychology of Men and Masculinities,* Advance Online Publication. http://dx.doi.org/10.1037/men0000208

Levant, R. F., & Williams, C. (2009). The psychology of men and masculinity. In J. Bray & M. Stanton (Eds.) *The Wiley-Blackwell handbook of family psychology* (pp. 588–599). Oxford, England: Blackwell.

Levant, R. F., & Wimer, D. J. (2014). Masculinity constructs as protective buffers and risk factors for men's health. *American Journal of Men's Health, 8,* 110–120. https://doi.org/10.1177/1557988313494408

Levant, R. F., Wimer, D. J, & Williams, C. M. (2011). An evaluation of the psychometric properties of the Health Behavior Inventory-20 (HBI-20) and its relationships to masculinity and attitudes towards seeking psychological help among college men. *Psychology of Men and Masculinity, 11,* 26–41. https://doi.org/10.1037/a0021014

Levant, R. F., Wimer, D. J., Williams, C. M., Smalley, K. B., & Noronha, D. (2009). The relationships between masculinity variables, health risk behaviors and attitudes toward seeking psychological help. *International Journal of Men's Health, 8,* 3–21. http://dx.doi.org/10.3149/jmh.0801.3

Levant, R. F., Wong, Y. J., Karakis, E. N., & Welch, M. W. (2015). Moderated mediation of the relationship between the endorsement of restrictive emotionality and alexithymia. *Psychology of Men and Masculinity, 16,* 459–467. https://doi.org/10.1037/a0039739

Levant, R. F., Wu, R., & Fischer, J. (1996). Masculinity ideology: A comparison between U.S. and Chinese young men and women. *Journal of Gender, Culture and Health, 1,* 207–220.

Liang, C. T. H., Molenaar, C., Hermann, C., & Rivera, L. A. (2017). Dysfunction strain and intervention programs aimed at men's violence, substance use, and help-seeking behaviors. In R. F. Levant & Y. J. Wong (Eds.), *The psychology of men and masculinities* (pp. 347–377). Washington, DC: American Psychological Association.

Lindsay, J. A., Keo, M. C., Hudson, S., Walder, A., Martin, L. A., & Kauth, M. R. (2016). Mental health of transgender veterans of the Iraq and Afghanistan conflicts who experienced military sexual trauma. *Journal of Traumatic Stress, 29,* 563–567. https://doi-org.ezproxy.uakron.edu:2443/10.1002/jts.22146

Liptake, A. (2019, January 22). Supreme court revives transgender ban for military service. *New York Times.* Retrieved from https://www.nytimes.com/2019/01/22/us/politics/transgender-ban-military-supreme-court.html

Liu, W. M. (Ed.) (2013). *The Oxford handbook of social class and counseling.* New York, NY: Oxford University Press.

Liu, W. M. (2016). Masculinities on the verge: An editorial. *Psychology of Men and Masculinities, 17,* 1–2. https://doi.org/10.1037/men0000020

Locke, B. D., & Mahalik, J. R. (2005). Examining masculinity norms, problem drinking, and athletic involvement as predictors of sexual aggression in college men. *Journal of Counseling Psychology, 52,* 279–283. https://doi-org.ezproxy.uakron.edu:2443/10.1037/0022-0167.52.3.279

Loiselle, J. (1980). *A review of the role of fathers in parent training programs.* Unpublished manuscript, Boston University.

Love, K. (2018, March 6). Everyone is going through something. *The Players Tribune.* Retrieved from https://www.theplayerstribune.com/en-us/articles/kevin-love-everyone-is-going-through-something

Lupton, B. (2000). Maintaining masculinity: Men who do "women's work." *British Journal of Management, 11,* 33–48. https://doi.org/10.1111/1467-8551.11.s1.4

Madkins, C. (2016, July 19). White, male privilege is killing us all [blog post]. *End Rape on Campus.* Retrieved from http://endrapeoncampus.org/eroc-blog/2016/7/19/white-male-privilege-is-killing-us-all

Mahalik, J. R., Burns, S. M., & Syzdek, M. (2007). Masculinity and perceived normative health behaviours as predictors of men's health behaviours. *Social Science and Medicine, 64,* 2201–2209. https://doi.org/10.1016/j.socscimed.2007.02.035

Mahalik, J. R., Lagan, H., & Morrison, J. A. (2006). Health behaviors and masculinity in Kenyan and U.S. male college students. *Psychology of Men and Masculinity, 7,* 191–202. https://doi.org/10.1037/1524-9220.7.4.191

Mahalik, J. R., Levi-Minzi, M., & Walker, G. (2007). Masculinity and health behaviors in Australian men. *Psychology of Men & Masculinity, 8,* 240–249. https://doi.org/10.1037/1524-9220.8.4.240

Mahalik, J. R., Locke, B. D., Ludlow, L. H., Diemer, M. A., Scott, R. P., Gottfried, M., & Frietas, G. (2003). Development of the Conformity to Masculine Norms Inventory. *Psychology of Men and Masculinity, 4,* 3–25. https://doi.org/10.1037/1524-9220.4.1.3

Mahalik, J. R., & Rochlen, A. B. (2006). Men's likely responses to clinical depression: What are they and do masculinity norms predict them? *Sex Roles, 55,* 659–667. https://doi-org.ezproxy.uakron.edu:2443/10.1007/s11199-006-9121-0

Majors, R., & Billson, J. M. (1992). *Cool pose: The dilemmas of Black manhood in America.* New York, NY: Simon & Schuster.

Malamuth, N. M., Heavey, C. L., & Linz, D. (1996). The confluence model of sexual aggression: Combining hostile masculinity and impersonal sex. *Journal of Offender Rehabilitation, 23,* 13–37. https://doi.org/10.1300/J076v23n03_03

Malamuth, N. M., Linz, D., Heavey, C. L., Barnes, G., & Acker, M. (1995). Using the confluence model of sexual aggression to predict men's conflict with women: A 10-year follow-up study. *Journal of Personality and Social Psychology, 69,* 353–369. https://doi.org/10.1037/0022-3514.69.2.353

Malamuth, N., Sockloskie, R., Koss, M., & Jeffrey, T. S. (1991). Characteristics of aggressors against women: Testing a model using a national sample of college students. *Journal of Consulting and Clinical Psychology. 59,* 670–681. https://doi.org/10.1037//0022-006X.59.5.670

Martin, L. A., Neighbors, H. W., & Griffith, D. M. (2013). The experience of symptoms of depression in men vs women analysis of the national comorbidity survey replication. *JAMA Psychiatry, 70,* 1100–1106. https://doi.org/10.1001/jamapsychiatry.2013.1985

Mayer, J. (2019, July 22). The case of Al Franken: A close look at the accusations against the former senator. *New Yorker.* Retrieved from https://www.newyorker.com/magazine/2019/07/29/the-case-of-al-franken

McBee, T. P. (2018, October 25). Men are socialized to act inhumanely [video file]. *The Atlantic.* Retrieved from https://www.theatlantic.com/video/index/573877/male-socialization/

McCreary, D. R., Newcombe, M. D., & Sadava, S. W. (1999). The male role, alcohol use, and alcohol problems: A structural modeling examination in adult men and women. *Journal of Counseling Psychology, 46,* 109–124. https://doi.org/10.1037/0022-0167.46.1.109

McElvain, J. P., & Kposowa, A. J. (2008). Police officer characteristics and the likelihood of using deadly force. *Criminal Justice and Behavior, 35,* 505–521. https://doi-org.ezproxy.uakron.edu:2443/10.1177/0093854807313995

McDermott, R. C., Kilmartin, C., McKelvey, D. K., & Kridel, M. M. (2015). College male sexual assault of women and the psychology of men: Past, present, and future directions for research. *Psychology of Men & Masculinity, 16,* 355–366. http://dx.doi.org/10.1037/a00395441524-9220/15/$12.00.

McDermott, R. C., Pietrantonio, K. R., Browning, B. R., McKelvey, D. K.; Jones, Z. K., Booth, N. R., & Sevig, T. D. (2019). In search of positive masculine role norms: Testing the positive psychology positive masculinity paradigm. *Psychology of Men & Masculinities, 20,* 12–22. http://dx.doi.org/10.1037/men0000160

McDermott, R. C., Smith, P. N., Borgogna, N., Booth, N., Granato, S., & Sevig, T. D. (2018). College students' conformity to masculine role norms and help-seeking intentions for suicidal thoughts. *Psychology of Men & Masculinity, 19,* 340–351. http://dx.doi.org/10.1037/men0000107

McGinnis, J. M., Williams-Russo, P., & Knickman, J. R. (2002). The case for more active policy attention to health promotion. *Health Affairs, 21,* 78–93. http://dx.doi.org/10.1377/hlthaff.21.2.78

Men adrift: Badly educated men in rich countries have not adapted well to trade, technology or feminism. (2015, May 23). *The Economist.* Retrieved from http://www.economist.com/news/essays/21649050-badly-educated-men-rich-countries-have-not-adapted-well-trade-technology-or-feminism

Mervosh, S. (2018, December 19). Nearly 40,000 deaths from firearms in 2017. *New York Times,* A19.

Messinger, A. M. (2011). Invisible victims: Same-sex IPV in the National Violence Against Women Survey. *Journal of Interpersonal Violence, 26,* 2228–2243. https://doi.org/10.1177/0886260510383023

Mikorski, R., & Szymanski, D. M. (2017). Masculine norms, peer group, pornography, Facebook, and men's sexual objectification of women. *Psychology of Men & Masculinity, 18,* 257–267. https://doi.org/10.1037/men0000058

Miller, B., & Irvin, J. (2017). Invisible scars: Comparing the mental health of LGB and heterosexual intimate partner violence survivors. *Journal of Homosexuality, 64,* 1180–1195. http://dx.doi.org/10.1080/00918369.2016.1242334

Mincey, K., Alfonso, M., Hackney, A., & Luque, J. (2014). Being a Black man: Development of the Masculinity Inventory Scale (MIS) for black men. *Journal of Men's Studies, 22,* 167–179. http://dx.doi.org/10.3149/jms.2203.167

Moore, T. M., & Stuart, G. L., (2005). Review of the literature on masculinity and partner violence. *Psychology of Men & Masculinity, 6,* 46–61. https://doi.org/10.1037/1524-9220.6.1.46

Mosher, D. L., & Sirkin, M. (1984). Measuring a macho personality constellation. *Journal of Research in Personality, 18,* 150–163. http://dx.doi.org/10.1016/0092-6566(84)90026-6

Munsch, C. L., & Willer, R. (2012). The role of gender identity threat in perceptions of date rape and sexual coercion. *Violence against Women, 18,* 1125–1146. https://doi.org/10.1177/1077801212465151

Murnen, S. K., Wright, C., & Kaluzny, G. (2002). If "boys will be boys," then girls will be victims? A meta-analytic review of the research that relates masculine ideology to sexual aggression. *Sex Roles, 46,* 359–375. https://doi.org/10.1023/A:1020488928736

Murphy, S. L., Xu, J., Kochanek, K. D., & Arias, E. (2017). *Mortality in the United States.* Retrieved from https://www.cdc.gov/nchs/data/databriefs/db328-h.pdf

Muthén, L. K., & Muthén, B. O. (1998–2008). *Mplus user's guide* (5th ed.). Los Angeles, CA: Author.

Najdowski, C. J., Bottoms, B. L., & Goff, P. A. (2015). Stereotype threat and racial differences in citizens' experiences of police encounters. *Law and Human Behavior, 39,* 463–477. https://doi-org.ezproxy.uakron.edu:2443/10.1037/lhb0000140

National Center for Health Statistics. (2017). *Health, United States, 2016: With Chartbook on Long-term Trends in Health.* Hyattsville, MD.

National Institute on Alcohol Abuse and Alcoholism. (2019). *Alcohol use disorder.* Retrieved from https://www.niaaa.nih.gov/alcohol-health/overview-alcohol-consumption/alcohol-use-disorders

Nixon, D. (2009). "I can't put a smiley face on": Working-class masculinity, emotional labour and service work in the "new economy." *Gender, Work and Organization, 16,* 300–322. https://doi-org.ezproxy.uakron.edu:2443/10.1111/j.1468-0432.2009.00446.x

North, A. (2019, February 13). Aziz Ansari actually talked about the sexual misconduct allegation against him like an adult. *Vox.* Retrieved from https://www.vox.com/2019/2/13/18223535/aziz-ansari-sexual-misconduct-allegation-me-too

Ojeda, L., & Brandy Piña-Watson, B. (2014). Caballerismo may protect against the role of machismo on Mexican day laborers' self-esteem. *Psychology of Men and Masculinity, 15,* 288–295. https://doi.org/10.1037/a0033450

O'Leary, P. J., & Barber, J. G. (2008). Gender differences in silencing following childhood sexual Abuse. *Journal of Child Sexual Abuse, 17,* 133–143. https://doi.org/10.1080/10538710801916416

Oliffe, J. L., Han, C. S. E., Drummond, M., Estephanie, S. M., Bottorff, J. L., & Creighton, G. (2015). Men, masculinities, and murder-suicide. *American Journal of Men's Health, 9,* 473–485. https://doi.org/10.1177/1557988314551359

O'Neil, J. M. (1996). The gender role journey workshop: Exploring sexism and gender role conflict in a co-educational setting. In M. A. Andronico (Ed.), *Men in groups: Insights, interventions, psychoeducational work* (pp. 193–213). Washington, DC: American Psychological Association.

O'Neil, J. M. (2008). Summarizing 25 years of research on men's gender role conflict using the Gender Role Conflict Scale. *Counseling Psychologist, 36,* 358–445. https://doi.org/10.1177/0011000008317057

O'Neil, J. M. (2012). The psychology of men. In E. M. Altmaier & J. C. Hansen (Eds.), *The Oxford handbook of counseling psychology* (pp. 375–408). New York, NY: Oxford University Press.

Oren, C. Z., & Oren, D. C. (2010). *Counseling fathers.* New York, NY: Routledge.

Orgera, K., & Artiga, S. (2019). Disparities in health and health care: Five key questions and answers. *Henry J. Kaiser Family Foundation.* Retrieved from https://www.kff.org/disparities-policy/issue-brief/disparities-in-health-and-health-care-five-key-questions-and-answers/

Oringher, J., & Samuelson, K. W. (2011). Intimate partner violence and the role of masculinity in male same-sex relationships. *Traumatology, 17,* 68–74. https://doi-org.ezproxy.uakron.edu:2443/10.1177/1534765610395620

Osland, J. A., Fitch, M., & Willis, E. A. (1996). Likelihood to rape in college males. *Sex Roles, 35,* 171–183. https://doi.org/10.1007/BF01433105

Parent, M. C., Gobble, T. D., & Rochlen, A. (2018, April 23). Social media behavior, toxic masculinity, and depression. *Psychology of Men and Masculinity, 20*(3), 277–287. http://dx.doi.org/10.1037/men0000156

Parkhill, M. R., & Abbey, A. (2008). Does alcohol contribute to the confluence model of sexual assault perpetration? *Journal of Social and Clinical Psychology, 27,* 529–554. http://dx.doi.org/10.1521/jscp.2008.27.6.529

Parnell, K. J., & Hammer, J. H. (2018). Deciding on couple therapy: The role of masculinity in relationship help-seeking. *Psychology of Men & Masculinity, 19,* 212–222. http://dx.doi.org/10.1037/men0000098

Parrott, D. J. (2009). Aggression toward gay men as gender role enforcement: Effects of male role norms, sexual prejudice, and masculine gender role stress. *Journal of Personality, 77,* 1137–1166. http://dx.doi.org/10.1111/j.1467-6494.2009.00577.x

Parrott, D. J., Peterson, J. L., & Bakeman, R. (2011). Determinants of aggression toward sexual minorities in a community sample. *Psychology of Violence, 1,* 41–52. http://dx.doi.org/10.1037/a0021581

Pence, E., & Paymar, M. (1993). *Education groups for men who batter: The Duluth Model.* New York, NY: Springer.

Peralta, R. L., & Tuttle, L. A. (2013). Male perpetrators of heterosexual-partner-violence: The role of threats to masculinity. *Journal of Men's Studies, 21,* 255–276. https://doi.org/10.3149/jms.2103.255

Petter, O. (2018, October 20). Caitlin Moran starts viral twitter discussion on toxic masculinity after asking "What are the downsides of being a man?" *Independent.* Retrieved from https://www.independent.co.uk/life-style/caitlin-moran-twitter-downsides-man-toxic-masculinity-feminism-reactions-a8593471.html

PettyJohn, M. E., Muzzey, F. K., Maas, M. K., & McCauley, H. L. (2019). #HowIWillChange: Engaging men and boys in the #MeToo movement. *Psychology of Men & Masculinity, 20*(4), 612–622. http://dx.doi.org/10.1037/men0000186

Picker, M., & Sun, C. (2008). *The price of pleasure: Pornography, sexuality & relationships* [Documentary]. Northampton, MA: Media Education Foundation.

Pitt, H. (2016, July 24). Three personality traits of aggressive people. *Sydney Morning Herald*. Retrieved from https://www.smh.com.au/national/nsw/the-personality-traits-that-help-you-spot-an-aggressive-person-20160723-gqc43k.html

Plan International USA. (2018). The state of gender equality for U.S. Adolescents. Retrieved from https://www.planusa.org/docs/state-of-gender-equality-summary-2018.pdf

Pleck, J. H. (1981). *The myth of masculinity*. Cambridge, MA: MIT Press.

Pleck, J. H. (1995). The gender role strain paradigm: An update. In R. F. Levant & W. S. Pollack (Eds.) *A new psychology of men* (pp. 11–32). New York, NY: Basic Books.

Pleck, J. H. (2010). Fatherhood and masculinity. In M. E. Lamb (Ed.) *The role of the father in child development* (5th ed., 27–57). New York, NY: Wiley.

Pleck, J. H., Sonenstein, F. L., & Ku, L. C. (1994a). Attitudes toward male roles: A discriminant validity analysis. *Sex Roles, 30,* 481–501. https://doi.org/10.1007/BF01420798

Pleck, J. H., Sonenstein, F. L., & Ku, L. C. (1994b). Problem behaviors and masculinity ideology in adolescent males. In R. D. Ketterlinus & M. E. Lamb (Eds.), *Adolescent problem behaviors: Issues and research* (pp. 165–186). Hillsdale, NJ: Erlbaum.

Pollack, W., & Levant, R. F. (Eds.). (1998). *New psychotherapy for men*. New York: John Wiley & Sons.

Popper, N. (2019, February 23). What baby formula does for fathers. *New York Times*. Retrieved from https://www.nytimes.com/2019/02/23/opinion/sunday/formula-breastfeeding-fatherhood.html?action=click&module=Opinion&pgtype=Homepage

Porter, T. (2010). A call to men. *Ted Talk*. Retrieved from https://www.ted.com/talks/tony_porter_a_call_to_men

Powell, W., Adams, L. B., Cole-Lewis, Y., Agyemang, A., & Upton, R. D. (2016). Masculinity and race-related factors as barriers to health help-seeking among African American men. *Behavioral Medicine, 42,* 150–163. https://doi.org/10.1080/08964289.2016.1165174

Precopio, R. F., & Ramsey, L. R. (2017). Dude looks like a feminist!: Moral concerns and feminism among men. *Psychology of Men & Masculinity, 18,* 78–86. http://dx.doi.org/10.1037/men0000042

Quart, A. (2018, September 25). #MeToo's hidden activists? Working-class women. *The Guardian*. Retrieved from https://www.theguardian.com/global/2018/sep/25/metoo-activism-working-class-women-sexual-harassment

Rabinowitz, F. E., & Cochran, S. V. (2002). *Deepening psychotherapy with men*. Washington, DC: American Psychological Association.

Ramaeker, J., & Petrie, T. A. (2019). "Man up!": Exploring intersections of sport participation, masculinity, psychological distress, and help-seeking attitudes and intentions. *Psychology of Men & Masculinities, 20*(4), 515–527. http://dx.doi.org/10.1037/men0000198

Ramsey, D. (2018, July 5). How to rehumanize our boys and young men. *The Goodmen Project*. Retrieved from https://goodmenproject.com/featured-content/how-to-rehumanize-our-boys-and-young-men-ndgt/

Reidy, D. E., Smith-Darden, J. P., Cortina, K. S., Kernsmith, R. M., & Kernsmith, P.D. (2015). Masculine discrepancy stress, teen dating violence, and sexual violence perpetration among adolescent boys. *Journal of Adolescent Health, 56,* 619–624. https://doi.org/10.1016/j.jadohealth.2015.02.009

Reiner, A. (2018, October 24). Boy talk: Breaking masculine stereotypes. *New York Times*. Retrieved from https://www.nytimes.com/2018/10/24/well/family/boy-talk-breaking-masculine-stereotypes.html

Rennison, C. M., & Welchans, S. (2000). Criminal victimization 1999: Changes 1998–99 with trends 1993–99. *Department of Justice, Bureau of Justice Statistics*. Retrieved from https://www.bjs.gov/content/pub/pdf/cv99.pdf

Rich, S. (2018, June 11) Today's masculinity is stifling. *The Atlantic*. Retrieved from https://www.theatlantic.com/family/archive/2018/06/imagining-a-better-boyhood/562232/

Roberts, S. (2012). Boys will be boys . . . won't they? Change and continuities in contemporary young working-class masculinities. *Sociology, 47,* 671–686 https://doi.org/10.1177/0038038512453791

Rogers, B. K., & Levant, R. F. (2018). *The development and evaluation of the Racist Gender Role Strain Scale to measure African American masculinities.* Manuscript submitted for publication.

Rogers, B. K., Sperry, H. S., & Levant, R. F. (2015). Masculinities among African American men: An intersectional perspective. *Psychology of Men and Masculinity, 16,* 416–425. https://doi.org/10.1037/a0039082

Rosin, H. (2012). *The end of man and the rise of women.* New York, NY: Riverhead Books.

Ross, L., & Nisbett, R. E. (2011). *The person and the situation: Perspectives of social psychology.* London, England: Pinter & Martin.

Rothgerber, H. (2013). Real men don't eat (vegetable) quiche: Masculinity and the justification of meat consumption. *Psychology of Men & Masculinity, 14,* 363–375. http://dx.doi.org/10.1037/a0030379

Rubin, J. (2018, October 23). Polls should come with an asterisk. *Washington Post.* Retrieved from https://www.washingtonpost.com/news/opinions/wp/2018/10/23/polls-shouldcome-with-an-asterisk/?utm_term=.330a35262d6a

Ruiz, R. (2018, June 16). You haven't heard of this masculinity movement, but it's exactly what men need right now. *Mashable.* Retrieved from https://mashable.com/2018/06/16/how-to-be-a-better-man-healthy-masculinity/#gKwSIsAJcaqi

Rummell, C., & Levant, R. F. (2014). Masculine gender role discrepancy strain and self- esteem. *Psychology of Men and Masculinity, 15,* 419–426. https://doi.org/10.1037/a0035304

Saad, G. (2018, March 8). Is toxic masculinity a valid concept? On the dangers of pathologizing manhood. *Psychology Today.* Retrieved on 7/22/18 from https://www.psychologytoday.com/us/blog/homo-consumericus/201803/is-toxic-masculinity-valid-concept

Santana, B. (n.d.) How Black boy joy is redefining the image of Black men in America. *Vix.* Retrieved from https://www.vix.com/en/pop-culture/527454/how-black-boy-joy-redefining-image-black-men-america

Sapolsky, R. D. (2014, August 17). The trouble with testosterone: Will boys just be boys? *A Voice for Men.* Retrieved from https://www.avoiceformen.com/men/the-trouble-with-testosterone-will-boys-just-be-boys/

Schaefer, R. T. (2001). *Racial and ethnic groups.* Upper Saddle River, NJ: Prentice Hall.

Schuhr, A. (2018, July 5). The terrifying potential for masculinity. *The Goodmen Project.* Retrieved from https://goodmenproject.com/featured-content/terrifying-potential-for-masculinity-phtz/

Seabrook, R. C., Ward, L. M., & Giaccardi, S. (2018). Why is fraternity membership associated with sexual assault? Exploring the roles of conformity to masculine norms, pressure to uphold masculinity, and objectification of women. *Psychology of Men & Masculinity, 19,* 3–13. https://doi.org/10.1037/men0000076

Schwing, A. E., Wong, Y. J., & Fann, M. D. (2013). Development and validation of the African American Men's Gendered Racism Stress Inventory. *Psychology of Men & Masculinity, 14,* 16–24. http://dx.doi.org/10.1037/a0028272

Seligson, H. (2018, December 8).These men are waiting to share some feelings with you. *New York Times.* Retrieved from https://www.nytimes.com/2018/12/08/style/men-emotions-mankind-project.html

Selin Davis, L. (2018, Decmeber 21). Scorn girlie girls? That's' sexist. *New York Times,* a25.

Seymour, W., Smith, R., & Torres, H. (2014). *Building a better man: A blueprint for decreasing violence and increasing prosocial behavior in men.* New York, NY: Routledge.

Shepard, D. S., & Harway, M. (2012). *Engaging men in couples therapy.* New York, NY: Routledge.

Shields, S. A. (2008). Gender: An intersectionality perspective. *Sex Roles, 59,* 301–311. https://doi.org/10.1007/s11199-008-9501-8

Silverstein, L. B. (2016). Feminist masculinities: The end of gender as we know it. In Y. J. Wong & S. R. Wester (Eds.), *APA handbook on men and masculinities* (pp. 145–172). Washington, DC: American Psychological Association.

Silverstein, L. B., & Auerbach, C. F. (1999). Deconstructing the essential father. *American Psychologist, 54,* 397–407. https://doi.org/10.1037/0003-066X.54.6.397

Sloan, C., Conner, M., & Gough, B. (2015). How does masculinity impact on health? A quantitative study of masculinity and health behavior in a sample of UK men and women. *Psychology of Men & Masculinity, 16,* 206–217. http://dx.doi.org/10.1037/a0037261

Smith, R. M., Parrott, D. J., Swartout, K. M., & Tharp, A. T. (2015). Deconstructing hegemonic masculinity: The roles of antifemininity, subordination to women, and sexual dominance in men's perpetration of sexual aggression. *Psychology of Men & Masculinity, 16,* 160–169. https://doi.org/10.1037/a0035956

Smith, S. G., Chen, J., Basile, K. C., Gilbert, L. K., Merrick, M. T., Patel, N., Walling, M., & Jain, A. (2017). The National Intimate Partner and Sexual Violence Survey (NISVS): 2010–2012 state report. *National Center for Injury Prevention and Control, Centers for Disease Control and Prevention.*

Sonmez, F. (2018, August 7). Donald Trump on John McCain in 1999: "Does being captured make you a hero?" *Washington Post.* Retrieved from https://www.washingtonpost.com/politics/donald-trump-on-john-mccain-in-1999-does-being-captured-make-you-a-hero/2018/08/07/a2849b1c-9a56-11e8-8d5e-c6c594024954_story.html?utm_term=.c2a955bce09d

Southall, A. (2018, January 7). Rape reports are up sharply, and Mayor points to #MeToo. *The New York Times,* p. A19. Retrieved from https://www.nytimes.com/01/06/nyregion/rape-reports-nyc-me-too.html

Spencer, S. J., Steele, C. M., & Quinn, D. M. (1999). Stereotype threat and women's math performance, *Journal of Experimental Social Psychology, 35,* 4–28. https://doi.org/10.1006/jesp.1998.1373

Statista. (n.d.). Number of mass shootings in the United States between 1982 and September 2018, by shooter's gender. Retrieved from https://www.statista.com/statistics/476445/mass-shootings-in-the-us-by-shooter-s-gender/

Stratmoen, E., Greer, M. M., Martens, A. L., & Saucier, D. A. (2018). What, I'm not good enough for you? Individual differences in masculine honor beliefs and the endorsement of aggressive responses to romantic rejection. *Personality and Individual Differences, 123,* 151–162. http://dx.doi.org/10.1016/j.paid.2017.10.018

Straus, M. A. (1979). Measuring intrafamily conflict and violence: The conflict tactics (CT) scales. *Journal of Marriage and the Family, 41,* 75–88. https://doi.org/10.2307/351733

Straus, M. A. (2008). Dominance and symmetry in partner violence by male and female university students in 32 nations. *Children and Youth Services Review, 30,* 252–275. https://doi.org/10.1016/j.childyouth.2007.10.004

Strauss, M. A., Hamby, S. L., & Warren, W. L. (2003). *The Conflict Tactics Scale Handbook.* Los Angeles, CA: Western Psychological Services.

Swartout, K. M. (2013). The company they keep: How peer networks influence male sexual aggression. *Psychology of Violence, 3,* 157–171. http://dx.doi.org/10.1037/a0029997

Sweet, H. B. (Ed.). (2012). *Gender in the therapy hour.* New York, NY: Routledge.

Tannenbaum, C., & Frank, B. (2011). Masculinity and health in late life men. *American Journal of Men's Health, 5,* 243–254. https://doi.org/10.1177/1557988310384609

Tavernise, S. (2018, December 20). Senator Claire McCaskill on losing Missouri and the politics of purity. *The Daily (New York Times)* [Podcast]. Retrieved from https://www.nytimes.com/2018/12/20/podcasts/the-daily/senator-claire-mccaskill-missouri-interview.html

Terman, L., & Miles, C. (1936). *Sex and personality.* New York, NY: McGraw Hill.

Tharp, A. T., DeGue, S., Valle, L. A., Brookmeyer, K. A., Massetti, G. M., & Matjasko, J. L. (2013). A systematic qualitative review of risk and protective factors for sexual violence perpetration. *Trauma, Violence, & Abuse, 14,* 133 167. https://doi.org/10.1177/1524838012470031

Thomas, K., & Levant, R F. (2011). Does the endorsement of traditional masculinity ideology moderate the relationship between exposure to violent video games and aggression. *Journal of Men's Studies, 20,* 47–56. https://doi.org/10.3149/jms.2001.47

Thompson, E. H., Jr., & Cracco, E. J. (2008). Sexual aggression in bars: What college men can normalize. *Journal of Men's Studies, 16,* 82–96. https://doi.org/10.3149/jms.1601.82

Thompson, E. H., Jr., & Pleck, J. H. (1986). The structure of male role norms. *American Behavioral Scientist, 29*, 531–543. https://doi.org/10.1177/000276486029005003

Tilbrook, E., Allan, A., & Dear, G. (2010). *Intimate partner abuse of men.* Perth, Australia: Men's Advisory Network.

Tillet, S., & Tillet, S. (2019). After the 'surviving R. Kelly' documentary, #MeToo has finally returned to Black girls. *The New York Times.* Retrieved from https://www.nytimes.com/2019/01/10/opinion/r-kelly-documentary-metoo.html

Timmel, N. (2018, September 22). A love letter to "toxic" masculinity: Defining masculinity on your terms doesn't mean you have to belittle other interpretations. *The Good Men Project.* Retrieved from https://goodmenproject.com/featured-content/a-love-letter-to-toxic-masculinity-ndgt/

Tjaden, P., & Thoennes, N. (2000). *Extent, nature, and consequences of intimate partner. violence: Findings from the National Violence Against Women Survey.* Washington, DC: National Institute of Justice/Centers for Disease Control and Prevention.

Tjaden, P., Thoennes, N., & Allison, C. J. (1999). Comparing violence over the life span in samples of same-sex and opposite-sex cohabitants. *Violence and Victims, 14*, 413–425. https://doi.org/10.1891/0886-6708.14.4.413

Toxic masculinity. (n.d.[a]). *Urban Dictionary.* Retrieved from https://www.urbandictionary.com/define.php?term=Toxic%20Masculinity

Toxic masculinity. (n.d.[b]). *Wikipedia.* Retrieved from https://en.wikipedia.org/wiki/Toxic_masculinity

Troche, S. J., & Herzberg, P. Y. (2017). On the role of dominance and nurturance in the confluence model: A person-centered approach to the prediction of sexual aggression. *Aggressive Behavior, 43*(3), 251–262. https://doi-org.ezproxy.uakron.edu:2443/10.1002/ab.21685

Turchik, J. A. (2012). Sexual victimization among male college students: Assault severity, sexual functioning, and health risk behaviors. *Psychology of Men & Masculinity, 13*, 243–255. https://doi.org/10.1037/a0024605

Ullman, S. E., & Filipas, H. H. (2005). Gender differences in social reactions to abuse disclosures, post-abuse coping, and PTSD of child sexual abuse survivors. *Child Abuse & Neglect, 29*, 767–782. https://doi.org/10.1016/j.chiabu.2005.01.005

Unger, R. K. (1979). Toward a redefinition of sex and gender. *American Psychologist, 34*, 1085–1094.

U.S. Department of Justice. Criminal justice information services division. (2016). Arrests by race and ethnicity. *Federal Bureau of Investigation.* Retrieved from https://ucr.fbi.gov/crime-in-the-u.s/2016/crime-in-the-u.s.-2016/topic-pages/tables/table-21

Uy, P. J., Massoth, N. A., & Gottdiener, W. H. (2013). Rethinking male drinking: Traditional masculine ideologies, gender-role conflict, and drinking motives. *Psychology of Men & Masculinity, 13*, 121–128.

Vagianos, A. (2018, February 21). How gun violence and toxic masculinity are linked, in 8 tweets. *Huffington Post.* Retrieved from https://www.huffingtonpost.com/entry/gun-violence-toxic-masculinity-tweets_us_5a85ead4e4b05c2bcac8ec08

Valenti, J. (2018, July 26). Boys need feminists' help too. *New York Times.* Retrieved from https://www.nytimes.com/2018/07/25/opinion/feminists-misogyny-patriarchy.html

Vandello, J. A., & Bosson, J. K. (2013). Hard won and easily lost: A review and synthesis of theory and research on precarious manhood. *Psychology of Men & Masculinity, 14*, 101–113. https://doi.org/10.1037/a0029826

Van Mulligen, A. (2018, December 21). There is no right way to be a man and that's what we should teach our sons. *Good Men Project.* Retrieved from https://goodmenproject.com/featured-content/there-is-no-right-way-to-be-a-man/

Vedantam, S. (2018, October 22). Can a child be raised free of gender stereotypes? This family tried. *Hidden Brain.* Retrieved from https://www.npr.org/2018/10/18/658449559/can-a-child-be-raised-free-of-gender-stereotypes-this-family-tried

Velasquez-Manoff, M. (2018, February 24). Real men get rejected, too. *New York Times*. Retrieved from https://www.nytimes.com/2018/02/24/opinion/sunday/real-men-masculinity-rejected.html

Vega, W. A., Rodriguez, M. A., & Gruskin, E. (2009). Health disparities in the Latino population, *Epidemiologic Reviews, 31*, 99–112. https://doi.org/10.1093/epirev/mxp008

Verona, E., Sachs-Ericsson, N., & Joiner, T. E., Jr. (2004). Suicide attempts associated with externalizing psychopathology in an epidemiological sample. *American Journal of Psychiatry, 161*(3), 444–451. https://doiorg.ezproxy.uakron.edu:2443/10.1176/appi.ajp.161.3.444

Wade, J. C. (2009). Traditional masculinity and African American men's health-related attitudes and behaviors. *American Journal of Men's Health, 3*, 165–172. https://doi.org/10.1177/1557988308320180

Way, K. (2019, January 13). I went on a date with Aziz Ansari. It turned into the worst night of my life. *Babe.net*. Retrieved from https://babe.net/2018/01/13/aziz-ansari-28355

Way, N., Cressen, J., Bodian, S., Preston, J., Nelson, J., & Hughes, D. (2014) "It might be nice to be a girl . . . then you wouldn't have to be emotionless:" Boys' resistance to norms of masculinity during adolescence. *Psychology of Men and Masculinity, 15*, 241–252. https://doi.org/10.1037/a0037262

The weaker sex. (2015, May 23). Blue collar men in rich countries are in trouble. They must learn to adapt. *The Economist*. Retrieved from http://www.economist.com/news/leaders/21652323-blue-collar-men-rich-countries-aretrouble-they-must-learn-adapt-weaker-sex

Weisman, J. (2018, January 16). American Jews and Israeli Jews are headed for a messy breakup. *New York Times Sunday Review*, p. 3. Retrieved from https://www.nytimes.com/2019/01/04/opinion/sunday/israeli-jews-american-jews-divide.html

Wellman, J. D., & McCoy, S. K. (2014). Walking the straight and narrow: Examining the role of traditional gender norms in sexual prejudice. *Psychology of Men & Masculinity, 15*, 181–190. https://doi-org.ezproxy.uakron.edu:2443/10.1037/a0031943

West, C., & Zimmerman, D. H. (2009). Accounting for doing gender. *Gender & Society, 23*, 112–122.

Wexler, D. B. (2009). *Men in therapy: New approaches for effective treatment*. New York, NY: Norton.

Whorley, M. R., & Addis, M. E. (2006). Ten years of psychological research on men and masculinity in the United States: Dominant methodological trends. *Sex Roles, 55*, 649–658. https://doi.org/10.1007/s11199-006-9120-1

Widman, L., Olson, M. A., & Bolen, R. M. (2013). Self-reported sexual assault in convicted sex offenders and community men. *Journal of Interpersonal Violence, 28*, 1519–1536. https://doi.org/10.1177/0886260512468237

Williams, D. R., (2003). The health of men: Structured inequalities and opportunities. *American Journal of Public Health, 93*, 724–731. http://dx.doi.org/10.2105/AJPH.93.5.724

Willie, T. C., Khondkaryan, E., Callands, T., & Kershaw, T. (2018). "Think like a man:" How sexual cultural scripting and masculinity influence changes in men's use of intimate partner violence. *American Journal of Community Psychology, 61*, 240–250. https://doi.org/10.1002/ajcp.12224

Wimer, D. J., & Levant, R. F. (2013). Men's issues, social class, and counseling. In W. M. Liu (Ed.), *The Oxford handbook of social class in counseling* (pp. 481–497). New York, NY: Oxford University Press.

Wong, B. (2019, February 22). This photographer asked men how they reject toxic masculinity. *Huff Post*. Retrieved from https://www.huffpost.com

Wong, Y. J., Ho, R., M., Wang, S.-Y., & Fisher, A. (2016). Subjective masculine norms among university students in Singapore: A mixed-methods study. *Psychology of Men and Masculinity, 17*, 30–41. http://dx.doi.org/10.1037/a0039025

Wong, Y. J., Ho, M.-H. R., Wang, S.-Y., & Keino Miller, I. S. (2017). Meta-analyses of the relationship between conformity to masculine norms and mental health-related outcomes. *Journal of Counseling Psychology, 64*, 80–93. https://doi.org/10.1037/cou0000176

Wong, Y. J., Nguyen, C. P., Wang, S.-Y., Chen, W., Steinfeldt, J. A., Kim, B. S. K. (2012). A latent profile analysis of Asian American men's and women's adherence to cultural values. *Cultural Diversity Ethnic Minority Psychology, 18,* 258–267. https://doi.org/10.1037/a0028423

Wong, Y. J., Liu, T., & Klann, E. M. (2017). The intersection of race, ethnicity, and masculinities: Progress, problems, and prospects. In R. F. Levant & Y. J. Wong, (Eds.), *The psychology of men and masculinities* (pp. 261–288). Washington, DC: American Psychological Association.

Wong, Y. J., Steinfeldt, J. A., Speight, Q. L., & Hickman, S. L. (2010). Content analysis of Psychology of Men and Masculinity (2000–2008). *Psychology of Men and Masculinity, 11,* 170–181. https://doi.org/10.1037/a0019133

Wong, Y. J., & Wester, S. R. (Eds.). (2016). *APA handbook on men and masculinities.* Washington, DC: American Psychological Association.

World Health Organization. (2002). *Gender and mental health.* Retrieved from https://www.who.int/gender/other_health/genderMH.pdf

Worthington, R. L., & Whittaker, T. A. (2006). Scale development research: A content analysis and recommendations for best practices. *Counseling Psychologist, 34,* 806–838. https://doi.org/10.1177/0011000006288127

Wu, R., Levant, R. F., & Sellers, A. (2001). The influence of sex and social development on masculinity ideology of Chinese undergraduate students. *Psychological Science, 24,* 365–366.

Yavorsky, J., Cohen, P. N., & Qian, Y. (2016). Man up, man down: Race-ethnicity and the hierarchy of men in female-dominated work. *Sociological Quarterly, 20,* 1–40. https://doi.org/10.31235/osf.io/74fhn

Zolla, A (2015, June 23). Is it finally time to put down "man up'? *The Good Men Project.* Retrieved from https://goodmenproject.com/featured-content/is-it-finally-time-to-put-down-man-up-fiff/

INDEX

Tables and figures are indicated by *t* and *f* following the page number

For the benefit of digital users, indexed terms that span two pages (e.g., 52–53) may, on occasion, appear on only one of those pages.